*Information
and
its users*

Information
and its users

*a review with special reference
to the social sciences*

by J. M. Brittain

WILEY

Wiley-Interscience
A Division of John Wiley & Sons, Inc.
New York — Toronto

SBN 900843 08 X
Library of Congress
Catalog Card Number 71-152735

Sole Distributors for the United States
Wiley-Interscience, A Division of
John Wiley & Sons, Inc.
New York — Toronto
Printed in Great Britain

Contents

FOREWORD   ix

PREFACE   xi

1.0   PRELIMINARIES

   1.1   Terminology
      1.1.1   Users and user studies   1
      1.1.2   Information needs and information demands   1
      1.1.3   Operational definitions   3
      1.1.4   Disciplines   5

   1.2   Information science and user studies   6

   1.3   The relevance of user studies in science and technology   12
      to social science user studies

2.0   METHODOLOGY

   2.1   Introduction   16

   2.2   Texts on methodology   18

   2.3   Other methods
      2.3.1   Case histories   19
      2.3.2   Self-reported observations at random periods   20
      2.3.3   Operations research study   20
      2.3.4   Some unconventional methods   21

   2.4   Evaluation of methods   22

   2.5   Problems of sampling   23

   2.6   Psychological and environmental variables related to
      information needs and uses   26

   2.7   Evaluation of user studies
      2.7.1   Rationalisation of methods   29
      2.7.2   User studies in context   30
      2.7.3   Some theoretical considerations   31

   2.8   Summary   33

3.0 STUDIES IN THE SOCIAL SCIENCES

3.1 General and conceptual
    3.1.1 Nature of social science research and literature   34
    3.1.2 Classification of social science literature   54
    3.1.3 The application of social science research   63
    3.1.4 Summary   70

3.2 Number of user studies   71

3.3 Language barrier   74

3.4 Informal networks of communication   76
    3.4.1 Characteristics of informal networks   78
    3.4.2 Informal communications, social structures and the research literature   80
    3.4.3 Gatekeepers and two-step flow of information   82

3.5 Informational, environmental, and personality factors associated with productivity   84

3.6 Requirements and demands for published material   88
    3.6.1 Primary material   89
    3.6.2 Secondary material and information services   92

3.7 Studies confined to specific social science disciplines
    3.7.1 The American Psychological Association studies   96
    3.7.2 Other disciplines and fields of study   99

3.8 Practitioners using social science information
    3.8.1 Social and community work   101
    3.8.2 Urban and regional planning   106
    3.8.3 Teachers   111
    3.8.4 Educational administrators   118
    3.8.5 Some omissions   120
    3.8.6 The poverty of usable material   122

4.0 THE SYSTEMIC APPROACH: STUDIES OF COMMUNICATION ARTIFACTS

4.1 General   125

4.2 Growth of social science literature   126

4.3 Citation studies of social science literature   129
    4.3.1 Obsolescence rate of literature   130

4.3.2   Characteristics of the literature used by
        researchers   133
4.3.3   Author and journal hierarchies   136
4.3.4   Scattering of references across journals   139

4.4   The relationship between primary and secondary
      literature   143

4.5   Summary   145

5.0   OVERVIEW

5.1   The number of social science user studies   146

5.2   The methodology of social science user studies   147

5.3   Neglected aspects of users and their information
      requirements   147
5.3.1   Aspects of use   148
5.3.2   Costing information services   150
5.3.3   The formal system   154

5.4   Future trends in the study of information requirements 156

5.5   Conclusions   161

REFERENCES   163

INDEX   198

Foreword

This book stands in its own right, but also represents a giant offshoot of the Investigation into Information Requirements of the Social Sciences. The author, Mr. J. M. Brittain, has since October 1968 been Senior Research Fellow in this Investigation, which is being conducted under my direction with the support of the Office for Scientific and Technical Information.

The origin of the Investigation lay in a belief that the information needs of the social sciences had received insufficient investigation, and that some data concerning them was urgently required if appropriate information systems were to be developed for social scientists. A review of relevant literature and work already conducted was obviously an essential ingredient of the Investigation. Mr. Brittain's review however goes well beyond the minimum requirements of the Investigation, and is likely to be of interest to all working in the treacherous field of information needs.

Grateful thanks are extended to all those who have contributed, wittingly or unwittingly, to the work of the Investigation, especially to OSTI, for their encouragement as well as financial support.

Maurice B. Line
University Librarian
Bath University of Technology

Preface

The study of the information requirements and needs of the social sciences has a short history. A few years ago Paisley (1965) attempted to review user studies in the social sciences, and quickly concluded that there were none to review. During the last five years there has been some interest in social science information, and one or two attempts to determine empirically information needs in the social sciences. But user studies on any scale approaching that in science and technology are not to be found in the social sciences.

In science and technology user studies are numerous and have a history of some twenty years. The relevance of the methodology of science user studies to the social sciences is considered in Chapter 2. The pressing need in user studies, in science as well as social science, is for a general body of theory about the flow of information in research and teaching communities. Some of the fundamental characteristics of social science research and its literature which have a bearing upon investigations of information needs and requirements are considered in the first part of Chapter 3, and the second part is devoted to a review of empirical studies in the social sciences. Other relevant material about the use made of information is discussed in Chapter 4 on systemic approaches.

Although this monograph set out, like Paisley's work, to review empirical studies of information needs and requirements in the social sciences, there are precious few to review. A good many of the references in the present monograph have appeared since 1965, and some of them are directly relevant to user studies in the social sciences, but a number of them are of marginal interest only. However, it seemed appropriate to place user studies in the context not only of information science as a discipline, but also in the context of the pressing demands which have been seen during the last few years for the application of social science knowledge.

I would like to acknowledge and thank my colleagues and friends for their help in the preparation of this book. Especially to Maurice Line for his constant help. I have relied so much upon his extensive knowledge of the subject and his tireless attention to detail. I owe a great deal to him: for his original foresight in making an application to the Office for Scientific and Technical Information for support of research that made the preparation of this monograph possible, for the many references that he brought to my attention, for the many suggestions he made after reading the first draft of the manuscript, for reading subsequent versions, and for many other constructive acts. Coming to an area of scholarship that was new to me I was fortunate in having many colleagues willing to read through the various versions of the work, making helpful suggestions, and bringing to my attention relevant references. Mrs. Brenda White, Miss Vi Winn, and Mr. David Dews have given me much help in this way; and Professor Don Swift looked through parts of the manuscript. My immediate colleagues at Bath, Mrs. Dawn Cunningham and Mr. Frank Cranmer, gave much time and attention to the first draft. Mrs. Joyce Line edited the bibliography and prepared the index. Mrs. Monida Harris and Miss Katharine Sawbridge spent many hours typing and retyping the manuscript. My wife Hilary spent many hours helping me prepare the first draft.

J. M. BRITTAIN

Bath University of Technology

April 1970

CHAPTER ONE

Preliminaries

1.1 Terminology

1.1.1 *Users and user studies*

Some of the terms to be found in the study of information needs and requirements are ambiguous and can easily lead to confusion.[1] Empirical studies of the use of, the demand or need for, information are usually called 'user studies'. Here 'user' can be read 'user of information', but from a reading of user study it is not obvious whether the study is one of demand, need, or use. Further, ambiguity resides in the term 'use': as most frequently found it refers to the study of the gathering stage of use rather than the use to which information is put once it has been collected or collated. The term is less frequently found in this latter context.[2]

1.1.2 *Information needs and information demands*

The definition of 'information demands' is relatively easy. It refers to the demands, which may be vocal or written, and made to a library or to some other information system. The definition of 'information needs' is more difficult. In some cases needs will be synonymous with demands: for example where the user knows of all the information that is relevant to his work, and makes a demand to an information source. At the other extreme is the user who makes very few demands but has many needs. He may have a felt but unarticulated need (perhaps because

---

[1]Some idea of the terminological confusion can be gauged from the many different terms used by different workers. For example Wysocki (1969) refers to 'the study of the needs of the users of . . . information'; Fishenden (1965) and Barnes (1965) to 'information use studies'; Martyn (1964a) to 'literature searching studies'; Paisley (1968) to 'use studies'; and the *Journal of Documentation* (1965) to 'information needs studies'.

[2]Wysocki (1969) suggests that this particular ambiguity could be avoided by adopting the term 'information needs studies' for investigations on the influence of information on the development of science, while 'user studies' or 'use studies' could be concerned with studying information processing activities of the user.

of inertia or because he does not have sufficient specific details about the felt need to translate the need into a demand) or he may have an unfelt need (in which case he may not be aware until this is pointed out, at which time he may readily agree that he has a need or he may not realise this until the need has actually been met). One of the problems in this aspect of user enquiry is terminological: there is no suitable word for 'potential user' or 'needer'.

The problem of terminology in this area has often been discussed[3] and there is general agreement about the value of distinguishing between needs and demands, but not about the possibility of empirically discovering needs by asking users. Bernal (1957, p. 197), for example, was not a great advocate of user studies (which he defined in a very limited way) and maintained that they had severe limitations: 'when it is realised that scientists are usually completely untrained in any matters concerned with the storage and collection of information and do not even know what services are available, far less what might be available, their opinion on these questions is probably of little positive value'. In another paper Bernal (1959) continues: ' . . . though the user may well know what he *wants* from an information service, he is in no position to know what he *needs* from it, namely what variation in the system would help most to further his work. Consequently, any action based on analysis of present user habits is unlikely to produce impressive results'.

For some time now information scientists have stressed the importance of investigating needs rather than uses or demands—the 'real' information needs as Dannatt (1967) puts it—and this direction of attention has

---

[3]Menzel (1967, p. 279) suggested that ' . . . "information needs" are not synonymous with either demands or the conscious wants of information users. It is not the information that users are aware of wanting that counts, not even the information that would be "good for them", but rather the information that would be good for science—the progress of scientific research'. Engelbert (1968) makes a distinction between the subjective needs and the objective needs of users. Subjective needs relate to the vague feeling that the researcher may have about the information he requires, and will be very strongly influenced by his style of working and his experience. Objective needs arise in the context of the social circumstances in which the user works. There is a definite correlation between the two. Objective needs are little more than the demands that the user makes upon information systems. One might ask why Engelbert's distinction between objective and subjective needs is necessary, if objective needs are little more than demands. Dannatt (1967) suggests that enquiries about needs may appear to the researcher to be superfluous. Dannatt notes that the information scientist has increasingly been concerned with 'real' needs and that the demand studies do not go far enough in this direction. To the researcher, Dannatt suggests, the needs arrived at by questioning are no more 'real' than the demands for documents. O'Connor (1968, p. 200) takes information scientists to task for speaking, writing, investigating, and attempting to satisfy information

taken place in spite of the doubts expressed by Bernal, O'Connor, and others, but in fact there is no agreement (Rees, 1963) that this movement has been successful in practice. Rees (1963) suggests that most studies which have purported to be of information needs have in fact been of information uses or, at best, demands.

The problems of terminology are not, of course, confined to the social sciences, although there may be special problems in the social sciences (see 3.1 and 3.2 and 3.3) requiring attention. Line (1969a) suggests that any study of need must include a study of use and demand. He supports the multi-method approach which he suggests can go a long way to overcome the difficulties of investigating needs. Line (1969a, p. 7) suggests that by obtaining data on uses and demands, and by carefully distinguishing intended and unintended use, some pointers to unarticulated needs can be obtained. Another approach mentioned by Line is to hypothesise about need from the nature of the activities in which individuals are involved. This is a less reliable, although perhaps a more valid approach than the others, and is perhaps best used to supplement the data obtained by the other methods—rather than adopted as a main method for investigation.

1.1.3 *Operational definitions*

When studies were limited to the demands that users made upon library services, the problem of defining 'need' did not exist. But when the information scientist turned his attention from observation and measurement of library borrowings to enquiries about user behaviour

---

needs without clearly defining what is meant by information needs. 'The expression "satisfying a requester's information need" is often used, but its meaning is obscure. The literature on "information need" in relation to retrieval suggests three different (though not inconsistent) possible interpretations. However, each of these interpretations is itself fundamentally unclear.' O'Connor goes on to attempt to clarify these three meanings. Line (1969a, p. 6) discusses the problems of defining information needs, and focuses upon another aspect of needs—what he calls 'unintended use'. He notes that '. . . little attempt has been made in use studies to distinguish "intended use" (= satisfied demand) from "unintended use". Now if it is true that much information seen as "relevant" is gathered in this way, there must be a great deal of "relevant" information that is not gathered at all, or sought in any sense. Some of this is likely to be of importance, in the sense that the activity (research, etc.) to which it is relevant would be furthered if it were known. Its importance is likely to be quite different from that of "sought" information; the latter being central to the activity, the former shedding new light, offering fruitful analogies, extending a conceptual framework, or suggesting possible lines of development. It may act merely as a stimulant; this function may perhaps be performed by almost any information— it does not need to be at all relevant or even related in subject content to set off a useful train of thought—and is perhaps of its very nature best left to chance.'

(using the verbal or written reports of users) he was faced with problems of subjective reports, unreliable data, and defining that which he was attempting to discover.

The usage of recorded material is easy to define and to measure. The behaviour of users in the library, in the laboratory, or in their own rooms when they are working, could be objectively observed; but there are many problems involved in this type of research and it has not been undertaken to any extent. The three most popular methods in user studies—questionnaire, interview and diary—all involve the participation of the user. As soon as the user is invited to participate to this extent the investigator is faced with exactly the same problem that faces the psychologist when he asks the subject for a verbal report. The problem is very familiar and remains a point dividing psychologists. The behaviourist, the exponent of the method of measurement and observation under controlled experimental conditions, demands objectivity and reliability of results; and may sometimes have to compromise on the question of the validity of data. The behaviourist adheres strictly to the operational definition, so that the variables to be studied have no ambiguity. The less strict behaviourist may today be just as meticulous as his more operationally minded colleague in the care he lavishes on the design of his experiment, the collection and the analysis of the data, but his variables are likely to be less tightly defined.

The librarian or information scientist dealing with circulation counts, or demands for information, hardly faces the problem of defining his variables: but the information scientist dealing with information needs and requirements faces the problem both in the design and the data gathering stages of his investigation.

The term 'information' can be ambiguous and lead to misunderstanding. In some cases this ambiguity can be avoided by 'documents' or 'location'—terms more clearly related to physical referents. Referring to the use of 'information' by librarians and information scientists Fairthorne (1968, p. 91) maintains that one cannot be too careful about invisible assumptions contained in the use of the term 'information'. He suggests that ' . . . we must get into our minds that we are dealing with records. Also we deal to a certain extent with interpretations of these records, but only inasmuch as interpretations affect people's behaviour when dealing with records. . . . Inasmuch as we inform anybody about anything in an information system, we merely notify them about records'.

Some such clarification of the ambiguity involved in using record, data, and information is required. Fairthorne's suggestion plays down the problems that face the information scientist or librarian when a 'translation' of a request is required in order to produce any document at all. Fairthorne's suggestion makes good sense when the demand is for a record or document, but many demands are very vague, and require the initiative and expertise of the supplier who must be able to transform a vague expression of a need into details specific enough to retrieve documents.

1.1.4 *Disciplines*

User studies attempting to cover the social sciences have the problem of defining their area of study. Few would disagree with the inclusion of sociology, economics, political science, and anthropology under the general heading 'social science'. There would be less general agreement about the place of psychology, history, education, jurisprudence, and management studies. Some prefer the label behavioural science to social science: but confusion is likely to arise whatever label is chosen. Many psychologists prefer to call their discipline behavioural science rather than social science, but the term can be used in a much wider context. For example, Handy and Kurtz (1964) in their *A current appraisal of the behavioral sciences* include anthropology, sociology, history, economics, political science, jurisprudence, psychology, and education under this heading.

When an investigation is directed to the study of the information requirements of more than one discipline a decision must be made at the outset about criteria of inclusion and exclusion. The disciplines mentioned above (e.g. sociology, economics) are accepted entities with some boundary delimitations, with professional associations, with identifiable activities that can be differentiated from the activities of other disciplines, and with different practical applications. However, there is a group of newer subjects which tend to cut across the established disciplines. Handy and Kurtz (1964) mention information theory, cybernetics, linguistics, sign-behaviour (semiotics), game theory, decision-making theory, value inquiry, and general systems. Handy and Kurtz group together, under the heading 'communication theory', information theory, cybernetics, linguistics and sign-behaviour; and under the heading 'preferential behaviour', game theory, decision-making theory, and value theory. Although some of these newer areas of study were more closely attached in the past to parent disciplines (e.g. game theory and economics) they are now interdisciplinary in nature. Other fields of an interdisciplinary nature, of longer standing, include criminology and conflict research. Some of the boundaries between disciplines are perhaps pragmatic and perpetuated by the existence of professional associations, university departments, and labels. These discipline boundaries are not always drawn according to the dictates of subject matter and the destination of the results of research, and user studies that are directed to goals other than the maintenance of the *status quo* have to consider carefully the boundaries that are dictated by information requirements and the provision of information, rather than the boundaries that are perpetuated by professional associations, university departments, etc.

1.2   Information science and user studies

User studies form part of a body of study and knowledge that come under the (generally accepted) name 'information science'. Although user studies are not tightly linked in any theoretical framework they are obviously related[4] to many of the activities that go on in information science.

There is general agreement that a science of information[5] is evolving and that it is in a state of rapid change, but less agreement about the form that this new science will take, or about the contribution that

---

[4]According to Bourne (1962a), for example, an information system requires: (1) definition of the problem; (2) a determination of user requirements; (3) synthesis and design; (4) evaluation.

[5]There are many definitions of information science scattered throughout the literature. A broad definition was given by R. Taylor in his letter of December 1st 1967, addressed to members of the American Society for Information Science (ASIS), which, with slight revision, was reprinted and distributed in ASIS brochures. Taylor suggests that 'As a discipline information science investigates properties and behavior of information, the forces governing the transfer process, and the technology necessary to process information for optimum accessibility and use'. Taylor states further that information science is 'derived from or related to mathematics, logic, linguistics, psychology, computer technology, operations research, librarianship, the graphic arts, communications, management, and similar fields'. Cuadra (1964) attempted to identify the richest and most essential references in information science (it is obvious from the text that Cuadra limited his attention to information retrieval— an established area from which he saw information science developing) and to determine whether the field had matured sufficiently to show common agreement on the most important conceptual, methodological or practical contributions to the handling of documented information. Cuadra asked three experts in the field to rank order the ten most important contributors. Some agreement was seen between the three lists, and nearly all the contributors mentioned have published since the 1950's. Cuadra analysed the citations in six texts on information retrieval-documentation. These texts contained 911 citations to authors. Of these 911 citations 788 (86 per cent) were unique: that is, they appeared in only

existing disciplines will play. Kochen (1969, p. 186), in a penetrating analysis[6] of the development of information science, maintains that a 'new intellectual discipline seems to be in the making. It is the study of processes by which knowledge grows'. Until very recently, at least in the United States and Western Europe, there has been little concerted effort to establish a conceptual framework for information science, or to define its boundaries (the position in the Soviet Union is slightly different, and this is mentioned below). Developments in information science have gone hand in hand with developments in library science (in fact the distinction between the two is not always made). Work in information science includes activities in traditional areas of library science; for example, classification and retrieval, and more recently, the development of thesauri, autonomic classification, and computer-assisted retrieval. Other activities include the development and assessment of information services (e.g. selective dissemination of information) and the development and assessment of new bibliographical tools (e.g. citation indexes and KWIC indexes). All these activities have been firmly based on library science, and it is only very recently that developments have proceeded so far as to call into question the focal point for these studies.

The orientation of Russian workers is slightly different. There is some confusion in translations from the Russian (and sometimes

---

one of the six texts. No single reference appeared in all the texts. Another analysis of four of the most comprehensive bibliographies in the field were examined in detail. The four texts mentioned a total of 7,550 citations. For all authors who were mentioned at least twice (in three of the texts; in the fourth text the authors had to be mentioned three times) in any one text, their publications in the other three texts were tallied. A total of 322 authors were included in the tallies. A list of basic readings was compiled from the published works of the 25 authors who appeared most often in the bibliographies. Kochen (1969) takes a more global view of the information sciences and maintains that the new discipline that is developing cannot as yet be characterised by pointing to some fundamental papers and books, although he suggests that works by Dessauer (1949) on stability, Garfield (1967) on citation indexes and bibliographic coupling, and by Glass (1965) on science and ethical values are first approximations.

[6]In the first 'Distinguished lecture of the American Society for Information Science' Kochen draws an analogy between the way in which a growing literature organises knowledge and the way a learner, by creating models of his environment, is able to take increasingly effective actions. A similar analogy, this time between information retrieval and education, was drawn by Heilprin and Goodman (1965). They suggested that both searching for information and the process of education are subject to, and shaped by, one basic constraint— the very limited human information processing capacity. The germinal theme common to both these papers concerns the user of information, with finite assimilation and processing capacities, in the context of an exponentially expanding universe of documentation.

German) when the term 'informatics' is used: it is often thought to be equivalent to 'information science'. However, Russian workers themselves are far from agreeing about the science of informatics.

Mikhailov *et al.* (1966, p. 39) defined informatics as 'a new science which studies the structure and properties of scientific information, the patterns of scientific information activity, its theory, methods and organisation'. The *Terminological Dictionary of Scientific Information* (1966, p. 329), for which Mikhailov and his colleagues are responsible, has a similar definition. 'Informatics is the branch of knowledge which studies the patterns of collecting, processing, storing and disseminating documentary scientific information and which determines the optimum organisation of informational work on the basis of modern technical means.'

Some other definitions are less broad. For example, according to Györe (1969) informatics is a branch of science dealing with the characteristics of users of information, especially their personality. Novikov (1969, p. 8*) is very much opposed to the inclusion of personality factors into the definition of informatics. He maintains that: 'The creator and consumer of scientific information is man. The processes of creation and perception of information by man belong to the class of mental processes. The book, *Bases of informatics* (by Mikhailov, Chernyi and Gilyarevsky, 1968), contains no chapters devoted to the psychological aspects of informatics. And this is proper. The study of mental processes is the subject matter of psychology. Hence informatics and psychology are bordering sciences . . .'. Novikov looks to established areas such as psycholinguistics, engineering psychology, and labour psychology (a Russian speciality) for the contribution they can make to informatics, but dismisses them all and proposes that a new branch of psychology should be developed, which would employ information specialists whose tasks would include the comparison of what is known in a discipline with what is available, the assessment of information needs and the amount of information required by users, and assessments of potential needs. In addition to these tasks this new branch of psychology, according to Novikov, would be responsible for Selective Dissemination of Information (SDI) services, long-term studies of patterns of utilisation of information by workers in science and industry, the nature and use of abstracts, channels of communication, problems of classification and the psychological factors associated with the use of

---

*Page number refers to translation.

information, creativity and productivity. These topics have received attention in the United States and Western Europe, and are generally assumed to be the subject matter of information science. Since these topics would be covered by the new branch of psychology (and this new sub-discipline would itself be a part of informatics) it is difficult to see what would be left for 'informatics'. It would appear from Novikov's analysis that informatics and the proposed new branch of psychology are very similar, perhaps indistinguishable.

Fairthorne (1969b, p. 26) objects to 'a dangerous tendency to bring in every and any science or technique or phenomenon under the "information" heading. Certainly hitherto distinct activities and interests should be unified, if indeed they have common principles. However, one does not create common principles by giving different things the same name'. Fairthorne refers to ISTA (Information Sciences, Technologies, and Activities) in an attempt to curb this tendency. He emphasises the poverty of theoretical developments in information science: he maintains that ISTA is more a federation of technologies than a set of specialist activities developed from common principles.

Schober and Wersig (1968) also object to the name 'information science' but for different reasons. They suggest that a theory of 'information science' is formed from information theory of the Shannon and Weaver variety, and that this has little to do with information in its other sense. They consider various compound names, none of which are suitable, and compromise with 'information and documentation science', following a suggestion by Koblitz (1968).

A good deal of the confusion arises from the usage of the term 'information science'. Perhaps when the evolving discipline referred to by Kochen develops a fully-fledged theory it will be, as Otten and Debons (1970) suggest, a metascience of information. Otten and Debons introduce the name 'informatology' for this metascience.

Rees (1965b, p. 72) asks: 'Can we not agree that, at the present time, information science has little connection with information handling and that to use information science interchangeably with information retrieval, science information, or documentation leads only to confusion?'.

During the past twenty-five years or so user studies have become an established field with some degree of cohesion. To some extent this may have been brought about by the development of identifying labels and bibliographical facilities. There are *Information Science Abstracts* (formerly *Documentation Abstracts*) and *Library and Information*

Science Abstracts. Both these abstracting journals include sections on user studies, as also does the 'Current Awareness List' published in *Aslib Proceedings.* Another unifying factor is the emergence of a first generation of students with training in information and library science.

The place of user studies within the body of knowledge that goes under the heading 'information science' is not firmly established, and it seems unlikely that the conceptual difficulties encountered in the study of information needs will be solved until information science has an acceptable theoretical backing which can accommodate user studies. It might be supposed that questions pertaining to the use of information, user behaviour, etc., would be the domain of the sociologist and the psychologist: the respective areas might be the sociology of information, and the psychology of information seeking and using behaviour.

Gushee (1968) noted that scientists themselves have been the most active in studying information requirements and the transfer of information between researchers; and that the earlier references came from chemistry, although recently physicists and psychologists have been researching into their own literature requirements.

In the 1969 *Annual Review of Science and Technology* Allen (1969) noted that the number of user studies concerned with the social sciences has increased over the past three years and is growing at a prodigious rate. He suggested that studies of information needs and uses have now become a recognised area of activity for social scientists although this trend is limited almost exclusively to psychology. User studies in the other social sciences have been slow to appear. Although the psychologist has recognised the need for knowledge in this area he has not been active in studying the information gathering and disseminating behaviour of researchers in other disciplines. Other commentators upon the information scene have outlined a central role for the behavioural scientist. For example, United States National Research Council Committee on Information in the Behavioral Sciences (1967, p. 2) Report on *Communication systems and resources in the behavioral sciences* suggests that behavioural scientists 'have an obligation not only to their colleagues but to all scientists, to establish a better understanding of the behavioral elements in a scientific information system. What they have contributed to this end so far, however significant, represent only a beginning'.

The advent of computer-based information storage and retrieval systems, the application of systems theory to the management and planning of information centres and libraries, and the sheer cost (and perhaps novelty) of these systems have played a part in drawing attention to the design (including user requirements) of systems. These systems involve a feedback from users that could not be incorporated in a non-computer-based system. There is, in short, a movement towards a receiver-controlled system and a movement away from source-controlled systems.[7]

The attention to user-orientated information systems is only one example of a growing phenomenon. Attention to, and a demand for, user orientated services is currently to be seen in a wide range of human activities. Examples of user enquiries, other than into information systems, include investigations of the users of public transport (with the object of reorganising transport systems to provide services that are required and used frequently), consumer research (although this pre-dates user studies of information requirements), and the redesign and creation of courses of instruction that are student, rather than teacher, orientated.

In the field of information studies investigations have usually been pursued for their practical value. Paisley (1968, p. 21) has pointed out that ' . . . the earliest studies of information needs and uses took place within libraries, information centres, and laboratories because librarians and administrators needed data for service decisions. Later, many studies were sponsored by professional associations, such as the American Psychological Association and the American Institute of Physics, because associations in general were examining their information programs in the light of the "information explosion" and the new technology. The centre of effort has now shifted again; government agencies are sponsoring studies of diverse scientific and technical groups that happen to be working in the same very general area (e.g. aerospace) and therefore receive funds from a single agency (e.g. NASA)'.

As the pattern of support for user studies has changed the idea of the 'responsible agent' has evolved. As research areas become identified more by mission orientation than by contributing disciplines (e.g. aerospace research rather than physics, chemistry, and engineering), each professional association will be able to supply only a fraction of all information needed by the mission. Decisions taken at a national (and even international) level have had an important influence on the direction of research in information science; and such influences are increas-

---

[7]See Paisley and Parker (1965) for an outline of a hypothetical information retrieval system that is receiver-controlled; and Cavanagh (1967), Connor (1967) and Meister and Sullivan (1967) for other work on user-orientated systems.

ing. The role of government in the initiation, support, and direction of research in the physical sciences has been well documented, but the relationship between research in the social sciences and government policies is not so well known. As Oppenheim (1966, p. 330) points out 'not all of us are sufficiently aware of the amount and type of research in the social sciences which is, or has been, government-sponsored. Project Camelot may have been the largest of its kind, but it is by no means unique'. A distinction must be made between overt statements of national policy[8] and the less direct effect that government-sponsored research[9] has upon a discipline and its information requirements. Also, a distinction is required between statements about policy and actions that result in national information services.

1.3 The relevance of user studies in science and technology to social science user studies

It is tempting[10] for those concerned with information and users in social science to look to user studies in science and technology, and this temptation is made greater by the relatively small number of studies in

---

[8]See, for example, the United States Federal Council for Science and Technology Committee on Scientific and Technical Information (COSATI) 1965 report *Recommendations for national document handling systems in science and technology;* Horowitz (1967), and the United States Senate Committee on Government Operations/Sub-committee on Government Research (1966). Alpert (1958, 1960) reports on the attitude of the United States Government towards the social sciences and the 1967 November issue of *American Psychologist* deals with 'Congress and social science'.

[9]A very comprehensive account of the relationship between government and social science research can be found in a collection of papers edited by Crawford and Boderman (1969) and in their extensive bibliography. This publication is biased a little towards political science, but it contains many references to government policy and support of social science research. See Carter (1967) and Riecken (1967) for estimates of the percentage of the total United States budget for research that is allocated to the social sciences, and Darley (1957) on financial support given to psychology. The views of social scientists themselves on government support were called for by the United States Government at a Conference on Research in the Social Sciences and Humanities (reported by Legters, 1967). Lundberg (1947) and Parsons (1946) discuss the reasons for not making social science part of the National Science Foundation.

[10]The student of the social science information system could be forgiven for assuming that the information systems in the physical sciences are well established, organised and operating effectively. This would only be a comparative judgement, for the information systems in the physical sciences are still in a period of transition, with problems of centralisation still unsettled. A report by the United States Government President's Science Advisory Committee (1963), commonly known as the Weinberg Report, found the existing state far from satisfactory. From the very first hearings on information conducted by the

social science. The information services in the physical sciences (e.g. bibliographical aids, SDI services, retrieval services) are themselves much more sophisticated than their counterparts (where they exist) in the social sciences, and these services and their users have been extensively studied. Depending upon how user studies are defined and how the number of studies are calculated[11] there exist some 400 to 800 such studies. User studies in the physical sciences are now numerous enough to call forth reviews and summary articles on the state-of-the-art, and the reader is referred to the principal reviews[12] for details of these studies.

Bisco (1967a) suggested that the first known empirical studies of the needs and uses of information, in contrast to the recorded uses of stored materials, were reported by Bernal (1948a)[13] and Urquhart (1948) at the Royal Society Scientific Information Conference during June and July of 1948. Since then the growth of empirical studies in this area can be represented by an exponential curve. Bisco, abstracting data from Menzel (1966a, 1966b) and Paisley (1965), tabulated the number of studies by four-year periods from 1947 to 1966. The total number of studies reported during this period, according to Bisco's calculation, is a mere 76 and this contrasts markedly with other estimations.

Committee in March 1958, the concept of a Federal and national 'plan'—of a 'system' or a 'network'—was stressed. At that time few of the Federal agencies were prepared to accept the thesis that an inter-agency plan was necessary, much less feasible. The committee emphasised, however, that nothing less than a plan would suffice to deal with what was already becoming a 'flood' of scientific and engineering information and data.

[11]See Davis and Bailey (1964) who list 438 references to user studies of one kind or another, and Auerbach Corporation (1965) who list 676 references. A good many have been carried out since: see *Annual Review of Information Science and Technology*.

[12]Menzel (1960) attempts a 'synthesising review of completed studies of the behavior, habits, usages, experiences, and expressed needs of research scientists with regard to the obtaining of available scientific information'. The review covers conceptual approaches, research methods, as well as the factual results of user studies. Menzel's review can be supplemented with some of his own publications (e.g. Menzel, 1957, 1958, 1959, 1964, 1966a, 1966b, 1968). Menzel (1967) considers the feasibility of empirically determining information needs. A review by Paisley (1965) started life as a review of the research literature on the flow of behavioural science information but Paisley quickly concluded that there was no such research literature to review (with the exception of the American Psychological Association studies) and turned to user studies in the sciences reported during the period 1948–1965.

[13]Bernal (1948a) reported the results of a survey, by questionnaire, on the use made of literature by scientists and engineers. A sample of 300 was used. Bernal's interest in user studies went much further than a number of his successors in the field. He was concerned with the use to which information was put, unlike so many subsequent surveys that have been satisfied with a listing of material used and of the sources from which it came.

Between 1947 and 1951 Bisco identified two studies, between 1952 and 1956 there were five, between 1957 and 1961 there were twenty-two and between 1962 and 1966 there were forty-seven studies. The last four years of the 1947–1966 period accounted for 62 per cent of the studies.

Bisco's estimates fall far short of many other estimates and the number of references contained in bibliographies of user studies by Davis and Bailey (1964), Auerbach Corporation (1965), and the United States Federal Council for Science and Technology Committee on Scientific and Technical Information (COSATI, 1965). Bisco (1967a) maintained that these bibliographies were not very selective and that they contained references to studies of doubtful value. For example, Bisco suggested that of the 450 publications relating to information needs and uses identified in COSATI (1965) only 58 (i.e. 13 per cent) based their conclusions on satisfactory empirical evidence. He also noted that 70 per cent of these 58 studies were based upon users in the United States. Bisco made another estimate from the records of research into information needs and uses carried out by the National Science Foundation. He noted that fifteen studies were recorded in 1957, one hundred in 1962, and seventy in 1966. These figures show much closer agreement with Bisco's estimates from Menzel (1966a, 1966b) and Paisley (1965) than to the much greater number included in the bibliographies referred to above.

The vast majority of user studies in science and technology fall into one of two categories: (1) they study the information requirements of particular disciplines, for example, chemistry, physics, zoology; or (2) they are limited to a particular research establishment or industry[14] where they may cut across subject boundaries.

Whereas the results of studies of the first type may be of general use to many scientists, the results of the second type are necessarily severely restricted in their general applicability, and may be confined solely to the establishment in which they are undertaken. Research workers in industrial establishments or special research establishments (including government supported ones), unlike their counterparts in universities, are often provided with special information services and information officers. Researchers in such settings are less likely to interact with researchers outside their own disciplines than their

---

[14]For example, surveys and studies by Fishenden (1959) at the Atomic Energy Establishment, Harwell; by Thorne (1954) at the Royal Aircraft Establishment; by Levy (1964) at the Western Electrical Company; by Scott and Wilkins (1960) of technologists in the electrical and electronic industry.

counterparts in the universities. Also their goals, objectives, and demands are likely to be appreciably different.

In the present context user studies in science and technology are of interest only in as far as they contribute to questions about (1) the flow of information in the social sciences, and (2) the design of user studies in the social sciences and the interpretation of results. The contribution that user studies in the sciences can make to methodological issues in the design of user studies in the social sciences is considered in chapter 2. There is general agreement that the science user study has much to contribute in this way but there are pitfalls associated with too close an adherence to the model of the user study in the sciences. However, at present there is no alternative source, and an enquiry into information needs and requirements in the social sciences has little alternative but to set the scene with studies in the sciences.

CHAPTER TWO

Methodology

2.1 Introduction

A good deal has been written about the problems of research into information needs and requirements, but much of the comment has not been related to, or backed-up by, empirical data. Furthermore, many of the contributions have not been related to any theoretical structure. There is a deficiency of good theory in the area of user studies (and in information science), and although empirical investigations can (and do) proceed in the absence of satisfactory theory—and generate a number of points that are treated as methodological—long term progress in methodology depends upon a strong theory.[1]

Paisley (1968) suggests, following Merton (1967), that theories of the middle range are required: that is, concepts and theorems that are neither too close to information-use data nor too far removed into systems theory and cybernetics. In any field of enquiry researchers begin with typologies: for example, in the field of information-use studies, scientists are contrasted with technologists. In the beginning these typologies are crude, and they can be transformed into scalar dimensions with the help of theory. Paisley (1968, p. 25) states: 'The study of information needs and uses is still in its typological phase, because we lack middle-range concepts that would specify how the

---

[1]Paisley (1968, p. 26) shows clearly the problem of explaining discrepant findings in a field with no strong theory. In a field with no strong theory consistent findings are fairly easy to deal with (although the process of confirmation is open-ended), but discrepant findings are much more difficult to deal with. They may be the result of poor or mistaken enquiries, or they may be of real significance and set the pattern of future enquiries. On the other hand, in a field with a strong theory, consistent findings provide additional precision and generality to the theory, and discrepant findings break the paradigm and provide an impetus for a better theory and subsequent further empirical verification. Paisley takes the idea of the 'broken paradigm' from Kuhn's (1962) account of the progress of science—a good paradigm (or theory) permits a test that breaks it and forces scientists to propose a better paradigm in its place. The fact that information science has not succeeded in breaking its first paradigm indicates that it has a long way to go.

types in a typology relate to each other. The progress that can be observed now is a refinement of typologies, with greater specificity of information needs, kinds, channels, etc. It has been the experience of other fields that some refined typologies strike almost accidentally upon underlying conceptual dimensions that establish order'. Paisley suggests that concepts such as perceived utility, perceived cost, uncertainty and psychological distance could supplant the *ad hoc* typologies which now exist.

Many of the empirical studies in science and technology have necessarily been concerned with methodological problems involved in the design of questionnaires and other tests, in experimental techniques, pilot surveys, sampling, analysis of results and the drawing and applicability of conclusions. In some instances sound methods are found but this is often not the case. Menzel (1966b), Herner and Herner (1967), and Paisley (1968), in their respective reviews of the preceding year's literature for the *Annual Review of Information Science and Technology*, have expressed concern about the failure of user studies to adopt the sound methods of its own best work. Mistakes of the 1950's are repeated in the 1960's. Inconclusive studies are conducted to fill gaps left by previous inconclusive studies.

Paisley noted that methodological defects were still apparent, and suggested the time had come to object more strenuously to poor conceptualisation. In particular, Paisley suggested that the context in which the scientist works has been neglected. Many user studies have concentrated upon one small part of the total information system. 'As a result, in many studies, it is hard to glimpse a real scientist or technologist at work, under constraints and pressures, creating products, drawing upon the elaborate communication network that connects him with sources of necessary knowledge.' (Paisley, 1968, p. 2). Theories of information-processing that will generate propositions concerning channel selection; amount of seeking; effects on productivity of information quality, quantity, currency, and diversity; the role of motivational and personality factors, etc., are required. 'Purely descriptive study of any set of behaviors has its point of diminishing return. Eventually (certainly not yet) we shall have sufficiently precise knowledge of how much information flows, to whom, through which channels, for what purpose, etc. The scattered findings cannot be combined into a coherent overview, however, without abstract concepts to replace the tired labels of current research, such as "basic" versus "applied", "scientist" versus "technologist", and "formal" versus "informal".' (Paisley, 1968, p. 24).

2.2   Texts on methodology

There are now a number of texts,[2] some of them of an introductory nature, that discuss the different methods of carrying out and evaluating user studies[3]. The principal reviews of user studies—Menzel (1960) and Paisley (1965), supplemented by the relevant chapters in the four volumes of the *Annual Review of Information Science and Technology*—contain commentary on methodological problems. Short articles by Jahoda (1966), Coover (1969), Slater (1968), and Wood (1969) provide useful general introductions. These authors all discuss such fundamental questions as sampling frames, survey methods, pilot studies, the analysis of the data (including the application of statistical techniques). A less well known review of user studies by Wysocki (1969) contains a section on methods of research.

The main methods (interview, questionnaire, diary, and case history) have been summarised by Parker and Paisley (1966), Borko (1962), Bourne (1962a), and many others. An earlier account of the main methods can be found in Egan and Henkle (1956). The interview and questionnaire techniques have been used much more frequently than any other method. The reader is referred to standard texts in the social sciences for a consideration of the technical points relating to survey techniques. Wuest (1965) gives details about the questionnaire method when applied to user studies, and there is now a good deal of literature (see, for example, Cahalan, 1951; Edgerton, Britt and Norman, 1947; Linsky, 1965; Franzen and Lazarsfeld, 1945; Longworth, 1953; Robin, 1965) dealing with the advantages and the disadvantages of the questionnaire method, although relatively little about the application of the questionnaire method to investigations of information requirements, needs, and uses.

There has been some evaluation of the results of user studies (Taube, 1959; Hanson, 1964; Barber, 1966), of methods (see 2.4), and of the practical value of user studies for the design and implementation of

---

[2]The serious student of user studies needs to consult detailed bibliographies. The standard bibliographies (now out of date and requiring supplementation with bibliographies in more recent papers and the reviews found in the *Annual Review of Information Science and Technology*) are by Davis and Bailey (1964) with 438 references, and Auerbach (1965) which lists 676 citations. These bibliographies require careful and discriminating use. Where an intending researcher has limited time and money to pursue in detail the literature of user studies, it is a little unrealistic to refer him to such detailed, and in some parts unrepresentative, bibliographies. These bibliographies list a large number of studies (usually library surveys) conducted between 1920 and 1940. The researcher unfamiliar with the field would have difficulty in deciding which

information storage and retrieval systems (Herner, 1958, 1962; Bourne, 1962a; Borko, 1962).

The student of social science information will look in vain for references on methodology that have come from this field. There are now some user studies in social science (see chapter 3) and some thinking about the special problems of social science information (see 3.1), but user studies were born in science and technology and it is there that the focus of attention has remained. And yet there are questions of fundamental importance that should be looked at before empirical enquiries are attempted. Menzel (1967) raised the question whether it is possible at all to determine, empirically, science information needs—as opposed to uses. Students of social science information have not so far been much concerned with this question.

2.3 Other methods

The main methods are well established and there is some danger that the interview and questionnaire techniques will be used to the near exclusion of other methods. The main methods have now found their way into user studies in the social sciences but a number of the less popular methods have not been tried out here.

Some of the infrequently used methods[4] have been developed in the context of the design and evaluation of information systems, including information storage and retrieval systems (e.g. Bourne, 1962a; Borko, 1962; Herner, 1958). The social sciences have not been endowed with many specially designed information systems and services, and therefore it is not surprising that these methods have not been introduced into social science user studies.

2.3.1 *Case histories*

The data obtained from a diary or tape-recorded self-observations during working hours give case history type material, but more

---

references were relevant to his immediate problem. More up to date and selective bibliographies (e.g. those contained in introductory texts) should be consulted first.

[3]Most studies have assumed *a priori* that empirical investigations of information needs are possible. Before embarking upon any investigation a reading of Menzel's (1967) article 'Can science information needs be ascertained empirically?' would seem to be a prerequisite.

[4]For example, traffic observation, postulation of a new system and the invitation of service requests, perturbation of user system and observation of user reactions. See Bourne (1962a) for more details.

commonly a case history refers to written material of an autobiographical kind. The collection and analysis of case histories has not been popular among information scientists, although material can be gathered at a level of detail impossible with the other methods. Case history material is difficult to quantify and is very time-consuming to collect and analyse; and these problems alone tell against the study of large numbers of users. But case histories can help in the understanding of the research process and although they may not provide the most objective data they increase understanding of the literature searching processes and contribute to the formulation of more precise and empirically testable hypotheses. An example of the method can be found in Kittel (1955).

2.3.2 *Self-reported observations at random periods*

The random alarm device was used by Martin (1962) in a study of the reading behaviour of chemists and physicists, to determine what was read, why it was read, and what differences there were between groups. A device which generated an audible alarm at random intervals was carried by scientists and used to signal the times at which observations were to be made.

Martin and Ackoff (1963) looked in detail at a study of the reading habits by the self-observation method; 300 chemists and 400 physicists recorded 30,000 observations of themselves. The participants carried alarm clocks during all waking hours for the fourteen consecutive days of the study. The alarms were sounded at random intervals at an average of 3.5 times per day. If a sounding occurred whilst the participant was reading a scientific journal, the participant noted down what he was reading by checking off a form.

2.3.3 *Operations research study*

An operations research method was used by Halbert and Ackoff (1959) to study the dissemination of information. Chemists were observed at random times during the day and the time spent on various activities was calculated. Another operations research and systems engineering study, this time of a university library, is reported by Johns Hopkins University (1963).

2.3.4 *Some unconventional methods*

The majority of studies have relied upon structured or semi-structured methods. An alternative method allows the user to comment spontaneously upon information services, his work or his requirements. This unstructured approach allows the user to highlight the areas of concern to him, uninfluenced by the investigator's questions.[5] Both structured and unstructured methods have their pitfalls: the more structured methods obviously highlight the areas that the investigator deems to be of importance and thereby run the risk of obtaining data (albeit reliable and sound) about those aspects of the information system that are of peripheral interest and concern to the user. Conversely, the unstructured approaches run the risk of obtaining a good deal of data that is of immediate interest to a single user, but that has minimal applicability to other users. Also personal grouses and completely irrelevant comments are more likely to be collected by this method, and the cost of processing—transcribing and tabulating—this type of material is great. Very personal and idiosyncratic material is irrelevant, and must be avoided.

Biographical and autobiographical works can be a source of information, uncontaminated by investigators' questions, about the way in which scientists work, the use they make of formal and informal channels of communication, etc. A recent example of interest is Watson's (1968) memoir of two years' pursuit of the molecular structure of DNA. Paisley (1968) suggests that information scientists will find that Watson's low-key account of conversations, letters, and international meetings presents a different picture of information use from the picture gained by enquiries using questionnaires. In such autobiographical accounts the writer structures his activities and presents a large amount of detail that may not be covered by the more formal methods of interrogation. However, there are a number of disadvantages: the subjectivity of the material, misleading emphases, and even the deliberate distortion. There is also the problem of generalisation. An idiosyncratic account, however detailed and interesting, will be of little use for institutions intending to design and implement new information systems, or improve existing systems.

---

[5]An example of a very unstructured approach is the method used by the American Society for Metals Documentation Service Conference, reported by Hyslop and Chafe (1967), where delegates at the conference offered their critical opinions and evaluations of the service provided, and suggested possible improvements. The best of both the unstructured and the structured methods can be combined in a single investigation. This was done by Parker (1967) who combined a secondary analysis of previously collected questionnaire data (from Libbey and Zaltman, 1967) with tape-recorded depth interviews of essentially the same population.

Other material about the way in which scientists work, and about the conditions (including the information) that are optimal for creative and inventive activity, comes directly from studies of creativity and inventiveness. However, the payoff from such sources for information scientists may be small unless the gap between one researcher and another is fairly narrow, and unless generalisations can be made.

The field of advertising and marketing, although well outside the domain of the information scientist, is another form of user study: the study of the preferences and needs of consumers. It is the goal of consumer research to produce new goods and modify existing goods and packages in a way that will encourage consumption of them. In short, marketing consists of (1) finding out what people really want, and (2) getting them to buy what there is to sell.

Pemberton (1969) suggests that publication programmes for social science material reflect to some extent demands that are emerging in the social sciences. Pemberton points to the microfilming of the *Annual Abstract of Statistics* from 1940–1950 by Micro Methods Limited, and the reprinting of *Documents on International Affairs* and the *Statesman's Yearbook* as indicators of a demand for official and quasi-official material. Obviously publication programmes are very inaccurate guides to demands. Publication programmes may be anticipatory, or responsive (after delay), to demands.

2.4 Evaluation of methods

The two basic aspects of evaluation involve measures of reliability and validity. Reliability is a measure of the degree to which the results on subsequent occasions match the results of previous studies when the population and the method are the same. In theory it is relatively easy to assess reliability, although it may involve some difficult technical problems (e.g. finding matched populations of users).

One of the few studies of reliability was reported by Shaw (1956). 105 participants were given a personal data form to complete as well as diary forms on which technical reading and library use were recorded. Each participant recorded the age of documents read, amount of time spent reading, and method of obtaining consulted documents. Shaw concluded that even with good co-operation and supervision the diary method was not reliable enough to justify further studies over extended periods of time. Over short periods the diary method could be recommended.

The measurement of validity is much more difficult. The object of user studies is the assessment of information demands, or requirements, or needs, or some combination of these three. In the absence of some objective criterion for the measurement of demand, or requirement, or need, a measure of validity is impossible. A method is valid in so far as it is a measure of the object measured.

Where comparisons between methods have been attempted[6] it is usual to find that different results are forthcoming. It is difficult to know if the results reflect merely the different methods or real differences. The advantages and disadvantages of the different methods have been enumerated[7] but in the absence of some external invariant criteria an absolute evaluation of methods is not possible.

The evaluation of user studies is discussed in 2.7.

2.5 Problems of sampling

User studies can normally draw upon only a small number from the target population. Where the object of the investigation is to make generalisations from the sample to the target population a representative sample must be drawn. But it is not sufficient to ensure that the sampling frame includes a representative sample of users. It is also necessary to ensure that states of research, types of data, types of information usage, channels of communication, and types of user behaviour are adequately represented in the sampling frame.[8] The problems of sampling encountered by user studies are basically similar to the problems of sampling encountered in social science research, and the reader is referred to the numerous relevant references in psychology, statistics, and experimental design.

Some idea of the problems involved in drawing samples can be seen

---

[6]For example, a survey by interview and diary cards of scientists at the Atomic Energy Research Establishment, Harwell (reported by Dannatt, 1967) showed that the diary card method was more successful than the interview in quantifying the relative importance of various sources of information in research. Hertz and Rubenstein (1953) used three methods in their investigations: questionnaire, interview and direct observation. The INFROSS investigation (see Line, 1969a) is using two methods—questionnaire and interview—with the same population. Wuest (1965) compared the questionnaire with other techniques, using the same population.

[7]See Jahoda (1966) and Wuest (1965).

[8]Menzel (1960, 1964) considers sampling problems, the comparability of data from different studies, and the general usefulness of the results of investigations.

from a breakdown of users by environment. Line (1969a) suggests that users can come from one of seven different environments: (1) academic institutions; (2) research organisations; (3) industry; (4) government; (5) professional associations; (6) trade unions and political parties; and (7) the press and broadcasting. Line also classified users according to eight functions: (1) research; (2) teaching and training; (3) management; (4) social work and administration; (5) the press and broadcasting; (6) politics; (7) business and commerce; (8) study and learning. Line's classification is specifically orientated to social science users. It serves to show the difficulties that face any investigation that attempts to sample any but a very tightly defined group (e.g. psychologists employed as college of education lecturers). In this example the problem of sampling is minimal. College of education lecturers as a category are self-explanatory, their function is teaching (as opposed to management, politics, or business) and their environment is an academic institution. The representativeness of a sample of such persons can be ensured by obtaining a list of all college of education lecturers. If an investigation attempts to study psychologists,

---

[9]A good example of the feasibility of classifying users according to their research (including information seeking) activities was reported by Mote (1962), who was able to differentiate groups of users according to their activities. This grouping was related to different information requirements. For example, in a group of researchers looking for the structure and method of synthesis of complex organic polymers, underlying principles were well developed: the literature was well organised and the width of the subject well defined. But in another group, studying the application of a lubricant, the study cut across chemistry and physics in an engineering environment, and the literature was not organised within discipline boundaries. Mote also identified a third group of researchers in which there was no organisation of the literature to speak of at all and in which the researcher approximated to the description offered by Bernal (1957) where the scientist does not know what information he wants, or enough to pinpoint his subject to make use of existing indexes. Further he does not know if information exists on the subject, or even that he really needs such information. Many social scientists may recognise this as a familiar picture, and the few user studies that have appeared in the social sciences suggest that social scientists may be closer, in respect to their information requirements, to Mote's third type of researcher than to the others.

[10]Slater (1963), for example, surveyed fourteen industrial libraries and found six main groups of users—working scientist, technician, administrative/executive, technical/executive, non-scientific specialist, and clerical/secretarial. These groups were differentiated by their use of libraries and their information requirements. Another approach contrasts researchers in basic research with applied scientists and/or technologists (e.g. Bernal, 1957; Flowers, 1965; Hanson, 1964).

[11]A discussion of some of the factors affecting response rate can be found in Champion and Sear (1969) who emphasise the effect of type of postage, length of questionnaire, and incentive of respondents as factors determining response rate. In general the more expensive type of postage increases response rate

or social scientists, the problems of obtaining a representative sample are much greater.

Sampling frames are best drawn in the presence of details about the target population(s). Users can be classified by environment, as in Line's analysis, by the type of work/environment (e.g. administration, research laboratory), by subject of research (e.g. chemistry, physics, sociology), or a finer classification by subject speciality (e.g. chemical engineering, research into polymers, research in solid state physics). Other classifications are by research activity[9] and type of researcher.[10]

Whatever attention is paid to sampling frames, the representativeness of the sample (and thereby the general usefulness of the results) is determined by the response rate[11]. Low response rates, especially where no attempt is made to follow up nonrespondents, make the generalisation of the results of user studies unwarranted. It is unfortunate that so many studies, characterised by a meticulous attention to detail and statistical analysis, have failed to obtain high response rates.[12]

Another technical aspect of user enquiry, and one that affects the representativeness of the results of enquiries, is the distribution of users'

(Kephart and Bressler, 1958). There is considerable inconsistency in the literature (see Wallace, 1954) regarding the effect of hand-stamped letters on response rate. Gullahorn and Gullahorn (1959) reported that the use of special delivery postage is worth the additional expense in eliciting responses from individuals who have not acknowledged any previous correspondence. Various incentives have been used to increase response rates but there is little agreement as to the effectiveness of a given incentive upon response rate (Levine and Gerald, 1958; Bevis, 1948; Greenberg and Manfield, 1957; Roeher, 1963). The effect of length of questionnaire upon response rate has been studied. Goode and Hatt (1952) reported a negative relationship between length and response rate, but Sletto (1940) found that length was not related to response rate when the respondents were university alumni. Champion and Sear (1969) found that nine-page questionnaires were returned significantly more often than three-page questionnaires in a survey of attitudes about various aspects of programmes sponsored by the National Aeronautics and Space Administration, where the target population was drawn from city directories. Champion and Sear noted that the relationship between questionnaire length and response rate is complex. ' . . . the effect of questionnaire length needs to be more systematically explored, while holding constant such factors as socioeconomic status, type of cover letter, and postage. It is quite apparent that blanket generalisations with regard to questionnaire length are, at this point, at least, unwarranted. We are inclined to agree with previous researchers who contend that special postage is preferred over bulk postage. And lastly, we feel that to maximise response rate, the researcher ought to gear his cover letter accordingly, depending upon the SES (schooling and socioeconomic status) of the target of this survey.' (Champion and Sear, 1969, p. 339).

[12]It is quite surprising that results have been presented when response rates have fallen as low as 20 per cent. For example, Groenman and Riesthuis (1967) circulated a questionnaire to 600 participants at the Congress of the International Union for the Scientific Study of the Population held at Belgrade in September 1965. They obtained a response rate of only 20 per cent.

behaviour. It is rarely recognised, Curnow (1968) points out, that little attention has been paid to the highly skewed nature of the distribution of users' behaviour; for example, that 10 per cent of the users of a given system account for 90 per cent of its output, and that 15 per cent of a given literature field may be cited by 75 per cent of all publications in that field. Curnow's observation is not entirely accurate. Although empirical user studies have rarely paid attention to the skewed nature of users' behaviour, a good deal is known about the skewed distribution of citations, etc., and it is argued in chapter 4 that user studies could with advantage be integrated with such studies because studies of the statistics of literature give some indication about information requirements.

User studies must be judged with these considerations in mind. Those that recognise, delineate, define, and systematically sample their target populations are to be judged in a more favourable light than studies that ignore problems of sampling and definition.[13]

2.6 Psychological and environmental variables[14] related to information needs and uses

Demographic (e.g. age, education, background, length of experience in research) and psychological (e.g. motivation, intelligence, extraversion) variables may well be related to information requirements, needs and uses. From the point of view of the information scientist it is necessary to know the variables that influence information seeking activities, and that must be taken into account in the design of information systems. If studies of users (of information) can be integrated[15] with a more general body of knowledge (e.g. psychological theory) then so much the better, but the primary concern must be with the information system. In the long term a theory of user behaviour may be developed; but this possibility is a long way ahead. There has been

---

[13]Good planning and methodology do not always ensure adequate sampling: pilot studies may be required. For example, the INFROSS investigation (see Bath University of Technology, 1968) included, in its preliminary stage, an enquiry in the British Library of Political and Economic Science to help establish whether any significant category of social science user had not already been identified. One substantial group of users (the Press and Broadcasting) of social science information, not already included in the planning of the investigation, was identified by this empirical survey.

[14]In the experimental setting, variables may be classified as dependent or independent. The independent variable is the one that is manipulated in order to establish the relationship the independent variable(s) has to the dependent variable. For example, from the area of animal experimentation, a classic experimental design would look at the relationship between hunger (independent

little work on the identification of individual differences (as opposed to group differences) in users' behaviour. Information scientists must know about such behaviour because inter individual variations may necessitate the inclusion of certain features in the design of information systems. It is possible that interindividual variations in information seeking and information using behaviour (e.g. assimilation capacity, 'threshold of intake') may be so great that any system, if it is to be viable, must take them into account.

Bourne (1962a) suggests that a study of user requirements must include reference to the psychology of the user. Aspects of user psychology, according to Bourne, include: (1) the search time that can be tolerated; (2) the amount of irrelevant material that can be tolerated; (3) time available for retrospective searching; (4) the preferred form of the search product; (5) user's input channel capacity; (6) work habits; (7) terminological idiosyncrasies; (8) prior knowledge of reference tools and information systems; and (9) user's judgements about the comfortableness of the physical aspects of the information system.

Line (1969a, p. 9) has stressed the importance of including individual variables in studies of information gathering and seeking behaviours. He enumerates fifteen characteristics that may influence information requirements and needs: (1) age; (2) experience in research, in a particular job; (3) background, qualification; (4) seniority; (5) whether solitary or team workers; (6) persistence; (7) thoroughness; (8) orderliness; (9) motivation; (10) independence, willingness to accept help from others; (11) breadth of approach; (12) a measure of information threshold which may be limited by factors of absolute capacity and rate of absorption; (13) awareness of sources of published information; (14) awareness of non-literary media of communication or means of storage; (15) languages understood. As Line points out this list does not exhaust the individual and personality variables that may influence

---

variable) and maze learning (dependent variable). Various levels of hunger (perhaps defined as the number of hours of food deprivation) would be imposed upon the experimental subjects and the effects upon maze learning observed. Strictly speaking, it is incorrect to use the terminology of the controlled experimental design in observational studies and surveys. In the observation study it is possible to demonstrate a connection between two variables (e.g. distance travelled to library and frequency of usage) but not usually possible to establish a causative connection from such a correlational study. Before the direction and extent of causation in such a relationship can be established it is necessary first to control and manipulate the variables involved. This is usually not possible in social settings.

15One of the few discussions of the place of user studies in a general body of knowledge about behaviour can be found in Cavanagh (1967).

information needs or uses. Line suggests that some of these variables may be related to existing theories about the structure of personality. For example, that persistence, thoroughness, and orderliness may be related to the introversion/extraversion dimension or the neuroticism/ stability dimension; breadth of approach to the convergence/ divergence dimension; and the capacity to absorb information to intelligence.

Where empirical studies[16]—and there are very few—have included individual and environmental variables they have done so in a piecemeal way. A few studies[17] in science and technology have attempted to identify psychological and organisational factors in scientific performance, but in the main they have been concerned more with productivity than with information seeking and using behaviour.

Information scientists have almost completely ignored the possible reinforcement of users. Reinforcement is a well explored area of human behaviour and an information system is well placed to apply reinforcement. Commentators on the academic scene have implicitly assumed that researchers have enough motivation to carry them through the mass of material which any information system can provide. The sources of reinforcement in academic activity are not well understood. At each step in the use of an information system there exists the possibility that the user is receiving negative reinforcement (in which case he will be less likely to repeat the operation again), positive reinforcement (in which case he will be more likely to repeat the operation again) or no reinforcement (in which case the information system will have little

---

[16]For example, Rosenberg (1967) reported that preference for information-gathering methods correlated significantly with ease of use, but not with amount of information expected. Allen and Gerstberger (1967) showed that frequency of library use is related to the distance of the library from place of work or place of residence.

[17]A survey by Smith (1966) of 418 scientists and engineers found that five sets of variables provided substantial predictions of scientific performance. The five sets of variables were: (1) group composition; (2) group age; (3) inter-member processes of consultation; (4) the scientist's role in decision-making; (5) organisational structural variables, consisting of information flow and communication practices, and the influence these variables exerted in decision-making. Pelz and Andrews (1962) looked at the relationship between organisational atmosphere, motivation, and contributions to research, and Pelz (1956) at social factors related to performance in a research organisation. Factors associated with creativity are discussed by Shapiro (1968), and economic and social factors associated with the rate and direction of inventive activity are mentioned in a report of the United States National Bureau of Economic Research (1962). Pelz and Andrews (1966a, 1966b) report the results of a five-year study of scientific performance in industrial, governmental and university laboratories.

effect upon future behaviour; this will be determined by other forces outside the information system).

It is not enough for an information system to provide the user with the required goods, irrespective of the means used to achieve this end. The means are very important. During the course of the provision or the material there may be thousands of contingencies open for reinforcement. In fact, nearly every conceivable variable in an information system can be the occasion—the heating and lighting of a library or computer centre, the format of the output, the typography and layout of the text, the physical attractiveness of books, the personnel dispensing the goods and services, the cost of the service, the distance travelled, the time required for retrieval. This list is by no means exhaustive. It would obviously require a mammoth research effort to obtain useful data, but when it is considered that there are hundreds of thousands of users performing hundreds of thousands of operations every day in libraries, research laboratories, and institutions, the problem is well worth considering.

A complete knowledge of an information system can be gained only when all the variables that are part of the system have been investigated. It is important to explore all the variables in order to know which are: (1) relevant, and (2) of practical applicability to the design of information systems. Methodology in information science is still not very well developed and the majority of studies have employed low-powered methods that are little more than observational studies. The controlled experiment, in which all the variables except the one under investigation are controlled, has received little attention.

2.7 Evaluation of user studies

Some of the technical points relating to the reliability and value of methods found in user studies are considered in 2.4. Questions about the validity of the results of user studies pose much greater problems, because a measure of validity is always an integral part of a general body of knowledge. In the absence of generally accepted theories in information science, assessments of validity are especially difficult.

2.7.1 *Rationalisation of methods*

If the results of user studies are to be implemented they must be capable of accumulation and synthesis, as well as having general applicability. And this will require a degree of compatibility between various studies that does not now exist. It is likely that most new information systems, for economic reasons, will either be national or extracted from national systems for local use, and for this reason alone the results of user studies should have general as well as local applicability.

Barnes (1965), examining the common ground between several surveys,[18] showed that while the results were not inexplicably contradictory, differences in principle and method made it impossible to demonstrate any close agreement. He suggested that further surveys could with advantage be designed to include a few features with a deliberate and carefully planned relationship to earlier surveys, so that a few valid comparisons could be made. A slightly different position is taken by Paisley (1968) who draws attention to the advantages of an eclectic methodology[19] and the multi-method approach that has an internal check against biases introduced by the methods themselves, and Herner and Herner (1967) who point to the paucity of techniques in user studies.

In the attempt to rationalise methods it is sometimes forgotten that a variety of types of users, environments, stages of research, and types of information requirements (i.e. demands, needs, wants, expressed and unexpressed) have to be studied. It is unlikely that any single method would be appropriate for the assessment of all these aspects of information seeking and using behaviours. If a rationalisation of methods is ever achieved, it is likely that it will come about only after information scientists have a better understanding of the objects of their investigations.

The rationalisation of methods alone would not ensure a unified body of knowledge. Herner and Herner (1967), for example, suggest that user studies have failed to build on past gains and to profit by past mistakes, and point to an absence of rigorous experimental designs.

2.7.2   User studies in context

Paisley (1968) suggests that the time has come to view the information-seeking and information-using scientist within the context of the total work and social situation. Paisley points out that a scientist may be

---

[18]That is, those conducted by Martyn (1964a), Fishenden (1959), Barnes (1964), the National Lending Library for Science and Technology (reported by Urquhart, 1965), and the Advisory Committee on Scientific Policy (1965).

[19]The multiple operationism of Webb et al. (1966) is cited by Paisley as an example of eclectic methodology.

considered within: (1) his culture; (2) a political system; (3) a membership group; (4) a reference group; (5) an invisible college; (6) a formal organisation; (7) a work team; (8) his own head; (9) a legal/economic system; and (10) a formal information system. Such a conceptual system provides a meaningful organisation of the large number of variables that can play a part in information seeking, gathering, and using activities. Within any of these systems a large number of both independent and dependent variables can be identified and studied. A similar suggestion is made by Borko (1968).

2.7.3 *Some theoretical considerations*

Some have doubted the validity, as well as the use and value, of user studies. For example, Taube (1958) questions the rationale behind user studies. He maintains that an information service is a professional service (such as medicine) as opposed to a consumer service (such as the packaging of a breakfast food), and that user studies cannot provide a measure of effectiveness, or a guide to the design of information systems. A similar dissatisfaction with user studies is expressed by Shaw (1959) who questions their utility as a firm basis for planning communication systems. He maintains that there is a great variation in the assumptions underlying different studies, and an inadequate statement of methodological problems and interpretations.

There is also doubt about the ability of users to express needs as opposed to information requirements. Rees (1963), Menzel (1964), Line (1968a, 1969a), and others have noted that the user may be in no position to specify completely his information requirements. It is argued by these writers that the user is able to give a rough guide to types and sources of information that he uses for research and teaching, but even here he often comes up with vague generalisations and is unable (perhaps sometimes unwilling) to relate the details of his information searches and information uses. The investigator can probe and stimulate the researcher in an attempt to elicit further details. The user may not be able to recall past activities in great detail, but he may be able to recognise them if they are suggested by the investigator.

It may not always be sufficient to use a retrospective method (e.g. interviews or questionnaires, after the event). It may be necessary to explore, with the scientist, his day to day work. This has been attempted; and the methods that have been used include diary and tape recordings of day to day activities. A short-cut method—the critical incident technique—has also been tried. These methods place a large burden of responsibility upon the user for completeness and accuracy; and this cannot always be assumed. These methods are therefore essentially unreliable, as well as difficult to operate and time consuming.

Most studies have done no more than look at the demands made upon information services, and the conscious requirements of users, by questionnaire and interview. Very little progress has been made in the study of information needs, which include, according to Menzel (1967), not only the information that users are aware of wanting, not even the information that would be good for them, but also the information that would be good for the progress of scientific research. No satisfactory, reliable and objective method has been used, or even proposed, that could be used to assess information needs. Menzel (1964) suggests that information needs can be defined only in association with developing knowledge which will be gained by a study of the experience of scientists in receiving and using information. All the information gathering habits of the scientist must be carefully examined.

Coover (1969) criticises the usual methods because they have been technique-centred: that is, they have put the method before the problem. In a developed field (e.g. element analysis by chromatography) this is very acceptable. The value of methods has been assessed over long periods, and new scientists, as well as experienced scientists coming to a new field for the first time, can afford to take on trust the existing body of knowledge. In information science this is not possible at the present time. Menzel (1964) has been careful to avoid a premature acceptance of existing methods of user studies. He stresses the importance of the unit of observation (along with all the variables that might affect information needs), and this raises again the question of the relationship of user studies to the body of information science.

One final point on the question of evaluation. There are a number of assumptions (often implicit) underlying investigations of information requirements and needs, and little has been written about them. For example, investigators usually proceed with a set of implicit assumptions about the rational and ordered nature of the behaviour of scientists. The same assumption is implicit in the design and operation of existing information services and aids—indexes, bibliographies, abstracting journals, and guides to the literature. These bibliographic tools, as well as the more recent services of information officers and selective dissemination services, usually assume that the information-seeking activities of researchers progress by a series of well-ordered and logical steps, from the initial introduction to the literature that is assumed to be obtained through guides, working steadily and systematically through all available bibliographical tools until, at some predictable point in the future, the researcher is in possession of all the information that is required for his work. The creation of a straw-man must be avoided.

2.8 Summary

From a methodological point of view the field of user studies is weak. A few methods have been used frequently (e.g. survey techniques). Many methods have been introduced, but used very infrequently. Few methods have been introduced to meet the special problems of user enquiry; and where such methods have been introduced they have arisen in the context of user enquiries that are required for the design of information systems and their evaluation. Nearly all methods that are found in user studies have been lifted, without much modification, from other disciplines and areas—especially from the field of social survey.

Contributions to methodology from user studies in the social sciences are non-existent; and investigations in the social sciences have necessarily had to make use of existing methods in user studies in science and technology.

The development of an adequate methodology goes hand in hand with theoretical developments, and until information science has an acceptable theoretical backing it is unlikely that a fully fledged methodology will exist. It will be possible, in the absence of good theory, to introduce new methods and to improve existing ones, but the satisfactory evaluation of the results of user studies must wait upon advances in theory.

CHAPTER THREE

Studies in the Social Sciences

3.1 General and conceptual

In the present chapter empirical studies of user information needs and requirements will be mentioned in some detail, but first it is appropriate to bring together certain theoretical writings that have a bearing on the nature, organisation, and use of social science information. In general, user studies in the social sciences, like their counterparts in the sciences, have been carried out in the absence of conceptual frameworks, although Kochen (1969) maintains that a new discipline is in the making and that user studies will form a part of this discipline: so it is possible that the state of theoretical poverty will not continue.

Theoretical writings about the nature of social science research are widely scattered throughout the literature: some of this material is brought together in 3.1.1. There are also some theoretical writings in the established area of documentation (particularly the classification of social science literature) and this work is mentioned in 3.1.2. And finally, in 3.1.3, it is seen that discussions about the application of the results of social science research have involved some fundamental questions about the nature and aims of the social sciences.

3.1.1 *Nature of social science research and literature*

Questions about the nature of social science research and literature are fundamental to assessments of information needs and requirements. Social scientists themselves have been very prolific in writing about the nature of social science research; and have usually been very occupied—perhaps self-consciously so—with the status of the social sciences as scientific disciplines. Many other contributions[1] have come from

---

[1]Contributions from the philosophy of science are numerous and cannot be summarised here. Two examples may be given of the type of problem attacked: discussions about individualistic *v.* societal methodologies in Mandelbaum (1955), Gellner and Lucas (1956), and Watkins (1957); and the nature of generalisation, and the ideological and normative problems that are peculiar to the social sciences are discussed by Northrop (1947, especially chapters 14, 15 and 16).

philosophers of science, although very often the social sciences have been mentioned only as contrasting disciplines. Both social scientists and philosophers of science have seen the social sciences as the poor (but developing) brothers of the physical sciences.

By far and away the greatest demand for information made by scientists is for the archival collections of serial publications, supplemented (as has more recently been shown) by unpublished reports and a variety of informal contacts and interchanges.[2] In science the serial paper remains the key medium for the construction of the archives of science: it is the vehicle used to establish private property of ideas and experiments; it forms the body of material to which any scientist can turn to acquaint himself with the accumulated knowledge that exists (an activity that must precede new research and enquiry); and certain parts of this archive (i.e. textbooks) are used in the instruction of subsequent generations of scientists. But social science disciplines (perhaps psychology apart) do not use their own archival collections in the same way. In science the researcher is primarily concerned with obtaining information about the research activities of other scientists, the results of research, and theoretical and conceptual developments; either by the informal network of personal contacts and pre-publication papers or through the formal system of published documents. In the social sciences the results of experiments and the published writings of other social scientists do constitute, especially in psychology, an appreciable amount of the total information available and required; but there are a number of other types of data that do not find a parallel in science. Some of the types of data that are specific to the social sciences may be generated, and collected, outside the confines of the social science disciplines (e.g. institutional data, historical archives, court records, tax returns, school records, birth and death records) for purposes unrelated to social science research. Data that is generated by researchers themselves form only a small proportion of the information required by social scientists. Of all the social sciences psychology comes closest to scientific disciplines in its information requirements.

In one sense the social sciences are distinguished from the sciences in that they can extract from, and use, raw data of almost any kind. When

---

[2]Falling outside these communications that are central to the scientific information system is information about apparatus availability and construction. A different set of contacts and behaviours may be required here, although there is bound to be a large degree of overlap with the system that transmits the results of experiments and theoretical writings.

attempts are made to collect and store data for use by social scientists problems of representativeness and inclusiveness are encountered. The simple solution, although it may be uneconomical, maintains the total amount of data ever collected intact, and thereby potentially retrievable. When this is undertaken and centralised (sometimes by national directive) the resulting system is a data bank.[3] A data bank collects survey data from academic, commercial, and governmental sources, in order to make it available for further analysis. The storage of institutional data also represents a data bank, although in this case especially, decisions have to be made about quantity and delimitation. There is a very extensive amount of institutional data, even if coverage is restricted to a single country. How many records should be retained? How long a run? How extensive should the cover be? Because national policies have only recently entertained the idea of centralising institutional data this area is not well developed.

Some idea of the range of material that is potentially of use to social science research can be gained from the eight[4] types of data specific to the social sciences enumerated by Madge (1953). They include: (1) personal documents, including letters, folklore, life histories, auto-biographies, diaries and letters; (2) records, including records of professional societies, committee records, government reports; (3) reports that are made after an event, e.g. newspaper reports; (4) observations, including mass observation where the investigator may penetrate into the environment he is observing; (5) data from 'action research'

---

[3]There has been a good deal of comment about the growing demand by social scientists for access to the type of material to be found in data banks, but few writers on this subject have mentioned the large number of social data libraries that are already in existence. In the UK the Social Science Research Council Data Bank at the University of Essex is fairly well known but one wonders if the others are so well known. A number of data banks and data archives are mentioned by Grose (1967) and a bibliography and review of the state of the movement has been compiled by Bisco (1966, 1967b). He points out that social science disciplines have in the past used a variety of data-gathering and manipulating tools and methods, much as their counterparts in the physical sciences. Bisco draws attention to the new resource for the social scientist—archives of machine-readable data about social phenomena. Bisco points out that the word 'archives' and such phrases as 'data bank' or 'data repository' have come to be applied to this form of data, and are to some extent used interchangeably. Bisco suggests that data archives have come into being because of: (1) commercial market and survey research organisations; (2) university-based social research institutions; (3) the increasing availability of machine-readable information produced by governments; (4) increasing demand for these data for secondary analysis and teaching purposes, and (5) the computer. Bisco notes that government produced data has always been available in some published form, but it has become accessible in machine-readable form only during the past decade or so. Nasatir (1967) provides a useful list of some of the most prominent social

where the investigator resides in the target area for a period to observe the group life, morale and productivity of a single community with the aim of developing effective ways of resolving social stress and tension and facilitating agreed and desired social change; (6) 'overheard' data from passive observation; (7) data from interviews such as gallup polls, opinion polls, scalogram analyses, and measures of attitude; (8) data from experiments, usually conducted in controlled environments in laboratories.

The United States National Research Council Committee on Information in the Behavioral Sciences (1967) report draws attention to the new types of data (raw data, preferably machine-readable) that have become prominent and are required in economics, political science, demography, geography, and parts of sociology. The report suggests that the newly acquired (computer-based)[5] capacities to manipulate such large masses of data are responsible for this new demand. The most direct use of data involves the computer in statistical analysis of the information. A more recent and growing use involves various forms of 'modelling' or simulation, and here the degree to which such activities are dependent upon raw data is enormously variable, ranging from the simulations of mass political opinion formation, based on very large assemblages of sample survey data, to modelling work that needs to touch base only occasionally. The NRCCIBS report predicts an exponential increase in the demand for data resources, given the spread of interest in quantification across the social sciences. User studies in

---

science data libraries in the United States and Europe. These include: the Bureau of Labour Statistics, the Bureau of the Census, the Roper Public Opinion Research Center, the Inter-university Consortium for Political Research, the International Data Library and Reference Service, the Social Systems Research Institute, and the Louis Harris Political Data Center in the United States; DATUM in West Germany; the Social and Economic Archive Committee (UK); the Steinmetz Institute (Netherlands); and the Zentralarchiv für Empirische Sozialforschung (West Germany). The proceedings of 1964 Paris Conference on 'Data Archives for the Social Sciences' are edited by Rokkan (1966). An information retrieval service in political science, the Inter-university Consortium for Political Research system, is discussed by Bisco (1964). In this system information is retrieved from data archives. The use of data banks in educational research is discussed by Denum (1960).

[4]Another type of data, not included by Madge, is mentioned by Garvin (1967): nontextual data, a type of data used especially in social psychology and psychiatry. Examples of nontextual data include gestural movements, facial expressions, folklore and psychiatric interviews. Garvin discusses the problem of storage and retrieval of such data. It is usually very extensive especially when subject-produced as in an interview, and it is non-repeatable.

[5]See also Pool, McIntosh and Griffel (1969) on the design of computer-based information systems.

social science, drawing upon the past body of user studies in science for their methodology, must take care to orientate the new studies to the type of data to be found in the social sciences. It would be very easy to adopt the methods of user enquiry prominent in science, and to concentrate upon published material, thereby neglecting important sources of social science material. In science the problem revolves around the flow of information (formal and published, or informal and perhaps undigested) from one scientist (or group of scientists) to another. Psychology is the only discipline in the social sciences that approximates to this model of information flow—where the data is generated within the discipline itself by experiment.

If it were only a matter of a very extensive scattering of social science information, perhaps across unusual sources, the classification and retrieval of information, as well as the fulfilment of information needs and requirements, would be relatively simple—at least in theory. But there is considerable disagreement, both amongst social scientists themselves and commentators upon the social science scene, about the nature of social science research, about the way in which knowledge and information accumulates and about the value and application of the results of research.[6] The only agreement appears to be a belief that social science material differs in some fundamental aspect from the material of the natural sciences. If this is the case it leads, as Kyle (1960a, 1960b) points out, to some important differences in the manner in which social scientists use the literature, the way they want it organised, and their information needs and requirements. Classification and retrieval systems extracted from the physical sciences and applied with the minimum of change to the social sciences will not do.

Very often attempts to analyse the nature of social science research

---

[6]There is also the assumption (often implicit) that the social sciences are (or will be) of value in the solution or amelioration of social problems. It is rarely suggested that the nature of social science material is ephemeral, topical, and of passing or historical interest only; and that the products of social science research cannot accumulate to form the building blocks of a science. Suggestions that social science has very limited values and applications are obviously un-palatable to most social scientists. Zetterberg (1963), for example, maintains that sociological material in business functions only to reduce anxiety: it takes part in a ritual where the decisions are made before the entry of the sociologist. The sociologist is a palliative. The ritual is needed because although the outcome is unaffected by his appearance the participants feel more comfortable about the decision than they would have felt in his absence. In the field of social planning Rein (1969) suggests that value-free social science research, capable of probing the etiology of social problems and presenting programmes for action based upon fact rather than ideology, can provide a basis for legitimacy of action. Where the information is used solely as a basis for legitimacy of policies already

and literature have done so by comparing the social sciences with the natural sciences.[7] This comparison is inevitable, albeit a rather false one, when there is only one 'standard': but in so doing the social sciences may be seen as the 'poor' and undeveloped brothers of the natural sciences when, at the outset, the assumption is made that the characteristics of science (e.g. the 'hardness' of the data, the operational definition) are valuable, and necessary prerequisites for all academic and practical pursuits. Maybe these are enduring characteristics of 'good' or 'successful' scientific practice but they cannot, *ipso facto*, be used to characterise or evaluate social science activities. Furthermore, science, as Kuhn (1959)[8] points out, has not always followed the methods and practices that are now acceptable. If a digression is taken to explore the nature of social science research and its literature it is not done in order to make unfavourable comparison with accepted (and proved) practices in science. It is to show that such differences that do exist will affect the demands for, and the use of, information.

It is only during this century that the social sciences have evolved as distinct and separate disciplines. During their period of growth they have all been characterised by a movement[9] away from speculation and unfounded subjective opinion to a method of enquiry that approximates to that of science.

In psychology the use of empirical data was in evidence from the earlist times. Psychology emerged in the last quarter of the 19th century from a fusion of German physiology and British empirical philosophy. The early workers in the field, really only retrospectively labelled as psychologists, included the physiologists Wundt, Helmholtz and Fechner. Even in comparison with the activities of present day psychologists their use of empirical data was very apparent. Although

---

made it has a very low-powered role, and one very similar to the sociologist in Zetterberg's example. But even in cases where social science research has been used as a basis for decision making and action, Rein (1969, p. 239) maintains that 'the contribution of value-free social science information to the development of social policy has been greatly oversold'.

[7]It is the social scientists themselves that have been attracted to the methods of the natural sciences. As Northrop (1947, p. 273/4) observes: 'Impressed by the success of the natural sciences, the social scientists hastily and uncritically assumed that the whole of social science can be put upon a scientific basis by applying the method of natural science to social facts . . . Scientific inquiry in any field must begin not with some method taken over *a priori* from some other field, but with the character of the problems of its own field and the analysis of these problems. A subject becomes scientific not by beginning with facts, with hypothesis or with some pet method . . . but by beginning with the peculiar character of its particular problems'.

their conceptual superstructure (introspectionism) would be un-
acceptable to present day psychologists, their methods of empirical
research would be acceptable.

M. H. Harris (1967) has pointed out that the behaviouristic approach
is relatively recent in political science research. According to Harris
the new approach is characterised by: (1) a rejection of political institutions as the basic unit for research in favour of a concentration upon the
behaviour of individuals in political situations; (2) an emphasis upon the
unity of political science with the other social sciences; (3) an emphasis
upon the methods for the collection, classification, and analysis of
data, with the use of statistical and other quantitative techniques; and
(4) a redirection of the goal of research in political science to construct
a systematic, empirically-based theory. In terms of these activities the
two basic categories of data are documentary sources (including all
published sources of information on legislative bodies and their
behaviour) and original sources (including all information obtained
through surveys, polls, personal interviews and questionnaires). This
emphasis upon the use of original sources of data has required the
establishment of data archives, where source materials are brought
together and made available. Janda (1968), for example, presents a
strong case for the use of computer-based retrieval systems in political
science, and argues that the data required by researchers in political
science is more suited to computer-based handling systems than the
data required by some of the other social sciences—a point of view that

---

[8]Kuhn mentions that from remote antiquity until the end of the 17th century
there was no single set of paradigms for the study of physical optics. Instead,
many men advanced a large number of different views about the nature of light.
Some of these views found few adherents, but a number of them gave rise to
continuing schools of optical thought.

[9]Changing patterns of publication give some objective data about the nature
of change of disciplines with time, but it is not possible to know the direction
and causative connection in this relationship: it is only possible to observe that
there is a connection between the publication trends in a discipline and the
changing emphasis that takes place. Louttit (1957a) suggested that during the
twenty-five years preceding 1957 there had been an increasing emphasis in
psychology on the social aspects of behaviour, including attention to socially
deviant behaviour, and in the application of psychology to a variety of problems.
Louttit maintained that this supposed pattern would be reflected in the literature
of psychology. He examined the sixty-one year period between 1894 and 1954.
It was seen that during this period a focusing of attention had taken place in
psychology: a focusing upon English as the chief language of publication, and
upon the psychology journal as the accepted place for publication. During this
period the proportion of publications in English steadily increased: the proportion of the literature in the French and German languages decreased from 1905,
and the proportion of articles published in 'other languages', absolutely very

would have sounded strange a few years ago. A case for data-based research in international politics is argued by Singer and his colleagues (1969).

There has undoubtedly been a movement, in all the social sciences, away from speculation and unfounded theory towards data-based research and experimentation. This movement has been apparent in psychology (i.e. behaviourism) since the beginning of the century. Similar movements appeared in the other social sciences by degrees, and political science is perhaps the last of the social sciences to see a great upsurge in the demand for data-based theory and empirical research. These new approaches have created new and pressing demands for information: some of the information has always been required (and available) to social scientists, but other information is now required for the first time.

Information scientists must always be alert to new trends and approaches in the social sciences which may radically alter information demands. It would be easy to concentrate upon those information requirements that appear to be the result of empirically and data-based research: information requirements that have already been established in the sciences and technology. But there are other movements under way. There is a good deal of dissatisfaction with the applicability of the results of social science research (see 3.1.3 and 3.8). As the social sciences have become empirically minded some would maintain that the relevance of research for the applied field has

---

small, showed an increase until 1934, a sharp fall from 1934 until 1944, and a rise again since 1950. From *Psychological Index* and *Psychological Abstracts*, for the period 1894 to 1954, 200 entries were taken at random for every fifth year. A record was made of the subject classification of each entry, the method of publication, the language in which it was written and, for entries from journal articles, the subject field of the journal in which it appeared. During the sixty-one year period entries under 'general', 'physiological', 'receptor function', 'response', and 'abnormal' decreased; but entries under applied fields—'clinical', 'education', 'personnel', 'applied and developmental'—increased. Citations from psychological and educational journals increased: from the fields of psychiatry and biological sciences the number of citations remained fairly constant, and contributions from medicine, general and philosophy decreased. There were wide oscillations, especially under the heading 'higher' and in the number of citations from subject fields of psychiatry and the biological sciences. This makes the prediction of future publication trends in psychology difficult and Louttit did so only tentatively. A straight line is not a good fit in some instances. Louttit did make some speculations: taking the data from 1894 and extrapolating the curve to 1994, 'physiological' will have disappeared and 'response' and 'receptor' will contribute no more than 2 per cent of the total entries between them. The applied fields will together account for 50 per cent of citations: 'clinical' 22 per cent, 'educational' 20 per cent, 'personnel' 6 per cent, and 'applied' 5 per cent.

D

decreased. Various solutions have been proposed (for example, the development of a new breed of social scientists called 'social engineers'). Criticism of existing social science research has come very often from practitioners rather than from those engaged upon basic research. However, Smoker (1969) argues that this dissatisfaction will eventually work its way back to the basic researcher.

Smoker (1969) introduces the idea of postbehaviourism. He suggests that a new breed of social scientists will view with concern the way in which a generation or two of behaviourists have ignored questions of relevance. Smoker maintains that behaviourists have given undue prominence to questions of validity and reliability (i.e. to the technical assessment of their research) and too little attention to the context in which their research takes place and its applicability. Illustrating his argument with the technique of simulation Smoker argues that data-based theories are likely to be theories of past behaviour and the predictions of future behaviour are merely extrapolations of the past into the future. Smoker (1969, p. 13) maintains that 'A different view of global simulations would stress the continuous creation aspect of human behavior in contrast to the steady state theory. This view would argue that data-based theories can imprison alternative futures in perceived pasts'. He suggests that in the future the most desirable should be made the most probable, rather than, as in the past, placing the most desirable into an unattainable Utopian mould.

Smoker does not dismiss, or disagree with, existing empirical approaches in the social sciences: in fact, he predicts that laboratory experimentation will increase. Rather, he suggests that empirical research should be tempered with studies of reality. The criteria used to assess validity should correspond to the experimental environment, so that people may progressively participate directly in the definition and creation of their own futures. 'Using models validated to correspond with realities, and realities validated to correspond with models, man might experience the way it is and create the way it could be. By continually up-dating models and realities, a public dialogue, or more appropriately, a public multilog, between realities and multiple alternative futures could be established.' It is perhaps at the interface (where empirical research has to continually interact with the context in which it is undertaken) that new information requirements will come into being in the social sciences. Perhaps Smoker's most important prediction relates to the demands that an interaction involving public dialogue will make upon information systems. In some areas (e.g. community development, see 3.8.1) a new kind of research in social science does seem to be appearing, where the relevance of any work is assessed by an on-going interaction between those undertaking the research and those at the receiving end of the results of the research. It is perhaps too early to specify in any detail the nature of the information required in this type of research. But it is not too early for information scientists to plan for a possible demand which existing bibliographical services could not meet.

Although something is now known about the types of data that social scientists require, there has been far less discussion about other aspects of social science research. Very few social scientists have written about these problems and it is necessary to turn to the natural sciences. Of the many scientists, and philosophers of science, who have made valuable contributions to the understanding of scientific research the contributions of three—Kuhn, Price, and Storer—are now considered, because they have been interested (unlike some of their colleagues) in the relationships between the sciences, including the social sciences.

Kuhn (1962) identified three kinds of scientific activity: pre-normal, normal, and applied. In pre-normal science there is no agreement on methods and procedures for conducting an enquiry whereas normal science is characterised by a consensus regarding paradigms. Kuhn named physics and chemistry as normal sciences, sociology and political science as pre-normal sciences, and engineering as applied. Clearly, if this theory is valid, there are important implications about the way in which students from different disciplines will use information. In the social sciences students will look for paradigms that match their interest for a particular subject of enquiry. They will need considerable opportunities to browse, and to cover a wide range of literature, both conventional and unconventional. The student in the natural sciences will need, primarily, the standard texts: he will not have the same requirement for access to the most recent research and he will not be interested in unconventional literature.

Kuhn (1959) found evidence for his classification of sciences from an analysis of educational practices, especially the use of textbooks, in the natural sciences. He suggested that the most striking feature in the natural sciences, totally unknown in other creative fields, is the reliance upon textbooks. Typically the undergraduate and graduate student of chemistry, physics, astronomy, geology, or biology acquires the substance of his field from books written especially for students. Kuhn (1959, p. 165) maintains that the student of science 'until he is ready, or very nearly ready, to commence work on his own dissertation . . . is neither asked to attempt trial research projects nor exposed to the immediate products of research done by others, that is, to the professional communications that scientists write for each other. There are no collections of "readings" in the natural sciences. Nor is the science student encouraged to read the historical classics of his field—works in which he might discover other ways of regarding the problems discussed in his textbook, but in which he would also meet problems, concepts, and standards of solution that his future profession has long since disregarded and replaced. In contrast, various textbooks that the student does encounter display different subject matters, rather than, as in many of the social sciences, exemplifying different approaches to a single problem field. Even books that compete for adoption in a single course differ mainly in level and pedagogic detail, not in substance or conceptual structure. Last, but most important of all, is the characteristic technique of textbook presentation. Except in their occasional introductions, science textbooks do not describe the sort of problems that the professional may be asked to solve and the variety of techniques available for their solution. Rather, these books exhibit concrete problem solutions that the profession has come to accept as paradigms and they then ask the student, either with a pencil and paper or in the laboratory, to solve for himself problems very closely in both method and substance to those through which the textbook or the accompanying lecture has led him'. Kuhn maintains that science progresses by a series of ordered and charted steps, as though there is only one world to discover. At various points in time these steps, by their very nature accumulative, are brought together and synthesised in the form of reviews, textbooks, and accepted practices.

When a paradigm exists new knowledge can be evaluated. Material that is worthless or discrepant can be disregarded, and valuable material left to accumulate. In the absence of a paradigm, a discipline must proceed by trial and error, never knowing whether unusual or discrepant research findings are adding to knowledge or side tracking major issues. In the social sciences there is no lack of important problems to study (many come from the practical fields), but it is doubtful, even when problems can be clearly identified, whether much progress will be made until the social sciences have their own paradigm. In the pre-paradigmatic stage the information requirements are particularly difficult to assess, and to meet. But this is not to say that work in a field without a paradigm is worthless. Kuhn (1962) points out that in all fields that now possess and use rigorous methods, important work was done before the achievement of the maturity produced by consensus. But, Kuhn maintains, without a firm concensus, the more flexible practices pursued in applied science which produced the rapid pattern of consequential scientific advance (to which recent centuries have accustomed us) will not be seen in the social sciences. Kuhn sees the social sciences as being largely in a pre-paradigmatic stage of development; and, while not denying the value of some of the work that is now done, would doubt the advancement of knowledge in these fields until such a time as paradigms come into existence.

Another view of science comes from Storer (1967). He attempts to order sciences according to their hardness or softness. Storer suggests that the degree of rigour of a discipline is directly related to the extent to which mathematics is used: the harder the discipline the more mathematics. Storer presents evidence to show that the hard sciences are characterised by: (1) an impersonal relationship between members, indexed by the frequency with which first initials are used in footnotes; (2) an accumulation of knowledge; (3) invariant concepts; (4) greater use of mathematics; (5) the degree of complexity of materials contained in the body of knowledge, which in human terms means the amount of *real-time* required to follow out and to grasp the logical relationships among several different facts; (7) an easy detection of error, irrelevance, or sloppy thinking; (8) high level of rigour; and (9) the degree of risk a scientist takes when offering a contribution. Storer presents some evidence to show that some of these characteristics are interrelated. For example, he is able to show that the impersonality of a science, as indexed by the frequency of citation of initials rather than full names, is greater for the hard sciences (as assessed by some of the other criteria such as use of mathematics) than for soft sciences. When various disciplines are ordered according to the frequency with which they use initials in citations they are as follows: three hard sciences— physics, chemistry and biochemistry; three medium-hard sciences— botany, zoology, and economics; and three soft sciences—psychology, sociology, and political science.

Storer also looks at the relationship between the hardness of a science and the obsolescence rate of its literature. He points to two types of obsolescence. The first type is a result of the knowledge contained in an original article appearing at a subsequent time to be blunt, wrong, or misguided and which has been excluded from the corpus of literature. Storer suggests that such bodies of forgotten literature stem from the softer periods of a discipline's history. He concludes that the softer sciences will continue for some time to produce large bodies of literature that become obsolete with the passage of time, because the criteria by which they are judged at the time of presentation are not rigorous enough to effect their rejection. The second type of obsolescence involves the superseding of an article or piece of knowledge by a subsequent article or piece of knowledge: the original article is no longer referred to but its contents continue to be important in present day work. The contents have been carried forward by a subsequent generation of scientists; they have been assimilated by the work of subsequent scientists.

What are the implications for information use? In a subject where a paradigm is in force, specific theories and models within this paradigm are accepted or rejected in terms of empirical data. A single demonstration of the existence of a phenomenon is adequate to prove the case, although the retention of a theory requires a number of replication experiments. In the hard sciences, where evaluation of an individual piece of empirical data is easy, and where the relationship between empirical work and theory is tightly enumerated, a limited amount of empirical work will serve either to reject or include the proposed theory within the paradigm. In a softer science the relationship between theory and data is less strictly defined and the evaluation of empirical results is more difficult. In such a situation the empirical work required may be open-ended. It is difficult to produce the crucial experiment, and scientists in these disciplines may resort to a process of 'weighing up' the evidence in favour and the evidence against, simply by counting the number of pieces of evidence for the theory and the number of pieces against. When this is the case the demands upon the retrieval system are great: a large number of supporting or non-supporting pieces of evidence are required (the more the better) and there is imprecision[10] in the language used for retrieval.

Published knowledge is enduringly available. Publication gives research an existence independent of the knowledge possessed by any particular individual or group of individuals: the research becomes part of the universal body of knowledge to which scientists refer. Storer points out that scientists are expected to have access to this knowledge and to know of its existence, although it is not assumed that they know something that exists only in personal files. Communication between

---

[10]In the context of classification Foskett (1963) comments upon imprecise terminologies that appear in the social science literature.

scientists must be based upon the assumption that both parties have a considerable amount of knowledge in common, so that they need not start from scratch on every occasion. Knowledge is cumulative in science and the information system must be geared to retrieving blocks of this accumulated record. The retrieval part of the information system must be capable of recalling any block in the accumulated corpus of knowledge, and on occasions it must be able to recall all the material, or, at least, a representative sample.

It is much more difficult to be certain about the accumulation of knowledge in the social sciences. Where a discipline is in a pre-paradigmatic stage the demands upon the information system will not include completeness or representativeness of recall. There will be an element of substitutability in the array of material acceptable. The criteria for the judgement of relevance of material, and the subsequent incorporation of the material into the body of research and theory will be different. Where there is an element of substitutability, opinion and subjective judgement will play a large part in determining the relevance of material, rather than logical methods of induction characteristic of scientific methods. Where information serves as a source for ideas, or for discussion and debate, the demands upon the information system are less rigorous.

It is not suggested that all scientific activity is characterised by tightly accumulated knowledge, easy assessment of relevance, and the use of logical and objective means for the assessment of relevance. The 'scientific method' talked about by philosophers of science has been overplayed. Detailed reports of scientific activity, case histories, auto-biographical-type data, and some investigations by information scientists have focused attention upon the irrational, the subjective, and the unsystematic aspect of scientific enquiry.[11]

---

[11]In spite of the wealth of information that is available to the scientist, including sophisticated retrieval and current awareness services, the research scientist frequently has to make decisions on the evidence of little or no information, doing something that he has never done before and not knowing exactly what to do. Barber and Fox (1958, p. 136) quote one of the scientists whom they interviewed with the object of obtaining a case history. 'Should you boil or freeze, filter or centrifuge? These are the kinds of crossroads you come to all the time . . . It's always possible to do four, five, or six things, and you always have to choose between them . . . How do you decide?' This is the type of information that can only be obtained with experience, or sometimes through informal contacts with colleagues. It is the kind of information that perhaps will always defy crystallisation, storage and retrieval. There are also reports of scientists undertaking an experiment knowing (or suspecting) that the required information is available, but uncertain about the possibility of retrieving it.

Guttsman (1966) discusses a very important difference between the physical sciences and the social sciences. In the physical sciences there is a pressing demand for evaluation of the results of experimentation and theoretical structures. An analytical evaluation of social science material is perhaps just as pressing, but it does not exist at the present time. If the social sciences are to be cumulative, so that each discovery and its validation is relevant to subsequent study, each step in the system must be evaluated as the structure is built up, and (ideally) each person working in a given field must be able to have access to the various components in any given structure.

Some penetrating analyses of the flow of information in the natural sciences come from Price, a historian of science, who has made heavy use of data on publication and citation practices. Price has been active in determining the useful life of science serial articles by citation analyses, and the degree of bibliographic coupling between articles. From this work has come the idea of the 'cutting-edge' of science, and the concept[12] of the 'invisible college'.

Price (1965a) showed that the useful life of the average scientific article is between ten and fifteen years; that 75 per cent of citations in scientific literature refer to only a small percentage of all published articles and that there exists an active research front consisting of papers tightly knitted together by the process of reciprocal citation. On average, according to Price, an article contains fifteen references, twelve of which are to serial publications. He also notes that multi-authorship is increasing.

Price contrasts the working of the information system in science with that in non-scientific scholarship. Science is differentiated from other creative activities because it alone acts as if there was only one world to discover. As scientific discovery proceeds each piece of progress is enshrined on paper in order to say that it is there and that it has been found, and, to some extent, to say that it is now the intellectual property of its discoverer. All scholarship has a corpus and an archive, but science has a cutting-edge too. While they are at the research front, papers behave, as is known from citation-network studies, as if they were pieces in a jigsaw puzzle. Each paper fits onto two or three closely related previous papers and, in turn, becomes the point of departure for new research, so that old knowledge breeds new knowledge at a constant and rapid rate. This results in an exponential growth of the total

---

12See section 3.6 for a note on 'invisible colleges'.

literature. But some papers die (i.e. receive only one or two citations soon after publication) very quickly. A small part of the total literature accounts for a large percentage of the citations. The older publications that get cited come to form the 'classical' work of a subject, and the rate of growth of this section of the literature is much less than for the total published literature. Papers become part of a supranational research front and eventually enter the archives and are shaken down into the corpus of knowledge that appears in books. According to Price the chief features of scientific activity are: (1) the scientific paper is the unit of scientific archives; (2) the scientific paper is an important part of the research front, but increasingly comes to account for less of the total front; (3) papers fit tightly together, and this is especially so at the research front; (4) science progresses by an accumulation of units.

The point to be made in the present context does not concern the validity of Price's analysis, nor the fact that the situation is changing. Price is aware of the former and his article is mainly concerned with the demise of the structure that he was able to identify. Price notes that the scientific paper no longer holds the unique position it did fifty years ago. But the fact remains that regularities can be identified in the way in which scientific research is conducted and in the flow of information. It has yet to be established whether this is so in the social sciences. It is not argued here that the social sciences proceed, unordered, with no established methodology: methodology is, in fact, a strong point of some of the social sciences. There are many accepted approaches to research in the social sciences, and the researcher engaging upon new research will often come to his work well prepared with a background of training and experience in methodological problems. It is argued, rather, that the products of social science research (e.g. periodical articles, informal communications) may not behave in the same way as their counterparts in the physical sciences.

In the accounts of the nature of social science research considered so far it is often assumed (sometimes implicitly so) that the social sciences are in some fundamental ways different from the natural sciences. A rather different position is taken by Pool, McIntosh and Griffel (1969) who maintain that there is no absolute distinction separating all social from all natural sciences. However, they do agree that there are differences between social and natural sciences of great significance in emphasis and degree, and that problems that are acute and central in one field of study may be peripheral and minor in the other. In short, they maintain that there are differences in the modal activities of natural and social sciences although philosophical statements about the logical differences between them cannot (or perhaps should not) be made. They single out four distinctive characteristics of the social sciences. Social sciences (1) generally describe multivariate systems; (2) are data-rich and theory-poor; (3) are generally phenomenological, describing natural environments rather than working in well-controlled experimentation; and (4) have a strong historical bias.

The majority of accounts, and speculations, about the nature of social science research and the relationship between the social sciences and the sciences, have been concerned only in passing (and in some cases by implication only) with information needs. Line (1968a) proves to be an exception because he views the social sciences, and their relationship to the sciences and technologies, from the standpoint of their information requirements rather than from the standpoint of social science methodology. Illustrating his analysis with examples from the social science literature, Line enumerates thirteen ways in which the social sciences differ from the sciences: (1) the subject matter of the social sciences is less stable than that of the sciences; (2) there are many types of approach, and it is not unusual (as it is in science) for a researcher to question the whole validity of a given approach; (3) methodological disputes are much commoner in the social sciences; (4) each discipline in the social sciences is much less clearly defined than in the sciences; (5) the scatter of potentially relevant information is much greater in the social sciences than in most sciences; (6) the relevance of information is harder to assess in the social sciences; (7) the solid factual content is probably quantitatively less than in the sciences and almost certainly less vitally important; (8) concepts and ideas are more important in the social sciences; (9) the unstable subject content and the strong conceptual element in the social sciences tend to make identification of information requirements difficult; (10) the nature of discovery in the social sciences is a different phenomenon from discovery in the sciences; (11) duplication of research can be almost impossible in the social sciences; (12) scientific information is superseded by subsequent discoveries and general laws but there is no agreement that this takes place in social science—Line acknowledges this as Medawar's (1967) idea; (13) the pattern of research may be quite different in the social sciences.

Line puts forward his analysis as a working hypothesis. It is, as he states, largely hypothetical and remains to be tested. He emphasises the fact that very little is known about information needs (as opposed to demands). Line suggests methods which involve finding out a great deal about the user, not merely as a user, but as a social scientist, and this does take an investigation into relatively unexplored territory. Unlike many writings on social science information needs and requirements, Line's analysis is really a prolegomena to an extensive empirical investigation. Line argues that, since next to nothing is known about information needs and requirements in the social sciences, an investigation which produces an aerial view of information requirements in all the social sciences is required in the first instance, followed at a later date by investigations in depth into those areas identified as requiring special attention.

At this stage in the discussion, and taking a general view, it can be seen that very little is known about the nature of social science research; and that what is known about the methods and practices in social science research has only an indirect bearing upon information needs and requirements. The social scientist concerned with the development of better methods for the transmission of information, or the information scientists given the task of designing and providing an information system for the social sciences, could be forgiven for showing a certain amount of impatience with talk about conceptual systems and generalities; and for calling a halt to this approach, however interesting it might appear, because it had little to contribute directly to the hardware of an information system. It seems reasonable for social scientists to point to the development of information systems and services in science and technology, and to request a similar degree of activity in the social sciences. Looking for an explanation of the lack of activity in the social sciences on a scale similar to that in science and technology one could point to the relatively recent emergence of empirical and numerical techniques in the social sciences, the relatively small amount of money invested in the social sciences, and the absence of unifying forces that professionalisation and organised research brings. For example, there has been nothing in the social sciences to match the interest in, and financial support of, information systems and services in science and technology by the United States Government (see 1.2 and 3.8.5).

Activities involving social science information lack direction and co-ordination. In the field of documentation, particularly classification, there has been some national and international co-ordination (see 3.1.2), but this apart there has been little co-ordinated effort to tackle the difficult problems that can be, and have been, identified. One noticeable exception to the piecemeal and unco-ordinated activities relating to information in the social sciences is the work of the United States

National Research Council/Division of the Behavioral Sciences. The NRC organised a Committee on Information in the Behavioral Sciences, and sub-committees were established to deal with information practices and needs among behavioral scientists, the social organisation of behavioural science information resources, and the potentials of computer technology for information systems. The products of the collective efforts of the Committee and its three sub-committees are presented in a report *Communication systems and resources in the behavioral sciences* published in 1967. The report paid particular attention to the application of new technologies to the transfer of information in the behavioural sciences, and also to the obligation which social scientists have, to all other scientists, to establish a better understanding of the behavioural element in information systems. In so doing the Committee put in second place questions about the nature of social science research and its literature. However, such questions were recognised, and the following quotation from the 'foreword' of the report makes this clear. 'In any field of science the problem of information reflects three major concerns. These, in logical order, are relevance, accuracy, and accessibility. If information is not relevant, we need not worry about its accuracy. If it is not accurate, we need not fret over its accessibility. In the social and behavioral sciences the first two concerns present abnormally serious problems. The relevance of alleged information is often non-existent or questionable because the bulk of available social data are collected for administrative and legal purposes, and even those obtained to answer scientific questions come in a bewildering variety. Similarly, accuracy is an unusually grave problem in the social disciplines because of the limitations inherent in dealing with human beings, especially with their motives and their social behavior. By contrast, the matter of accessibility is simpler and more like that of other fields of scientific endeavour.'

The report suggests that research into information requirements and the provision of information services in the social sciences will require the development of a strategy with the kinds of concerted co-operative efforts that have not been undertaken in the past. In particular, it recommends that individual academic research centres, professional societies, and relevant departments and agencies of the government give priority to various kinds of studies that will produce knowledge essential for the formation of sound communication and information policies. These should include user studies in each of the social science disciplines, studies of the way in which effective means can be provided for indexing ind abstracting services and of packaging and delivering information in each of the disciplines, and studies of the relationship between information input to research activities and research outputs, designed to iscertain how research processes and productivity might be affected by changes in information services and forms. The Committee also reports on conventional documentation practices in the social sciences, and points to the need for the development of documentation if the newer forms of data that are now of use to social sciences are not to be under-utilised. Most of the remainder of the report is taken up with a consideration of the application of computer technologies to the retrieval of information.

The report is very timely, but it is a pity that it did not tackle some of the problems relating to relevance and accuracy of social science data to which the report addressed itself in the 'foreword'). The impression is given that the Committee assumed that these problems will look after themselves when the more practical aspects of information systems are investigated. The report states: 'Not only is there an opportunity to make significant progress in the communication apparatus itself through the use of modern technology, but there is also the extremely promising possibility of using an improved system to help overcome the worrysome handicaps connected with relevance and accuracy. If an investigator knows what is likely to be relevant, any communication system that increases his power of selectivity—that allows him to sift, rapidly and painlessly, the grain from the chaff—will greatly improve research productivity. Indeed, the very act of addressing himself to a system that can discriminate with extreme fineness will force the researcher to define his problem meticulously. Furthermore, since the accuracy of one piece of information is tested by reference to other information bearing on the same matter, a system that increases accessibility will lead to improved accuracy. It thus seems strategic to tackle the communicative problems of the social disciplines and to try to solve them'.

Although one can be fairly certain that empirical investigations into the information requirements and needs of social scientists, and into the structure of social science literature, will make contributions to an understanding of the research process in the social sciences it is naïve to assume that some of the fundamental questions about the nature of social science research will be brought together and formed into a general theory of information transfer by empirical studies alone, if there is no general direction and conceptual development.

3.1.2 *Classification of social science literature*

The classification of knowledge in the natural sciences has a long history, with scientists themselves playing a large part in the development of acceptable systems. In contrast, classification in the social sciences[13] has a very short history, and that which does exist is mainly the work of bibliographers and documentalists, rather than social scientists, although they do impose a structure upon social science knowledge in their publications.

Problems encountered in classification include fundamental questions about the nature of social science research—and these are also fundamental to enquiries about information needs and requirements and their satisfaction.

Foskett (1958, 1963, 1964, 1969a, 1969b) has attacked the information problem of the social sciences largely from the point of view of the classification of its literature. Foskett (1958) drew attention to the need for the international control of documentation in the social sciences and noted that activities on this front in the physical sciences, largely initiated by a series of international conferences, had been reasonably productive. Writing in 1958 Foskett saw the documentation, retrieval, and dissemination of social science information still within control but suggested that those responsible for social science information (e.g. the production and distribution of abstracts, retrieval services and facilities) might learn from the mistakes of the scientists. Foskett mentioned the work of UNESCO and the International Committee for Social Science Documentation as active in laying the foundations for the introduction of standard practices in the documentation of social science material, and the work of Kyle (1958a, 1958b) on methods of bibliographical control of social science material.

The classification of scientific literature is well established and Foskett (1969a) pointed to the impetus in this direction that came from

---

[13]Short summaries of the development of classification systems in the social sciences are given by Kyle (1957, 1958b, 1960a, 1960b) and Foskett (1963). Kyle (1958b) traces the work of the International Committee for Social Science Documentation from its meeting in 1953 when it was agreed to study the relative merits of adapting an existing classification or creating a new system appropriate to social science literature. As a result of this study work began on a classification specifically for the social sciences and the results of this study were reported by Kyle (1958b). Foskett mentions the enquiry by the Graduate Library School and Social Sciences Division of the University of Chicago into 'The desirability and feasibility of an abstracting system for the social sciences', reported in the *Library Quarterly*, April 1950, and the work of UNESCO (see *UNESCO Chronicle*, Number 5, 1955). Fellows (1957) provides an annotated

pecialist libraries and from industry where current awareness and SDI ystems are well established. These developments have taken place in he scientific community which has the sure conviction that progress s cumulative: researchers build upon data already established by others ind no longer begin to study every problem *de novo*. This in turn has iighlighted the importance of teamwork in scientific research. Foskett iistinguished two types of cumulation: the one, which is usually held o be a characteristic of scientific activity, where knowledge accumulates o form building blocks which are then used by subsequent researchers; ind the other, the accumulation of research literature. The accumula-ion of social science literature in this latter sense is not in question and is Foskett pointed out social science literature is longer lasting than icience literature (see section 4.3 for studies of the life of literature as issessed by citation studies). It is the accumulation of knowledge rather :han the accumulation of literature in the social sciences that is in question. At the present time there is no satisfactory answer to this question.

The conceptual vagueness of much of the social science information is responsible for many of the problems in the classification of its literature; ind this same conceptual vagueness makes for terminological difficul-ties. Shera (1951) remarks that 'The maturity of an area of knowledge is reflected in the degree of standardisation of its nomenclature ... In sociology and economics such consensus is ... lacking, with disastrous consequences for communication within the disciplines'. At the present time classification and retrieval of social science literature has to proceed in the absence of such consensus: it has to deal with subject matter that is emotive in content, vague in definition, and imprecise in terminology. Foskett (1963, p. 27) suggests that a 'great deal of the subject matter of the social sciences demands the expression of attitudes, of approval and indignation; and if this involves the imputation of incompetence or

---

review of selected references on documentation in the social sciences. Also relevant is the report by the United States National Research Council/Division of Medical Sciences (1967) on the revision of the indexing systems used by the National Library of Medicine for literature in the behavioural sciences. This indexing system is geared to medical science users and it provides an opportunity to contrast the classification of social science literature found applicable to users outside social science with the classifications that have developed within the social science disciplines. Some Eastern European work on classification and termin-ology in the social sciences is mentioned by Szwalbe (1969). Dutch work on documentation is discussed in Hogeweg-de-Haart (1967) and Netherlands Koninklijke Akademie van Wetenschappen Sociaal-Wetenschappelijke Raad (1968).

moral turpitude to one's opponents, then it must be accepted that such categories rightly find a place in the literature'.

Kyle (1958a) also highlights questions of terminology when she compares the social and natural sciences. Kyle notes that the literature relevant to social science differs from that of science and technology by virtue of (1) quantity, variety, and scatter; (2) imprecision and great size of vocabularies; and (3) the unstable character of its subject-matter. When material is required for general reading or for stimulation the demands made upon the information system are not so precise as when information is required for a quick answer to specific questions. These different needs may require the adoption of different methods in the provision of documentation and bibliographic organisation. For obtaining exact information on specific subjects precise tools for coding and retrieval are required, and these presuppose precise terminology. Kyle suggests that at present only a very small proportion of social science literature[14] is worth treating in this way, and that no attempt should be made to attach precise coding to imprecise language. Kyle is very strict in her criteria for the selection of material that should be coded for precise retrieval; and the evaluative nature of the process must rule out, for many, the adoption of Kyle's proposals for the organisation of social science literature. Where research literature in the social sciences is like scientific literature in its precise terminology, Kyle suggests existing methods for the classification and retrieval of material are inadequate. But she recognises that there is a need to retrieve items of information from less precise as well as from purely scientific literature and this is difficult to do by classical hierarchical methods of classification. Kyle (1958a, p. 196) suggests 'that the solution lies in matching frequencies of concepts in combination in different contexts, on the assumption that certain words (and their synonyms) in one piece of writing will, if found in another piece of writing, be concerned with related subjects'.

In the social sciences the absence of accepted classification systems that have evolved from the disciplines themselves is conspicuous. In the physical sciences the main classificatory systems were introduced by

---

[14]Kyle enumerates five types of information that may be classified, coded and retrieved: (1) accurate and detailed subject information; (2) generalised and speculative information; (3) historical and descriptive material; (4) information identifiable by author's name, language, nationality, source, etc. only; (5) information identifiable by proper nouns, or other words so widely accepted as to be almost unambiguous when cited in a particular context. Kyle suggests that only a small proportion of social science literature is amenable to analysis and coding.

the scientists themselves, and although the advent of computers onto the classification scene has brought in many outsiders and shed new light (e.g. automatic language generation, the possibility of automated classificatory systems and use of computers in retrieval) the pattern in the subject matter of science still prevails (Foskett, 1965). The scientist attempts to unravel and identify this pattern of regularities and in so doing he must structure his thinking. At the same time he is using the literature, not in terms of a preconceived classificatory system or of computer-imposed structures but in terms of his conceptual framework of his subject and this will form the basis of his requests for information.

The way in which social scientists structure their thinking is essential to classification systems, although those responsible for classificatory systems may be tempted to propose their own derived order of the way in which the material of the social sciences is structured. This danger was never very real in the development of classificatory systems in the physical and biological sciences, where there was greater agreement as to the underlying physical structure (e.g. Mendeleef's classification of the elements), theoretical schemes (e.g. Newtonian laws of motion), and scientists themselves were responsible for the development and verification of classificatory systems. Such classificatory systems in science 'work' in the sense that scientists can, by and large, retrieve what they want, and they have the additional attraction of high face validity (e.g. taxonomy in botany). If a superstructure were to be imposed upon social science information, from outside, it would be of little use to social scientists in their attempts to supply their disciplines with conceptual systems of their own; and it would make the retrieval of information (where a match has to be made between a classification scheme and the concepts spontaneously used by the scientist) more difficult. Chall (1966) makes the point that documentation people have not prepared classifications and symbolic languages in science and technology. This has been done by scientists themselves, and Chall doubts the wisdom of attempts, by those outside the discipline, to supply sociology with a classificatory system.

Although formal work on classification (both by professional librarians and social scientists themselves) in the social sciences has a very short history there is in every type of publication a structuring of material. Usually writers have not made explicit the nature of the structure, and indeed, many writers are perhaps quite unaware that the organisation of their material involves a rudimentary classification system. In addition to written material the conversations and thoughts of researchers serve to structure their material. All written and verbal communications in the social sciences are potential contributors to the structuring and classifying of knowledge, although it would be extremely difficult (and perhaps impossible) to measure the effect that such communications have upon classificatory systems.

One of the foremost contributions to the documentation of the social sciences in the 1930's was the *Encyclopaedia of the Social Sciences*. According to Lewis (1965) it had a great influence on taxonomy in the social sciences and did much to foster interdisciplinary approaches. Another work that appeared in the formative years of the social sciences was the *London Bibliography of the Social Sciences* and, as Lewis points out, the later volumes of this publication are virtually the current catalogue of the British Library of Political and Economic Science at the London School of Economics. Most of the classificatory systems found in indexes, abstracting journals, reviews of the literature, year-books, and all other bibliographical tools in the social sciences have developed in a piecemeal way. Specialised bibliographies coming from international organisations have provided some rationalisation in social science documentation and perhaps the best known of these is the four annual volumes on economics, political science, sociology, and anthropology which comprise the *International Bibliography of the Social Sciences*. On an international front UNESCO and the International Committee for Social Sciences Documentation have devoted some of their resources to widening the area surveyed for the *International Bibliography of the Social Sciences*. There are abstracting journals in most social science disciplines and a great variety of indexes and bibliographies. In psychology, for example, *Psychological Abstracts* dates from 1927. In addition to the major abstracting journals serving a whole discipline some specialist groups are also served by other abstracting/indexing journals (e.g. *Excerpta Criminologica, Language and Language Behavior Abstracts, Poverty and Human Resources Abstracts*) and also abstracting journals that focus upon a regional area rather than a subject field (e.g. *Tropical Abstracts, African Abstracts, South Asia Social Science Abstracts*).

More recently there have appeared many guides to the literature (e.g. *Guide to the World's Abstracting and Indexing Services in Science and Technology*, White's *Sources of information in the social sciences: a guide to the literature*), directories (e.g. Research Centers Directory), and data repositories (e.g. Project TALENT, Data Bank, Public Opinion Survey Unit) all of which have to structure the field with which they are dealing. In short, there are many bodies, institutions, libraries, and persons that have at one time or another been concerned with organising social science knowledge, and although their practices may be irregular and non-standardised they do, by their very activities of classifying the literature in one form or another, structure the field with which they are dealing.

Lewis (1965) notes that few of the large number of learned societies and professional institutions within the social sciences seem to have attached a high priority to the task of assembling information about the current output of relevant published material in their fields. Lewis highlights in particular the poor record of the Royal Statistical Society. He suggests that the American Economic Association, with its recently completed *Index to Economic Journals,* its current series of surveys on economic thought in various countries, its systematic listing of new books in the *American Economic Review,* and its part in the formation of the *Journal of Economic Abstracts,* provides an exception to this criticism. Since 1965 the American Economic Association established a Committee on the classification of economic literature (see Leftwich, 1968) which made a number of recommendations. It was suggested, among other things, that (1) the American Economic Association should work for the co-ordination of its bibliographical and indexing systems— at the time the recommendation was made three different classificatory systems were in use by the AEA; one for the *Index of Economic Journals,* one for the *AEA Handbook* and the *National Register,* and one for the listing of current economic literature and economic abstracts; (2) the scope of bibliographical indexing and classification should be extended to cover all economic literature contained in the major journals, books, and collective volumes; (3) the classifying and indexing of economic literature should be computerised; and (4) research to produce a new classification system should be undertaken with the aim of an integrated, co-ordinated, and mechanised system of classifying and indexing all information of concern to the American Economic Association.

There has also been comment about information requirements and classificatory systems in the social sciences from those concerned with documentation problems in specific disciplines. For example, a by-product of the work of indexing and retrieval in the social sciences carried out at the CNRS Section d'Automatique Documentaire was the creation of the special classificatory system in anthropology. And in a paper to a conference[15] on 'Documentation in criminology', held at Aslib in 1964, Andry (1965) identified some of the future needs for information in criminology. He gave a detailed account of the needs of researchers in criminological research, casual users and practitioners (e.g. probation officers), and producers of secondary material (e.g. journal editors, writers, lecturers, librarians), and made suggestions about various bibliographical services, abstracts, SDI systems, citation indexes, journals, and translation services that are needed to support any further progress in criminological documentation. Andry's analysis is very coarse and unlikely to make much contribution to an integrated information system: for example, he suggests that material on criminology could usefully be gathered together in one place in the library. It is also noted that Andry's analysis was not based upon empirical investigations.

Many of the computer-based information services[16] have generated an interest in classificatory systems and user studies. The number of information services that are in existence in the social sciences is small when compared with the number in science and technology, but wherever they exist some enquiry, however rudimentary, into user requirements (if only feedback from users) is required, and storage and retrieval of information necessarily involve questions of classification.

A fusion of interest in classification and retrieval is found in the work[17] of the Centre National de la Recherche Scientifique (CNRS) Section d'Automatique Documentaire created in 1961 to deal with the theoretical problems of documentation and information retrieval irrespective of application to any specific field, although most of the work has been physiology, psychology, sociology, and other social sciences; because, as Gardin (1964, p. 15) says 'it was assumed that the difficulties of document indexing and retrieval were greatest in that (i.e. social science) area of science, owing to the relative imprecision of terminology, the absence of accepted taxonomies, and so forth. Any general system which "worked" for the social sciences would then be *a priori* acceptable to the natural sciences as well. However, a by-product of that provisional concentration on the behavioral sciences was the creation of

---

[15]Also at this conference Tapper (1965) considered the application of mechanised methods to the documentation of material of interest to criminologists.

[16]Computer-based information services include data archives and retrieval of information from them (see section 3.1.1). The development of social science information and documentation services is reviewed by Bisco (1967a): services include bibliographies to meet special needs, lists of current acquisitions, computer-produced indexes, and the provision of data for secondary analysis. Levy (1966) outlines two information storage and retrieval systems in the social

specialised classifications which were found readily adaptable to the needs of existing documentation centers in some branches of anthropology'. Gardin's theory of classification is one of the few that has had a beginning in the social sciences.

Garfield (1964, p. 58) considering the application of citation indexing to the retrieval of information in the social sciences takes a rather unusual view of some aspects of indexing and classification. From the standpoint of indexing and classification, at least, Garfield believes that the literature problems of both science and social science can be treated with equal success: 'Special difficulties may arise insofar as each particular research field allows or requires different degrees of indexing specificity, depending upon the methodological precision of that field. However, as an information scientist, I find that even the informational problems of Biblical research are comparable to those of chemical research. In some aspects of both fields one deals with highly specific informational or data elements which are clearly defined and prescribed. Where such elements are not clearly defined, whether in the social or natural sciences, one encounters difficulties'. Garfield emphasises the multi-disciplinary, linguistic, and quantitative factors common to all fields of research. Unlike most commentators on the nature of social science research and its terminology, Garfield maintains that the linguistical and terminological problems in both areas are essentially similar: in fact, he suggests that citation indexing will probably find greater popularity in the social sciences and humanities than in most of the sciences because conventional language-orientated indexes are much more difficult to use in the social sciences.

Garfield argues that conventional indexing systems quickly obsolesce because they rely heavily upon quickly changing nomenclatures. It is quite impractical to constantly up-date them since this would require constant re-indexing of all the literature by trained subject specialists. However, Garfield suggests that this re-indexing is what is achieved routinely in a citation index. Each new reference to an 'old' paper

---

sciences—the general enquiry system at the Department of Social Relations, Harvard, and the History of Education System, University of Michigan. In the retrieval system at the Center for Documentation and Communication Research, Western Reserve University, the needs of users have been very palpably met in an education project where a 'user group' of specialists were sampled who submitted the questions and evaluated the replies (see Cleverdon, 1962; and Rees, 1965a).

[17]See Cros, Gardin and Levy (1964) for a report on the CNRS work, and also Gardin (1964) for an account of applications of the work to the social sciences.

re-indexes it. The citation index, as a self-organising system, is constantly being upgraded by the feedback of more current information. Advances in science are quickly reflected in the index, thereby bringing old information up-to-date. Garfield has outlined the way in which citation indexing can be used in research in sociology and history (Garfield, 1963; Garfield, Sher and Torpie, 1964), and the use of citation indexes in defining fields of study. And also the use of citation indexes in providing information services (Garfield, 1967) where, for example, users would receive, in addition to a conventional bibliography, details about the interrelationship of each item with every other item in the bibliography and a graph illustrating these relationships (see chapter 4 for more details on citation analysis).

Finally, on the subject of classification, a rather different viewpoint is taken by Altman (1968) in his account of classification in psychology. Altman shows that at least one of the social sciences has already begun to concern itself with problems of classification, although this is not usually recognised. He refers to factor analysis, content analysis, and propositional inventory approaches that have important implications for classificatory systems. These techniques are concerned with producing a structure from unstructured material. For example, in factor analysis the scores obtained from a large array of aptitude tests may be submitted to analysis with the object of identifying a number (sometimes the least) of factors that will account for the variance in the scores. In content analysis a mass of material from (say) an interview is broken down into categories and scored. These techniques involve questions about the unit of analysis. In content analysis it is very important to decide upon the unit of analysis before scoring can commence (and this usually requires a preliminary skimming of the entire material to be analysed). In factor analysis the unit is the object of the analysis.

Altman suggests that these beginnings, stemming from the subject itself, are of importance in the development of a classification system. He points to the example of the natural sciences where classification systems were developed over long periods of time and involved feedback and interaction between bibliographers and scientists. It would be unwise to suggest that an acceptable classification system in the social sciences could grow up overnight, and in the absence of substantial contributions from social scientists themselves. Altman maintains that this important task cannot be left to the bibliographers. Drawing upon examples from sciences Altman (1968, p. 56) notes the agreement that existed amongst scientists themselves about units of analysis that formed the basis of their classification systems. The sciences use a common set of dimensions to order subject matter (for instance, atomic number and atomic weight in chemistry, structural characteristics in zoology) in library classification. 'Users of these systems "knew" many important dimensions to use by virtue of a wealth of empirical knowledge and a history of attempts at classification and had "most" of the facts about their phenomena at hand. Our situation in the behavioral sciences is totally dissimilar. Replication of empirical findings is rare, and our data are often noncomparable from situation to situation. Moreover, the phenomena occur in situational contests which are extraordinarily complicated and need description as much as behavior itself. And the potential dimensions for describing behavior are multitudinous, and there is little consensus as to which are important. Thus, the other sciences had a good concept of their appropriate unit of study. . . . In the behavioral sciences, we have . . . not yet established consensus on relevant units and their structural-functional properties, which make the task of synthesis quite difficult (and) we are . . . not yet wholly confident about the reliability and validity of our findings.'

The existence of an acceptable classification system(s) would be of great help to the study of information needs and requirements: it would enable users to be more articulate and precise when specifying their information needs and requirements, and it would facilitate the retrieval and satisfaction of the needs.

3.1.3 *The application of social science research*

There are a large number of persons who require, and sometimes make use of, social science information—especially the results of research. These practitioners may be social scientists themselves (e.g. social workers, clinical psychologists, college of education lecturers) or non-social scientists (e.g. architects, administrators). Practitioners are concerned with the application of the results of social science research and theory rather than with the creation of more material—although some social scientists may take on the roles of both researcher and practitioner.

Although there is a certain amount of impatience and disillusionment in the practitioner community with the progress of research in the social sciences and with its relationship to practical problems, the expectations of the practitioners may be at fault. It may be that practitioners (and researchers) have misconstrued, in their criticisms, the relationship between pure and applied research. At least in science, the literatures of pure and applied research find little overlap, and similarly communication channels are rarely shared by the two groups.[18] In the social sciences applied research is not a clearly defined field; and perhaps as a result the demands made upon the researcher have been unrealistic.

There is little agreement about the nature of applied social science research or about the application of basic research to social problems. To take sociology as an illustration, the increasing amount of research and activity in this discipline has gone hand in hand with a rising demand for sociological knowledge to assist in decision-making processes. And at the same time there has been a growing concern as to whether, or in what manner, sociology should serve social goals outside science itself (see, for example, Gouldner, 1957; Horowitz, 1968; Lazarsfeld et al., 1967; Sjoberg, 1967; Etzioni, 1968). There has perhaps been far too much debate, as Heiskanen (1969) suggests, between the protagonists of different viewpoints and not enough investigation of how social science information is used by decision-makers and especially whether in fact it is used at all.[19,20]

The relationship between basic research and the applied field in the social sciences has been discussed by many including Cherns (1969), Riecken (1969), Bloom (1969), Eidell and Kitchel (1968), Leeds and Smith (1963), and the Department of Education and Science Committee on Social Studies (1965). Some of these views are considered in a little more detail.

Riecken (1969, pp. 101 and 108–109) defines the social sciences as intellectual subjects directed primarily towards understanding rather than action. 'It would, of course, be a curious kind of "understanding"

---

[18]Price (1965b) attempts to assess the interrelationship between science and technology from a study of the literature. In brief, he notes that science is primarily a literature-producing institution and technology a literature-demanding institution; but the literature produced by science is not the literature that meets the needs of technology. Science has a cumulating close-knit structure where knowledge flows from highly related and rather recent pieces of old knowledge. Technology also has a similar, cumulating, close-knit structure but this is a state-of-the-art knowledge, and is not always embodied in the literature. Where it is to be found in the literature it is fairly compact and readily available to those who require it. Science and technology each have their own cumulating structures. The structures are separate, and only in special cases involving the breaking of a paradigm can there be a direct flow from the research front of science to that of technology or vice versa. Price suggests that research-front technology is strongly related only to that part of scientific knowledge that has been packed down and accepted as scientific treatises and used in education and training of scientists, and not to research-front science. Similarly, research-front science is related only to the ambient technological knowledge of the previous generation of students, not to the research front of the technological state-of-the-art and its innovations. This reciprocal relationship

hat had no implications for action, and this is perhaps especially true or the social sciences. Nevertheless, there is a difference between nlarging one's understanding of human behaviour and society on the ne hand and trying to solve a social problem on the other. The social ciences are distinct from social problem-solving, but each activity ontributes to the other. . . . The production of recommendations for action goes beyond research and indeed beyond science, into what is properly termed "development" rather than "research"; or "engineering" rather than "science". The distinction is more than verbal—it is a whole complex: a state of mind, institutional auspices, cross-disciplinary elations, interaction with non-scientists, and employment of non-scientific . . . skills.' At the present time, Riecken continues, 'We have a social science but not social development or social engineering, except n very limited and spotty areas. Examples of social engineering can be ound in economics, in the development of fiscal and monetary policies, and in psychology, in new forms of psycho-therapy (especially behavior herapy), programmed instruction, human relations training, in the raining of managers and in the social organisation of production units n firms. . . . Most of these latter innovations in management come from a new breed of intellectual-scholar-engineer whose background is likely to be in economics, psychology, mathematics, business administration, or computer science, and who are active in the field of systems analysis, operations research, or "organisational development". . . . Most of the leading practitioners of systems analysis and "organisational development" have had interdisciplinary training, or at least mixed backgrounds, are associated with non-academic departments in the social sciences, and

---

between science and technology, involving the research front of one and the accrued archive of the other, is nevertheless sufficient to keep the two in phase in their separate growths within each otherwise independent cumulation. Price suggests that it is naïve to regard technology as applied science or clinical practice as applied medical science. Storer (1966) makes a similar point. He suggests that only recently have scientific progress and technology become related. In the past, and in many areas today, technological change is almost entirely independent of progress in science. Storer points out that developments in architecture, navigation, industrial processes, and armaments have come from those interested in solving immediate practical problems rather than in building a body of generalised knowledge.

[19]See Zetterberg (1963) for a discussion of the sociologist as a decision-maker, educator, researcher, consultant, commentator, and critic.

[20]There is no dearth of documentation about the possible uses of sociological knowledge (see, for example, a collection of readings edited by Lazarsfeld, Sewell and Wilensky, 1967, on 'The uses of sociology'); but when some of these writings are examined in detail it often turns out that the uses referred to are potential rather than actual.

are quite often found entirely outside academic institutions. Their orientation is toward the world of work—most often in industry or government agencies—and they seem to find their satisfaction in the application of econometric, psychometric and related quantitative methods and concepts to the analysis. . . . In education, one can see the engineering process at work in design and installation of computer based instruction systems, and, in a more limited and primitive way, in the design of new secondary school curricula in the sciences. The standard engineering steps of design, mock-up or trial version, pilot run and assessment, re-design and preparation of specifications for a reproduction model are followed to some extent in educational curriculum designing'.

Cherns (1969, pp. 209–210) suggests that at the root of the problem of application of basic research 'lies a misconception of the processes whereby research gets translated into action. A reading of the process in the natural sciences has provided us with a model in which pure research leads through applied research to development, and from development to application. Our misconceptions begin with the words "pure", "applied" and "research". The distinctions that are frequently made between pure and applied, theoretical and empirical research in the social sciences are not only unhelpful but often downright mischievous'. In his analysis of social science research Cherns proposes a four-fold division: 'pure basic' and 'objective basic' (taken from the classification proposed by the Office of the Minister for Science—Committee on the Management and Control of Research and Development, 1961), 'operational research' and 'action research'. Cherns illustrates these types of research with examples taken from the field of social research, and then looks at the respective channels of diffusion.

Many others have commented upon the basic/applied dichotomy in the social sciences (Carter and Williams, 1967; Cartwright, 1949; Gouldner, 1957; Helmer, 1965; Zetterberg, 1963), and upon the absence of specially trained persons for the application of social science knowledge (Carter, 1968; Herring, 1947). The Department of Education and Science Committee on Social Studies (1965, p. 39, paragraph 124) drew attention to this aspect of social science: ' . . . there are few people whose functions correspond to the engineering or development function in the physical sciences, and nowhere are such people trained. If anything approaching the full potential value is to be obtained from research in the social sciences, an attempt must be made to define and analyse this function and train people to perform it'.

In the field of education Eidell and Kitchel (1968), Guba (1968), and Leeds and Smith (1963) have discussed such questions as the utilisation of knowledge in educational administration and practice, and the gap between knowledge production and knowledge utilisation. These authors, and many others, have concluded that there is a need for the development of new organisations, new roles, and new training programmes to facilitate research and the application of research findings.

Bloom (1969, p. 16), like many commentators, paints a pessimistic picture for the practitioner. He refers to an information crisis: a *poverty of usable knowledge*, and contrasts it with another information crisis, familiar to all, a crisis of *abundant information*. Bloom suggests that 'We can agree that knowledge is essential to effective social work practice. The better the knowledge, the more effective should be the practice. But the question is how can we resolve the paradox of the availability of vast amounts of scientific information and the paucity of adequate scientific knowledge distilled from this information and necessary to guide practice?'

Finding himself with practical problems to solve, a need for suitable information, and taking such an analysis seriously, what does the practitioner do? Does he abandon social science research (that is the part that filters down to him) and await the advent of 'usable knowledge' or 'social engineering'? Certainly he has little direct contact with basic research. Bloom cites an empirical study by Rosenblatt (1967) on the use of social science research to show that social work taps only a few of the formal channels of communication and makes even less use of available informal channels. A study by McCulloch and Brown (see 3.8.1 for details) on the reading habits of social workers confirms the suspicion that social workers have little exposure to the literature reporting the result of research in the social sciences.

An analysis of bibliographic coupling,[21] similar to Price's (1965b) analysis in science and technology, of the basic and the applied literatures of social science would almost certainly demonstrate a one-way citing practice—social work journals citing basic social science research (albeit infrequently), but not the reverse. This would not be surprising; but it would contrast with the situation in science and technology where neither the 'applied' nor the 'pure' literature cite each other to any great extent (Price, 1965b).

---

[21]Bibliographic coupling refers to the relationship between articles (or books) as measured by the degree to which the bibliographies overlap. The standard reference on bibliographic coupling is Kessler (1963).

Notwithstanding such citation practices that do exist practitioners still speak as though there was much to be gained from the literature of basic research—if only it could be communicated to them. And information-conscious commentators make suggestions about the way in which this could be effected. There is the sure feeling that something of value exists in the literature of basic research. And this is understandable in the absence of a well developed applied literature. After all, the technologist or the applied scientist would no doubt have a greater interest in the literature of basic science if he had little literature of his own.

The conclusions reached by Bloom and Riecken are a little unusual: in general few have doubted the extent and volume of information in social science that is of some relevance to practitioners—although there has been no reluctance to point to the poor record to date of social science in solving or ameliorating social problems.[22] Judged by rigorous standards of usefulness, usability, goodness or relevance the amount of usable information may be small. This will be contained in the context of masses of publications, and if the practitioner is to find relevant information he must sift through mountains of material. The alternatives are to delegate this activity to research assistants, or to rely upon professional communicators and information officers.

In the practical field the question of selection is uppermost. In basic research the problem is perhaps not so crucial. The researcher is trained for this type of work and has more time (and perhaps inclination) to expose himself to masses of material—although even here the researcher can benefit from the services of information specialists. The practitioner, with neither the time, training, or inclination, may require some filter placed between him and the vast amounts of published literature. The use of some filtering device brings into focus again the question of the nature of social science information. How much is of use to the practitioner? How can the useful part be extracted? Can it be directly applied? Is further research (on application of 'pure' research findings) required? Bloom (1969), for example, favours the development of information services and specialists as positive steps that the social work profession can take in order to bring itself closer to new developments in the social sciences. These include scanning widely for relevant information and getting closer to the knowledge-creating sources for more recent information. Such specialised activities

---

[22]See, for example, Hoffer (1967), Cohen (1964), Rein (1969).

would perhaps have to be undertaken by a new group of workers, modelling themselves on information officers. But it is not just a question of selection: the thorny problem of evaluation is always present; unless it is decided that nearly everything in the social sciences is relevant. Bloom refers[23] to 'application criteria'. These would ask such questions as: how can the theory be used with a particular client-centred problem, and ought the theory to be used at all?

In concentrating upon questions of selection and evaluation of existing basic research Bloom loses sight of the central problem to which he addressed himself: a poverty of usable knowledge. And this is a problem of very great importance to the practitioner and the information scientist interested in, and responsible for, the flow of information in, and to, the applied field. The practitioner is in a position to assess the relevance (but not the validity) of the information he receives from the standpoint of his practical work, but he is not in a position to know whether there is other (perhaps more valuable) information around; the information specialist should however be in this position. This is a very difficult order (and one that many would disagree with), and if this requires more research into the application of knowledge, into 'social engineering', etc., then this must be done.

When the practitioner has looked (and continues to look), and finds little usable knowledge, he is tempted to initiate 'practically minded' research, where the motivation and guidance come from the field and from practical problems rather than from the laboratory and theoretical issues.

In the last decade there has been a movement towards problem orientated (rather than discipline orientated) research. Some examples of problem orientated research (and its information requirements) are mentioned in 3.8. In the light of such developments comments about the need for 'social engineering' appear a little out of date. The new developments in applied social science research proposed by such writers as Bloom and Riecken are already in existence. It is a characteristic of this type of research that it is not closely tied in with the existing bibliographic system, and it is, therefore, difficult for those relying upon the formal communication channels to get to know about it.

The disadvantages of problem-orientated research are well known: results are severely restricted in their general applicability, and the idiosyncratic nature of research not guided by conceptual frameworks or

---

[23]See also Gouldner (1957) and Thomas (1964) for an enumeration of application criteria'.

paradigms produces results that are of little use to other social workers. Problem orientated research in the social sciences appears to require information from basic research (see 3.8.1 for an example of a problem orientated project that drew upon the body of psychological knowledge for information about attitude, aptitude, and intelligence tests) and this can result in a very familiar information problem. The practitioner can never be sure that some very important piece of information is not already in existence. The way in which some practitioners in the social sciences have come to rely upon the literature of basic research for some of their information requirements contrasts with the position in applied science. Applied scientists and technologists rarely make use of the products of basic research before the products are transformed into forms that are acceptable to the research in the applied field. And even then the amount of basic research that ever finds its way into the literature of the applied field is small (Allen and Cohen, 1969; Price, 1965a; Medawar, 1969).

Whatever type of research develops, the practitioner, like the basic researcher, will find that the way in which knowledge accumulates in social science is crucial to his profession. If it does so only in the trivial sense (i.e. collections of published material soon relegated to unstructured archives) and not in any hierarchical fashion then the 'do it yourself' practitioner has a strong case. The building blocks of his discipline have not been (and perhaps cannot be) established; and the beginnings of one practitioner are as good as anyone else's.

The issues discussed in this section can be ignored in the relatively simple (from a conceptual point of view) task of assessing current information use patterns and when charting available data, information sources, and services; and also when bringing these to the attention of potential users. But these issues cannot be ignored when attempts are made to assess information needs.

3.1.4   *Summary*

In this section it has been seen that there is no generally accepted theory about the nature of social science research and the information requirements of social scientists. Empirical studies (to be reviewed in the remainder of this chapter) of the information requirements of the social sciences have made few references to conceptual issues.

Where theoretical and conceptual issues have been raised they have occurred in the pursuit of activities in traditional areas of documentation, classification, and retrieval. The fact that the beginnings of a heory have emerged from these established areas (the position in the soviet Union is slightly different) is bound to influence the future development of theory and experiment in the study of social science information and its users.

It has been suggested (Kochen, 1969) that a new discipline is in the making. When, and if, this discipline is crystallised user studies will form but one small, albeit important, part. Many of the present studies that go under this heading, with very limited horizons and using unsophisticated methods, will be relegated to the pre-scientific history of this field. Because of its relatively late arrival on the scene the social science user study has escaped the worst defects that characterise the early user studies in science, where, for example, data were happily presented in abundance, with no mention of statistical significance.

.2 Number of user studies

A theme recurrent in this review is the dearth of user studies in the social sciences. There is a poverty of detail about the social science information system and its users at all levels. Little is known about the growth and decay of the literature or about the coverage of its abstracting and secondary tools, and there have been few studies of user requirements and needs. The research process in social science has received little attention and no theoretical structure about the flow of information has emerged. Where attention has been focused upon the information scene in the social sciences it has often been limited to an introductory analysis of the problem; to suggestions for study, and changes that could be made to the system. The field is characterised by a paucity of well-designed empirical studies. A very notable exception is the series of studies conducted by the American Psychological Association (APA) and some of these are considered in detail in sections 3.7 and 3.8.3.

The first attempt to review user studies in the social sciences was made by Paisley as recently as 1965. He considered the literature on the flow of behavioural science information. He concluded that there was no literature to review and then attempted to extrapolate from the findings of user studies in the physical sciences. 'A review that attempts to represent the flow of behavioral science information must cull studies of promising generality from the large, diffuse, sometimes poorly executed and duplicative body of research focusing on physicists, chemists, zoologists, engineers, etc. As it happens, information-gathering and disseminating behavior of scientists does not seem to be affected *greatly* by their specific fields of research, whereas other factors in their research environments and in their professional backgrounds do seem to be influential. We shall infer that information flows to and from behavioral scientists in much the same way that it flows to and from physical scientists until we have better data on the former group' (Paisley 1965, pp. 1–2). Paisley was a little optimistic in assuming that studies in science would have great relevance to the social sciences, although as seen in chapter 2 many of the methodological problems encountered in user studies in science are similar to the ones in social science.

Reviewing the 1968 literature on user studies Allen (1969, pp.3–29) maintained that an extrapolation from the results of studies in science to social science was no longer necessary. 'The number of studies concerned with social and behavioral scientists has become quite large in the past three years and is growing at a prodigious rate.' Allen would seem to over-estimate the number of studies that have been conducted since Paisley's 1965 review. In the following sections it can be seen that the number of studies in the social sciences is still very small, especially when compared with the number in science. Certainly very few studies of the social sciences have found their way into the four volumes of the *Annual Review of Information Science and Technology*, published annually since 1966. Each volume has included a chapter on information needs and uses. In the first volume Menzel (1966b) mentioned some of the APA studies, but with the exception of a reference to Paisley's (1965) review, all the other references were to studies in science. In the second volume Herner and Herner (1967) also referred indirectly to the APA project,[2] but to only one other social science study. In the third volume Paisley (1968) again mentioned the APA studies, a study of psychology journals, a study of information exchange at a meeting of the American Sociological Association, the United States National Research Council Committee on Information in the Behavioral Sciences (1967) study of communication systems and resources in the behavioral sciences, and three other studies. The National Research Council report mentioned the APA studies, the studies of sociologists under way at Johns Hopkins University (1967, 1968b), and the study of researchers in the interdisciplinary area of communications by Parker, Lingwood and Paisley (1968) at the Institute of Communication Research, Stanford University. The NRC report concluded that there was little more documented about information needs and

---

[24]By reference to Garvey and Griffith (1966).

use patterns in the behavioural sciences, and only a few of the existing studies had direct relevance to the question of information needs and requirements. The Johns Hopkins University (1967, 1968a) studies of sociologists were limited to the information–exchange activities at a professional meeting and the Stanford study was concerned with the relationship between communication activities and research productivity. Allen's (1969) review of the literature on user studies in the fourth volume of the *Annual Review of Information Science and Technology* includes ten references to studies in the social sciences, but not all of them are user studies.

It could of course be that the *Annual Review* does not achieve a complete coverage of social science studies. Certainly in the past the *Annual Review* has been science-orientated; but this is because information science has been concerned in the main with science and technology. There are many other sources[25] where studies of social science information needs and requirements may be reported, and these have been used in the preparation of this chapter. Nearly all the social science studies are of very recent origin and some of the studies mentioned are on-going.

Before empirical user studies in the social sciences are mentioned in detail, brief reference must be made to the large number of library surveys,[26] of one sort or another, some of which have included social science users. These surveys include straightforward counts of circulation records, studies of the use of card catalogues, and studies of borrowers and their reading habits. These library surveys, beginning[27] in the late 1930s, have rarely attempted statistical analysis of the data, and their methods, especially the earlier ones, were often rudimentary. Many of the studies were conducted by students for higher degrees, and often the target population was the one closest to hand. Other library surveys have been conducted by, or on behalf of, university and public libraries. Sometimes social scientists have been included.

---

[25]In social science monographs and periodicals, in abstracting journals, indexes; and in information and library science publications, especially *Information Science Abstracts, Library and Information Science Abstracts,* the current awareness list in *Aslib Proceedings,* and in various newsletters (e.g. *SSRC Newsletter,* American Society for Information Science *Newsletter of the Special Interest Group in Behavioral and Social Sciences*).

[26]See Line (1969b), McDiarmid (1940), Tauber (1964), Tauber and Stephens (1967), Wight (1937) on library surveys.

[27]Stevens (1969) discusses three early academic library surveys, including one conducted at Williams College in 1915.

F

A library survey, of whatever kind, is not a user study, or indeed a prototype for a user study. Library surveys focus attention upon the artifacts of communication, and not upon the information-gathering and information-disseminating behaviour of scientists. But these artifacts of communication, like those included in chapter 4 on citation patterns and bibliographic coupling, throw some light on a poorly lit subject: the flow of information in the social sciences It is interesting to note that the standard reviews of user studies in the sciences (e.g. Menzel, 1960; Paisley, 1965) do not mention library surveys, and cite no material older[28] than 1948, the date of the 'founding' papers of user studies presented to the Royal Society Conference on Scientific Information by Bernal (1948a) and Urquhart (1948).

3.3   Language barrier

The language barrier is not a problem that is peculiar to the social sciences. There have been many studies in science but only a few in the social sciences. From the studies that exist it can be seen that social scientists do not draw upon the world's literature for their work. Researchers from all countries draw far more heavily upon material written in their own language than in other languages. It would be naïve to assume that scientific information contributes[29] to scientific progress regardless of the language in which it is written.

Louttit (1955b) looked at the use of foreign language material by psychologists. Taking 1,814 references from psychology literature contained in English language publications, he noted that 60 per cent of the references cited were in English, 15 per cent in German, 12 per cent in French and 9 per cent in other languages. Of the abstracts analysed, 77 per cent were in English, 6 per cent in German, 8 per cent in French, and 9 per cent in other languages. Psychologists used less

---

[28]With one exception of a citation by Paisley (1965) to Patterson (1945).

[29]It is tempting to equate the variable of translation with the variable of importance (or relevance), and to suggest that only the important articles get translated. Some evidence for this equation comes from the citation studies of Barinova *et al.* (1968) who looked at the half-lives (defined as the time during which half the cited works in the study were published) of articles in eight Russian chemistry journals. They noticed different half-lives for domestic and foreign works. It was suggested that the trivial factor of age of article upon receipt by the researcher making the citing would account for this difference: as a rule workers become acquainted with foreign works later than with domestic works. But Barinova suggested an alternative explanation: that foreign scientists deal with more important topics and that their work is executed on a higher level.

foreign material than chemists and physicists. In a citation study of 22 psychology journals published in 1950, Boll (1952) noted that with few exceptions foreign language sources accounted for less than 5 per cent of all citations. Of the 381 references in the 1950 issue of the *Journal of Personality* 22 per cent were to foreign language material, and of the 333 references in the 1950 issue of *Psychoanalytic Quarterly* 17.4 per cent were to foreign language material. In the other journals the percentage of citations to foreign language material was much smaller.

Groenman and Riesthuis (1967) analysed the footnotes of the papers prepared for the European demographic conference held at Strasburg under the auspices of the Council of Europe in 1966. References to works in languages other than the language of the publication were counted. The degree to which authors of different countries restricted their citations to references written in their own language was tabulated. It was seen that English and French authors were the worst offenders for excluding references to other languages.

There are some exceptions to the general tendency to restrict citations to material written in the researcher's own language. As would be expected the exceptions are found in the languages that are not associated with large populations in Europe. Hogeweg-de Haart (1967) analysed the citations in eight Dutch social science journals.[30] The 1965 issues of these journals contained 624 citations to journal articles. Only 33.6 per cent were to articles published in Dutch, whereas 51.7 per cent were to publications in English. German and French accounted for 9.5 per cent and 3.7 per cent of the total citations respectively.

In the sciences, where the problem of a language barrier has been acute for some time, the provision of a translation service does not automatically guarantee the use of foreign material. Shilling, Tyson and Bernard (1963) mailed a questionnaire to authors of papers in the biological sciences published in 1961. The study examined the availability of translation services, the characteristics of the authors, and the value placed on Russian literature: these factors were related to the extent to which Russian articles were cited. Those scientists who cited Russian articles tended to be more wide-ranging in their interests than those who did not cite Russian work. The national isolation of some

---

[30]*Man and Society; Sociological Guide; Social Sciences; Geographical Journal; Journal for Economic and Social Geography; Dutch Journal for Psychology; General Dutch Journal for Philosophy; Psychology and Pedagogical Studies.*

scientists has often been attributed to the language barrier, but this study suggests that other factors must be considered. In the cases where a scientist did not have a good opinion of Russian work in the biological sciences, neither availability of translation nor the interest factor of the scientist was associated with the citation of Russian work.

3.4   Informal networks of communication[31]

It is only recently that serious study has been made of informal networks in research communities. It has come as a surprise to some to find that informal communication plays such a large part in research activities. Most of the commentary upon the informal system has come from the sciences, and the reader is referred to these sources[32] for a general picture of the informal system and its function in the total information system. The studies conducted by the American Psychological Association (APA) have done much to make clear the extent and importance of the information that is conveyed by informal channels, at least in psychology, although there is now little doubt that informal communication plays a large part in the flow of information in the other social sciences—but this activity has yet to be documented. Perhaps in the

---

[31]In the context of informal communication mention should be made of Price's concept of the 'invisible college'. Price (1965a, 1966b) suggests that groups of scientists are closely knit together by way of their (largely) informal networks of communication. There exist below the palpable surface of the published material (and the regularities and degree of bibliographic coupling that can be identified by, for example, citation analyses) groups of researchers that form 'colleges' initiated and perpetuated by a flow of information through exchanges of pre-publication papers, unpublished reports, correspondence, telephone conversations, and the interpersonal contacts made and continued at conferences, society meetings, committee meetings and social activities and personal contacts. Some unfavourable comment upon the concept of an 'invisible college' has been made. This has not been directed to informal networks—there is now ample evidence to show their ubiquity and importance—but to the idea of *stable* informal networks: in the absence of some stability in the informal networks they would be no more than temporary contacts and communications. In his work on the communication patterns among biochemists Mullins (1966) found that whilst each scientist had his own circle of colleagues with whom he stayed in touch regarding his and their work, no two scientists had exactly the same group in mind. Storer (1968) suggests that this finding casts a shadow of doubt over the concept of the 'invisible college'. The associations and contacts that scientists demonstrably have—and that Price uses as support for his concept—may be no more than custom-made reference groups. Crane (1969) has produced empirical evidence to test the 'invisible college' hypothesis. Using a mail questionnaire, sociometric data on different types of scientific relationships were obtained from scientists, all of whom had published in a particular problem area. Respondents chose scientists who had not published in the area as often as they chose scientists who had. Analysis of direct and indirect ties revealed that a tie with one or more of the highly productive

other social sciences informal systems play a greater part in the communication of ideas rather than, as in psychology, ongoing research.

In general the informal network of communications has been judged favourably, but because documentation of this activity is recent an assessment of growth is difficult. Informal networks are seen to complement and sometimes to enhance the existing array of formal activities in the communication of information, although some doubts have been expressed about the efficiency of the informal network for conveying and disseminating information and about its cost (APA Report Number 21). The APA study suggested that a number of the functions of the informal system could be fulfilled, at less cost, by a new and planned formal system. Another comment upon the negative aspects of the informal system comes from the United States National Research Council Committee on Information in the Behavioral Sciences (1967) report on the communication system in the behavioural sciences, where it is noted that the existing communication systems (including the large part that is informal) work very well for some scientists most of the time, but are inadequate for others. The scientists that find the existing systems adequate are more likely than others to be older and established, to have many professional contacts, and to sit on committees and

---

scientists brought other scientists of less productivity into a large network of influence and communication. Crane concluded that the 'invisible college' concept (defined as an élite of mutually interacting and productive scientists within a research area) cannot account for two aspects of the social organisation of research areas which emerged from the study: (1) the interaction between the most active and influential members of the area and the 'rank and file' and (2) the role of 'outsiders' in the organisation of the area.

[32]Menzel (1968) discusses the advantages of informal communication in science. Some of the characteristics of informal networks in specific environments have been enumerated by Pelz (1956) in a study of the organisational and social factors related to performance in a research centre, and by Orr, Coyl and Leeds (1964) in a study of oral communication among biomedical scientists. Herner (1954) looked at the informal communication activities of pure and applied scientists, Herner (1959) at medical scientists, Shilling, Bernard and Tyson (1964) at informal communication among bioscientists and Rosenbloom, McLaughlin and Wolek (1965) at the communication of technical information in a large industrial corporation. Allen (1964, 1965, 1966a, 1966b, 1967, 1968), Allen, Andrien and Gerstenfeld (1966), Allen and Cohen (1969), Allen and Gerstberger (1967), and Allen, Gerstenfeld and Gerstberger (1968) have been active in tracing the flow of communications in industrial research laboratories, in the identification of key persons in the informal communication networks, and the relative effectiveness of channels (including informal) of communication. A study by Graham, Wagner, Gloege, and Zavala (1967) explored and defined the boundaries of informal communications behaviour, based on five kinds of scientists and engineers in four types of employing organisations. This study also includes a review of the literature on informal communications. As in so many other aspects of the flow of information in research, the social sciences, with the exception of the APA studies, have rarely been studied.

governing councils of professional bodies: in short, to be active and successful members of invisible colleges. In contrast, the younger and less experienced researcher is unlikely to be in a position to make use of informal systems, and consequently his information exposure is incomplete and inadequate to the extent that the formal channels (to which he has an equal chance of access) do not duplicate the functions of the informal ones.

3.4.1 Characteristics of informal networks

The most obvious advantage of interpersonal communication is its speed in bringing word of new developments to those who are tuned in to the appropriate scientific grapevine. In recent decades the time gap between experiment and publication has increased and this has made informal communications more attractive. Garvey and Griffith (1968) suggest that the increasing reliance placed upon informal communication is the scientist's way of adjusting to the information explosion and satisfying those information needs which formal channels do not or cannot fulfil.

Secondly, the interpersonal network performs a kind of current awareness service. By a process of selective switching it routes scientific news to the scientists to whom it is relevant. Information that is obtained from a fellow scientist is screened, evaluated, and synthesised. The colleague performs these services which traditional retrieval and formal systems do not. The colleague will deliver information rather than documents; he will have exposed himself to a wide variety of documents in his area of interest and will have selectively remembered some and not others. Another activity of a colleague, of special importance to practitioners, is the 'translation' he may be able to perform. Information originally reported in the language of the research report is 'translated' into applied or action terms. Also colleagues may be able to collate information from a wide variety of sources. Although certain handbooks, manuals, and practically-orientated reviews exist, these media are less successful than colleagues when it comes to collating basic-science information and translating it into action terms and imparting a sense of judgement. Some of the better formal systems attempt to incorporate these aspects of information flow in their design, but there remains a certain type of information that is more amenable to transmission through the informal network: know-how information is of this nature. This includes unpublished minor details of research already published, information about the use of techniques, information about the adaptation of apparatus and the availability of materials; in general, the fruits of experience and know-how. Information of this kind often fails to find its way into the literature, and even if published, it is difficult to retrieve.[33]

Thirdly, and contrary to what might be expected, the audiences for some informal communications may be equal to, or exceed, the number who examine articles shortly after publication.

Fourthly there is considerable redundancy in the informal system because information from a single study may appear in a variety of forms (e.g. by word of mouth, by an informal presentation of material at a small gathering, or by correspondence).

Fifthly, information disseminated by the informal channels is current. The information reaches audiences which contain a high proportion of active researchers involved in work in the same area.

Sixthly, scientists interacting informally are willing to speculate about their work, to discuss their mistakes as well as their successes and range over a broad area of interests which in a more rigorous framework may appear only tangential to their specific findings. In this way the 'art' of scientific research has a chance of being communicated.

Informal channels allow the scientist to direct a communication and select for himself the specific information he needs. In doing this he is trying to select from a particular source enough information to decide whether further pursuit is likely to provide him with fruitful information and also to select the channel which will allow him to obtain the most information with the least noise in the quickest manner and with the least effort. Informal channels allow for feedback, including critical feedback, which in turn may provide reinforcement. From the point of view of personal motivation informal communication may provide stimulation, facilitation and encouragement which are not to be had through the formal channels. It is the large number of opportunities for instantaneous feedback provided by interpersonal contacts that furnish contingencies for reinforcement. Feedback also provides opportunities for the modification and clarification of questions and for the exposition of difficult messages.

Lazarsfeld and Leeds (1962, p. 734) suggest that informal contacts

---

[33]Reports of studies of the transmission of this type of information can be found in Menzel (1959), Rosenbloom, McLaughlin and Wolek (1965) and in the APA (1965) Report Number 11.

gained at international meetings present a variety of benefits which cannot be had otherwise. 'Personal contacts often permit one to assess the merits of a man with greater ease than his published work. . . . These contacts themselves facilitate subsequent correspondence about professional matters which otherwise could not be initiated with the same ease. . . . The foreign colleague can also give his estimation of the work being done and the persons who are doing it. This provides one with some basis for judging whether it is worth establishing contact with a particular foreign group'.

Informal communication channels are created and perpetuated by scientists themselves to satisfy information needs which are not being fulfilled by formal channels. Informal channels are unstable and temporary: they do not provide permanent and public records. Garvey and Griffith (1968) suggest that the overriding disadvantage of information communication is its cost: both in terms of time and effort required on the part of researchers, and the technical software (e.g. extensive correspondence and telephone calls) required. If the advantages of the informal system cannot be replicated by less costly means then they are justified. A number of attempts to create formal systems which retain the advantages of informal systems and which can serve far greater numbers than any informal system have been investigated and evaluated.[34]

3.4.2 *Informal communications, social structures and the research literature*

One of the APA reports (Report Number 21) compares the structure of the research literature in psychology when based upon subject classification with the social and communication structures, identified through questionnaires and interviews. These two structures were compared in five specialised areas (audition, psycholinguistics, behavioural effects of drugs, social perception and speech perception). A summary of the findings in three of the five specialised areas can be found in Griffith (1969).

It was noted that communication patterns and social organisations vary from one area to another. A research literature may be the product

---

[34]The Interferon Scientific Memoranda (ISM), for example, represent an attempt to develop more advanced media for the transmission of informal communications. The desirable characteristics of informal communications (e.g. speed, direct feedback) are maintained at the same time making the services available to all members of a particular research community. Details of ISM are given in a report by the Aries Corporation (1969).

f a well organised group (audition) or of individuals operating completely independently (social perception). But even in the most isolated
type of research environment some interpersonal interaction takes place
(see APA Report Number 11). The relationship between social organisation and communication patterns varies independently. A high degree
of organisation is associated with: (1) a limited number of institutions
having research facilities; (2) a single specialised organisation containing
most researchers in the field; (3) many student-teacher relationships;
(4) long-term commitments to research in the area; and (5) the area
being the principal research interest of most researchers. A small
highly technical field (such as speech perception) seems likely to have a
large number of informal exchanges, but not necessarily a high degree of
social organisation. The absence of both informal communication and
social organisation can probably occur only in a field such as social
perception, which most researchers regarded as a subsidiary interest and
which did not generate its own conceptual framework. The report
considered the implication of the findings for the organisation of
research groups, and for indexing and classifying literature, and suggested that an attempt to align the classification of the literature with the
social structure of a field is only worthwhile in a highly organised field.
In general, the report concluded, one is forced to question whether the
classification of the literature can or should ever be matched to the
structure of systems that can be identified by the communication
patterns of advanced researchers. Many groups, especially those
created by conferences and committees, may have a very short life, and
even groups found in special centres for advanced study are unstable.

The findings of this APA study suggest that a clear distinction should
be made between 'organisation' and 'communication' although the
effect of one on the other is not clearly established. But it is clear, the
report concluded, that a highly organised and coherent group does not
come into existence primarily to meet communication needs.

The status of the initiator and the receiver of communications appears
to play a larger part in informal than in formal communications. A. G.
Smith (1966) looked at the relationship between communications and
status in the Center for the Advanced Study of Education Administration,
at the University of Oregon. The study dealt with the networks of interactions among the staff of the Center, with special attention to the influence
of position upon communication networks. Smith interviewed thirty-five
(75 per cent) members of the staff of the Center. The disciplines
represented included the behavioural sciences and educational

administration. The interviewer asked questions in a conversa-
tional tone and all the questions were open-ended. Each interviewee
was asked about his communications with each of the other members of
the staff. The interviewer gave the name of a staff member and asked
'Do you know him?' 'Who is he?' These questions were designed to
elicit the perceived status of the person named. The second question
was always of the order: 'Have you communicated with him during the
last couple of days?' Then it was determined how the communication
took place—by telephone, in person, by memorandum or by what other
medium. The interviews also produced data about: the initiator of the
contact, the content of the communication, the typicalness of the
communication, and social contacts. Preferences for title—last name,
first name, or epithet—were recorded.

From the interview material perceived statuses were charted and
individual members of the Center grouped in terms of their shared
statuses. It was found that group boundaries determined communication patterns, and that little communication took place across group
boundaries. As the Center had grown and become bureaucratised, it
had developed more distinctions of rank and division of labour. These
hierarchies presented barriers to the free flow of information; they also
provided shielding and prevented jamming in the communication network. Two status-sets (the organisation man and the research man) cut
across the officially established ranks and functional divisions of the
Center. Much of the communication network paralleled this division.

3.4.3 Gatekeepers and two-step flow of information
Menzel (1968) draws an analogy between the processes involved in the
flow of information through the informal communication channels and
the diffusion of innovations (e.g. Day, 1968; Rogers, 1962). From
studies of the mass media has come the idea of the two-step—sometimes
multistep—flow of information. In such a process the message is
generated from a source, which may be a single official document or a
doctrinal message embodied in some theoretical discourse. This
message is communicated by formal channels to the 'disciples', who are
already believers in the message, who are set to receive the message,
and who have the skills necessary to transmit the message to its final
destination, the public. It is this last stage in the multistep chain where
face-to-face communication is essential: personal influence about an
issue is often exerted unexpectedly as a marginal topic in a casual
conversation; face-to-face contact is more flexible, provides feedback

and instantaneous modification of the message, it is more likely to raise issues and arguments of immediate personal influence in making a decision and the receiver of the message is more likely to be rewarded by approval. The communication of information takes place in a series of interlocking steps. At each stage in the chain there exists the possibility of omission and/or addition to the message received.

In research communities all members are not exposed to equal amounts of information. There are differential exposure rates according to status and function within a community, and individual differences in preference for types of information seeking and gathering activities. Allen (1965), and Allen and Cohen (1969) have shown that within a technological research community the majority of workers have little direct exposure to outside sources and rely heavily upon a single member of the community for direction of attention to significant external information. These persons, called 'gatekeepers' by Allen, are atypical in technological research teams, and can be differentiated from other members of the team by a number of characteristics including their predilection for high exposure to external information.[35]

Menzel (1968) has also drawn attention to those characteristics of the informal communication network in mass communication that have their analogies in the field of scientific information flow. Although some of these characteristics are very attractive they can hardly suffice to account for the great part played by interpersonal communication in science. Whereas the mass media campaign involves persuasion, the material that diffuses throughout the communication network in science by interpersonal communication is cognitive. Menzel attempts to account for the prevalence of interpersonal communication in science. He enumerates six characteristics of the interpersonal network. If

---

[35]Lasswell (1960) has drawn attention to a similar differentiation of roles in animal communities where certain members perform specialised roles in surveying the environment. Individuals act as 'sentinels', standing apart from the others and creating a disturbance whenever an alarming change occurs in the surroundings. Lasswell (1960, p. 127) describes some of the activities of relay links in communication chains: 'Whoever performs a relay function can be examined in relation to input and output. What statements are brought to the attention of the relay link? What does he pass on verbatim? What does he drop out? What does he rework? What does he add? How do differences in input and output correlate with culture and personality? . . . It is useful to consider the attention frame of the relay as well as the primary link in terms of media and non-media exposures. The role of non-media factors is very slight in the case of many relay operators, while it is certain to be significant in accounting for the primary observer'.

other forms of communication were to be substituted they would need (1) promptness; (2) selective switching; (3) screening, evaluation and synthesis; (4) extraction of action implications; (5) transmitting the ineffable; and (6) instantaneous feedback.

3.5 Informational, environmental, and personality factors associated with productivity

The factors of communication associated with productivity, as assessed by the numbers of publications, were studied by Parker, Lingwood and Paisley (1968), in a group of workers in the interdisciplinary area of communications research. Two samples were drawn from many different disciplines. The total number in the first sample was 629 and the total number in the second sample was 506. Questionnaires were mailed to all members of each sample. There were slight differences in the information requested from the two samples. Demographic data was collected for the first but not from the second group, since this data was available from the National Register. Data about the education, the employment and the professional activities of the respondents were tabulated. There was a response rate of 84 per cent for the first sample and of 78 per cent for the second sample.

The multiple correlations predicting productivity from a set of nine independent variables ranged from 0.47 to 0.55, depending on which measure of productivity and which replication was reported. For the various correlations some 22 per cent to 31 per cent of the total variances were accounted for, leaving more than 70 per cent to be explained by error variance in the measure of productivity itself, or to be accounted for by variables not included in the analysis. The strongest predictor of productivity was the extent to which interpersonal contact with other researchers was utilised, as a primary source of information. The index of interpersonal contact was made up from assessments of receipt of preprints and unpublished papers, telephone conversations, personal contacts, visits, telephone or correspondence contacts with the major research personnel in own speciality, and unpublished papers of recent useful information. This index correlated 0.32 with productivity. However, when the other seven predictors of productivity were partialled out from the correlation relating the index of personal contact and productivity this relationship fell to between 0.21 and 0.27, depending upon the analysis in question. An index of impersonal contact (which included journal readership, use of reprints, contact with major research facility through journal articles and journals or formal meeting presentations) also correlated 0.32 with productivity There was a correlational coefficient of 0.31 between the indexes of interpersonal and impersonal contact. However, when both were included in the multiple regression analysis, interpersonal contact was the major predictor of productivity.

Other predictors of productivity included number of professional memberships, level of education (e.g. PhDs produced more), recency of highest degree (younger scientists produced more), number of immediate colleagues and physical access to them, individual *v.* teamwork, and attendance at conventions. The number of unpublished papers read at meetings and conventions also correlated strongly with productivity.

The study also included a principal components (varimax rotation) factor analysis of the 55 variables from the primary analysis. Twenty factors were derived, but no single factor accounted for more than a small percentage of the total variance. For example, Factor I accounted for 9.16 per cent, Factor II for 11.56 per cent, and Factor III for 9.15 per cent of the total variance. The first factor grouped together those variables measuring informal activity, the second factor accounted for the variables of exchange of written material, and the third factor loaded highly on those variables measuring sources of information and the nature of information.

In the introduction to their report Parker, Lingwood and Paisley 1968, p. 1) state: 'One of the reasons—perhaps the major reason—for research agencies to sponsor studies of the communication behavior of scientists is to learn the nature of the relationship between communication behavior and research productivity. The apparent hope is that funds invested in improved scientific communication will lead to a more efficient over-all use of funds invested in science. If this hope is to be realised, we need to know, first, whether there is a demonstrable relationship between scientific communication and scientific research productivity, and second, what kinds of communication should be supported to achieve increased productivity'.

Not all commentators upon the communication and publishing scene have been so concerned with productivity alone—in the absence of any concern with evaluation of scientific activity and the quality of published material. Although the use of informal channels of communication is the factor most clearly related to productivity it is not the only one, and the relationship is not all that high. The Parker, Lingwood and Paisley study commits a cardinal sin in statistical analysis by suggesting that the reported correlations can be used to show a causative connection. It is naïve to suppose that a complex human activity like the production of scientific papers could be systematically increased by facilitating the use of the informal communication channel alone. Parker, Lingwood and Paisley overstate their case.

Other investigators have looked at the correlates of productivity although most of these studies have been in science and technology including studies of productivity in industrial research laboratories. Cole and Cole (1967) have demonstrated that quantity and quality of published material are strongly correlated and that both these aspects in turn are correlated with the rewards obtained by scientists. A multiple measure of research productivity (e.g. peer-judgements of contribution to knowledge and usefulness of the organisation carrying out its responsibilities, unpublished reports) was used by Pelz and Andrews (1966a) as an index of productivity, and they reported similar results to those studies using the amount of published material as the sole indicator of scientific activity. Pelz (1956), Pelz and Andrews (1962), and C. G. Smith (1966) have looked at the relationship between organisational (including social) factors and performance in industrial and scientific research settings. Shilling, Bernard and Tyson (1964) found higher productivity in laboratories which permitted unrestricted use of long distance telephone calls and encouraged travel to other laboratories with more restricted travel policies. Paisley and Parker (1967) developed an index of 'communication input' and included this index along with ten other predictors in a multiple regression analysis of research productivity. C. G. Smith (1966) identified five sets of variables associated with scientific performance in an industrial research laboratory.

The American Psychological Association Report Number 19 identified a positive relationship between productivity and possession of a doctoral degree; and noted that age had little to do with the productivity factor. Also APA membership tended to increase with productivity. At the highest level of productivity research was ranked as the first or second most information-demanding activity. Research, research guidance, and writing and editing increased in time-consumption and information-demand as productivity increased. Applied and clinical activities plus administrative work and graduate study decreased as these measures of productivity increased. Journal use, meeting attendance, and the use of information contacts all increased as the productivity level increased.

There is some evidence to show that scientists who are highly productive come from different academic backgrounds and have different personality characteristics than scientists who are relatively unproductive. Crane (1965) looked at the productivity of biologists, political scientists and psychologists. In total the sample included 150 scientists located at three universities of varying prestige. The scientists at the major schools were more likely to be productive and to win recognition than scientists at minor universities. It was seen that the high status graduate schools selected the good students, the best of whom were trained by top scientists and became the next generation's most productive scientists. Scientists trained and later hired by minor universities had difficulty developing continuity in their research activities and tended to be differently motivated from scientists trained and hired by major universities. In terms of his chances of obtaining recognition, a scientist gained more from affiliation with a major university which provided better opportunities for contacts with eminent scientists in the same discipline.

The relationship between productivity and information requirements and use is likely to be very complex, and involve a fairly large number of variables. To the extent that each new unit of published material relies upon previous work (e.g. it is known that in science the mean number of citations per article is around ten, see Price, 1965a) highly productive scientists will use more material than unproductive scientists. The only observable measure here is use: the unproductive scientist may be exposed to the same amount of information as his more productive colleague: in fact, the unproductive colleague may be exposed to, and may seek and assimilate, *more* information and this may account for his unproductivity. Another factor working against a direct relationship between productivity and use of information is the tendency for the bibliography of one paper to repeat, or to bear a very close relationship to, the bibliography of past articles by the same author. However, the productive scientist is certainly more likely to make a greater mark on the information scene: he will appear more frequently in indexes, citations, abstracts, publishers' lists, etc., and will figure prominently in citation counts.

3.6 Requirements and demands for published material[36]

Most user studies include a section on the requirements of researchers for primary and secondary bibliographical material. Some user studies have investigated only requirements for published literature (leaving aside, for example informal communications). Such studies of the social sciences are considered below.

Very few studies have attempted to relate information requirements and demands to the available material in a discipline or to local conditions of availability and access. At the present time this would be a difficult, and perhaps impossible, task to complete because very little is known about many aspects of social science literature (e.g. coverage of primary journals by secondary tools, growth points). The ideal use study should, among other things, relate findings about the way in which researchers/teachers go about reference searching to a model representing the ideal searching method. Any attempt to assess the thoroughness of literature searching methods or the completeness of a user's searching methods or the completeness of a user's knowledge of secondary bibliographical tools can only be made in the context of details about the primary literature and the secondary tools.

---

[36]Some additional material about the demand for published material can be gained from studies of the circulation and use of monographs and serials in libraries (see 3.2). This type of study is sometimes referred to as 'use study' and is in fact sometimes mistaken for 'user study'. Such studies look at only the artifacts of communications between scientists, and do not, as do user studies, enquire about these communications. However, artifacts of communication provide valuable additional material about information requirements and a number of such studies are included in chapter 4.

[37]For purposes of illustration some examples of information sources, guides to the literature, and special information centres in the social sciences are given. This list is not intended to be comprehensive as this aspect of social science information falls outside the scope of this monograph. In the social sciences (and in education especially) there are very many guides to the literature, and special services and centres for information. In fact, it is possible that there are far too many and this may work against their usefulness. It would appear that it is a very hit and miss affair whether or not a researcher/teacher comes across the relevant part of this superstructure. Perhaps the best general guide, although now somewhat out-of-date, to sources of information in the social sciences is White (1964). Guides to the literature include Lewis (1960), Hoselitz (1959), Walford (1968), a recent French bibliography of the social sciences (Desrochers, 1969), and the American Behavioral Scientist *Guide to the published literature in the social and behavioral sciences* with supplements published each year since 1966. There is now also at least one guide to the guides (Schutze, 1968), and the better known UNESCO *World list of social science periodicals*. Each discipline in the social sciences also has its own guides, bibliographies, and lists of recent publications. There is an uneven coverage across the different disciplines, and perhaps education is better endowed with such documents than the other social sciences. In psychology there is the Harvard University (1967) *Harvard list of books in psychology;* in politics there is a guide to the literature by Harmon (1965), a guide to reference material by Wynar (1968), and an annotated guide to research resources in international relations by Mason (1968); in sociology there is a guide to the literature by Bottomore (1962); in statistics there are bibliographies going back as far as 1940 by Kendall and Doig (1962, 1965, 1968) and guides to the

There are many[37] secondary (e.g. abstracting journals, reviews) and tertiary (e.g. directories of research institutions, guides to the literature) sources of information in the social sciences, but their interrelationship with one another, coverage, and topicality are not always known.

3.6.1 *Primary material*

A study by Uytterschaut (1966a) was directed towards the methods used by researchers in searching the literature. It is one of the few studies in the social sciences that could properly be called a user study. Uytterschaut attempted to find out if researchers went about literature searching according to some general and uniform programme, and to assess researchers' attitudes towards assistance from documentalists. This study sampled only twenty researchers in law and economics, and it is therefore not possible to make generalisations from its results. It is unfortunate that it has this defect of sampling because otherwise it is an

---

sources of statistics by Harvey (1969) and Wasserman, Allen, and Georgi (1965), as well as the Central Statistical Office (1965) lists of principal statistics; in geography there is a reference handbook by Lock (1968); and in education there is a guide to periodicals by Camp (1968), the UNESCO list of education periodicals, and a good many bibliographies of special aspects of education.

There are abstracting journals that serve the major social science disciplines (e.g. *Sociological Abstracts, Psychological Abstracts*) and ones that have more specialised or interdisciplinary interests (e.g. *Sociology of Education Abstracts, Language and Language Behavior Abstracts*). There are special articles and monographs dealing with reference and bibliographical material in each of the disciplines: for example, information sources in applied social studies (Crossley, 1969; National Council for the Social Studies, 1963), in economics and commerce (Maltby, 1968), an annotated bibliography on the teaching of economics (Lee and Szreter, 1966), and documentation services in psychology by Elliott (1970). Scattered about the literature in each discipline are specialised bibliographies; for example, a bibliography on political élite by Beck and McKechnie (1968), a bibliography on primary education by UNESCO (1963), a bibliography on teaching machines and programmed learning by Gee (1965) and a bibliography on adolescent behaviour in urban areas by Gottlieb and Reeves (1963). In the literature of the social sciences there are many hundreds of bibliographies on specialised topics, although it is fairly difficult for the researcher/teacher to retrieve these bibliographies because there is no central listing. There is a guide to unpublished literature by Staveley (1957) which includes chapters on psychology and sociology.

In addition to the bibliographical tools a number of specialised information centres in the social sciences exist (e.g. School Research Information Service, The American Management Association Management Information Service, and the various Clearinghouses of the Educational Resources Information Centre. These specialised information centres are organised primarily to select, acquire, store, and retrieve documents pertaining to one specific discipline or field of interest, and to disseminate in response to user request. One recent publication, by Gates and Altman (1968), attempts to bring under one cover a large number of guides and directories, information centres, data repositories and abstracting and indexing services in education and the behavioural sciences.

G

interesting piece of work. It covers a wide range of information seeking activities and related topics—aspects of user behaviour not always covered by investigations that are more technically sound.

The method of investigation was rather unusual because the interviewer attempted to restrict the variability of answers by imposing artificial conditions under which literature searching could take place (e.g. a search that was not restricted by a time schedule, a thorough search, a new start to a field of research). Uytterschaut (1966a) argued that this method of interviewing avoids contamination of the answers by local conditions of availability and facilities for research. During interviews the interviewees were shown a chart in which all categories of literature searching were brought together (e.g. a listing of bibliographical tools). This was done to facilitate the recall of literature searching activities (as it is well known that recognition scores exceed recall scores).

Uytterschaut (1966a) found that the location of leading authors and standard works in a given field was the main concern of most respondents. Researchers often relied upon leading authors to provide suitable and selective bibliographies from which relevant material for an investigation could be taken. Respondents mentioned that such bibliographic material was often out-of-date and had to be supplemented by more recent references from several secondary sources and also from main periodicals. Many respondents mentioned that their literature searching had to pass through a trial-and-error period. Most respondents mentioned several kinds of bibliographical sources that were consulted at the same stage in research. Uytterschaut suggested that most respondents were uneasy about their trial-and-error beginnings and as a result mentioned several bibliographical sources. Literature searching did not appear to be dictated by the methodology of the investigation in hand; rather the methodology grew out of the literature searching methods.

Different information seeking behaviours were used in central and peripheral areas. In peripheral areas respondents were predisposed at the very beginning to contact experts. There were also differences in literature searching methods between those respondents with little experience in their field of research and subject specialists. Although all researchers planned to locate rapidly the leading material, the novice felt much less certain about how to proceed. He was less sure of his selections and less likely to skip over sources of information. The experienced researcher was much more certain of his ground and tried to avoid redundancy at the outset. However, Uytterschaut concluded that the experienced researcher sometimes deliberately neglected valuable bibliographical tools. These were consulted only occasionally to fill gaps in an experienced researcher's knowledge about documentation available in his nearest surroundings.

Researchers were questioned about the possibility of delegating literature searches, but there was no unanimous agreement. It was often remarked that the scattering of relevant information over a large number of bibliographic tools was a major barrier to research, although as Uytterschaut pointed out the term 'bibliographic tool' was almost always understood to mean a list of titles. None of the respondents had at hand a solution to documentation problems and usually, after some hesitation, a workable solution was seen to consist either of a co-ordination between existing services, or the creation of a central documentation service (perhaps central library or a bibliographic tool) which could stand for one specific social science, or a main sub-field of each social science. There was disagreement about where a central specialised service should be located geographically. Respondents did not think in terms of sophisticated documentation and information centres: rather they tended to think in terms of a central browsing room where they could find quickly, for themselves, by means of a major catalogue, all references to the topic of their interests.

For keeping abreast of their subjects nearly all respondents proceeded in much the same way: that is, primary attention was given to the main journals in their field and to book reviews in journals. Placed second in importance were lists of library acquisitions and catalogues from book publishers. Occasionally contacts with specialists, and other informal sources.

A methodological point well worth attention is the limited documentation vocabulary of social science researchers. Uytterschaut noted that respondents were usually unable to make a clear distinction between, on the one hand, the actual piece of information that was extracted from available knowledge, and on the other hand, the documentary itinerary by which the piece of information was located.

Uytterschaut suggested that this confusion was perhaps related to the constant attempt made by respondents to justify the logic of their literature searching methods, which they thought should parallel their approach to their subject. The way in which respondents saw their literature searching methods was often dominated by the 'logical' concept of the research process rather than by documentary considerations.

As a general rule, the results of this investigation suggest that investigators should not assume that researchers have a detailed or accurate vocabulary for documentation. According to Uytterschaut the documentation vocabulary of researchers could easily be reduced to 'list of titles' and 'standard works'. Uytterschaut suggested that information scientists should not start an investigation from the documentary point of view of the way in which knowledge is processed, but from the point of view of the production and processing of knowledge in social science research. Borrowing an idea from Maruyama (1962), Uytterschaut suggested that it may be important to get the 'feel' of research, and that to do so would require a good deal more than a theoretical knowledge of the research process.

Other user studies in the social sciences have looked at requirements and demands for published material (see 3.7.2 and 3.8) but no other study has concentrated solely on published material, as did Uytterschaut's investigation. Usually investigations explore information requirements involving many types of communication.

3.6.2 *Secondary material and information services*

A user study will generally include a section on the use of, and need for, secondary bibliographic materials—bibliographies, indexes, abstracts, etc. Some of these part-studies are brought together here. Also studies of the use made of information services (e.g. SDI, Current Awareness) are included.

In a pilot study of the bibliographic needs of social and behavioural scientists, Appel and Gurr (1964) reported that the location of material for research and teaching was regarded by social and behavioural scientists as a very time consuming task. But during literature searches users made little use of special resources. They were much more likely to track down material through footnotes and journal bibliographies than to use abstracting journals, special bibliographies, research assistants, or librarians. All economists included in this study used *American Economic Review*, 90 per cent used *Journal of Economic Abstracts*, and 75 per cent used *Index of Economic Journals*. All the psychologists in the sample used *Psychological Abstracts* and *Psychological Bulletin* and 80 per cent used *Contemporary Psychology*. 89 per cent of all respondents indicated that they did not know the UNESCO *International Bibliography of the Social Sciences:* where this bibliography was used it was often judged to be irrelevant and seldom useful.

The fact that the social scientist feels his literature searching is inadequate, that information is passing him by, and that he often fails to learn about relevant work that would have made a difference to his research and/or teaching (60 per cent of the social scientists in the Appel and Gurr study made this comment) supports the suspicion long held amongst librarians, and substantiated by empirical investigations in the sciences, that researchers are very unknowledgeable about bibliographic tools.

The fact that secondary bibliographic tools are not used extensively by the majority of social scientists can be attributed to a number of factors. It may be that (1) the tools are in some way inadequate for the requirements of the users; (2) the tools are unknown to users; (3) users have no habit of using them and no tradition of instruction in the use of bibliographic tools; or (4) a combination of these factors. In the absence of reliable data about the causes of the infrequent use of secondary sources it would be premature to attempt drastic alterations in the nature and format of secondary tools or a massive course of instruction in the use of them.

Those responsible for the production and editing of secondary tools in the social sciences have not in the past made many enquiries about the requirements of users. There are at least two exceptions: (1) the American Psychological Association study of *Psychological Abstracts* (see 3.7.1 for details), and (2) an investigation[38] of the users of *Sociology of Education Abstracts* (SEA).

The SEA investigation is concentrating upon the physical form of the journal, the coverage and classification of the abstracts, and the effectiveness of different kinds of document representation. To date, the investigation has included enquiries into the needs, requirements, and preferences of users (see 3.8.3 for details about this part of the investigation), an experimental bibliographic enquiry service, and contacts with SEA users (see Winn 1969a, 1969b).

It is interesting to note, in the context of studies of requirements for published material, that the (American) Institute for Scientific Information (ISI) first published in 1955 *Current Contents of Social and Management Sciences*, a semi-monthly publication consisting of facsimile reproduction of contents pages of some two hundred journals. It was discontinued in 1962. According to Albright and Glennon (1963) this publication was popular among those who used it, but never gained wide support (Garfield, 1964). Similar publications in physics, chemistry, and the life sciences have been on the market for a number of years,

---

[38]Currently being carried out with the support of OSTI by the editor of SEA, Professor D. F. Swift, and Miss V. A. Winn, Department of Educational Studies, Oxford University.

and towards the end of 1968 the ISI introduced a weekly *Current Contents of the Behavioral, Social, and Management Sciences,* and in 1969 *Current Contents in Education.* It is always very difficult to assess the relationship between publication policies and frequency of usage, and statements such as made by Garfield about the publication of *Current Contents of Social and Management Sciences* must be viewed with caution. In his article Garfield gave no empirical data to support his suggestion. As a method (see 2.3.4) of enquiry into information requirements publication policies are of marginal interest only.

In order to provide information services (e.g. SDI, current awareness) it is necessary to enquire first about the information needs and requirements of users, and this usually requires the construction of an interest profile, a trial period of service, feedback from users to evaluate the service, and a modification of the profile to regulate the flow of information to the user. In science and technology information services have been provided in some areas for a number of years (see Bivona and Goldblum, 1966; Cooper, 1968; Connor, 1967). Where interest profiles are limited to a listing of topics of interest, key words, or subject areas, they give little data about information needs, but where an information officer has a good deal of contact with users of information services, perhaps over long periods of time, and especially where the information officer sets out to record the interaction, valuable data can be gathered about user information needs and requirements. This type of data can provide a valuable supplement to the data gained from interview and questionnaire, which typically tap the needs and requirements of a user at a certain point in time, whereas the interaction of a user and an information officer can provide a longitudinal picture of the information needs of a user. Only very recently have information services been provided for social scientists, and some of these are mentioned below. They can provide valuable data about the information needs and requirements of social scientists, especially so at the present time when so little is known about them. Even if in the future user studies provide a body of knowledge about the information needs and requirements of social scientists, data from field observations and interest profiles made by information officers may provide valuable additional data to that gathered by survey techniques. In fact, in order to establish needs (as opposed to demands or requirements) it will perhaps always be necessary, at least in the social sciences, to include field observations.

A computerised SDI system was operated at Northwestern University (see Janda and Rader, 1967) for notifying social scientists of new journal articles relevant to their interests, and provision was made to obtain feedback from users who were asked to judge the relevance of the information they received, to report on articles they already knew about or would have discovered through other means, and to note articles they may have missed completely (perhaps because the article appeared in unfamiliar journals) in the absence of the service. Interest profiles of users were established and incorporated into the 'search command', which included specific keywords and logical connections that had to exist between keywords before an abstract qualified for retrieval. Janda and Rader reported that considerable experience and imagination were required to effectively establish a user's interest profile that could act as an appropriate search command. The usual procedure was for a SDI staff member and user to meet in conference, followed by a trial run using the search command that resulted from the first meeting, and a second conference to review the output and improve the command if necessary. Further opportunities were provided for modification and revision of interest profiles and search commands. As a by-product of this service a good deal of data was collected about the information needs and requirements of social scientists.

At Durham, as part of an OSTI-supported Project for the Evaluation of Benefits from University Libraries (PEBUL), an experimental current awareness service (CAS) was evaluated (Durham University, 1969) by interviewing the 31 university staff (drawn from economics, economic history, politics, and the Business School) who had participated. The service, preceded by the construction of interest profiles, consisted of cards containing references to current serials and recent acquisitions at the local libraries. During the time the service operated provision was made for informal feedback. A follow-up study attempted to evaluate the service. It was found that the service had little effect upon frequency of library use, but it did save time in compiling bibliographies. The service was judged to be more useful for research than for teaching, and index cards were preferred to other communications. 20 per cent of the respondents knew about the information before they were notified, but only 16 per cent had read the articles or ordered books at the time of the survey. 32 per cent had filed the information for future use. Only 8 per cent found the information irrelevant. When asked to choose between the CAS, a research assistant for five days per year, an additional book grant, or a visit each year to a London or Oxford library—services of approximate equal cost—20 of the 29 respondents chose the CAS.

A current awareness service to social scientists, involving the construction of user interest profiles, is being provided by the OSTI-supported Information Officer at Bath University of Technology —the first university in the United Kingdom to have an information officer in the social sciences. The impetus for the appointment came partly from the requirements for field observations to supplement the data gathered by interview and questionnaire in the Investigation into the Information Requirements of the Social Sciences (INFROSS). It became clear to the INFROSS investigators that no one method of investigating information needs would by itself be adequate. It was envisaged that an information officer, observing users over relatively long periods of time, would be able to provide data in depth about users' needs, and that this data would be of a different kind, and perhaps of greater validity, than the data obtained from the main INFROSS survey.

The Information Officer at Bath made an initial contact with social science users by letter. There followed a short, unstructured interview, where data was collected about sources of information. Subsequent contact with users was informal, and the construction of interest profiles was a continuous, rather than a single, operation. A report (Bath University of Technology, 1970) on the first year of operation of the service gives details about the construction of interest profiles, their modification, evaluation of the service, its extension to social scientists at Bristol University, future plans, and a brief review of selective dissemination of information and current awareness services. Details of the field observations will be included in the INFROSS reports to be submitted to the Office for Scientific and Technical Information during 1970.

3.7 Studies confined to specific social science disciplines

3.7.1 *The Americal Psychological Association studies*

By far the most thorough and extensive investigation of the information requirements of a social science discipline (perhaps of any discipline) has been undertaken, since 1961, by the American Psychological Association (APA). An over all picture of the study can be gained from an article in *Science* by Garvey and Griffith (1967), and from a paper read to the 19th International Congress on Psychology, London (Griffith, 1969). Earlier accounts can be found in Garvey and Griffith (1963, 1964a, 1964b) and Griffith and Garvey (1964), and details of specific parts of the project, on the communication of innovations

(Garvey and Griffith, 1966) and on the characteristics of the informal network of communication (Garvey and Griffith, 1968). Reports covering the work in great detail have been published by the APA since 1963, and these are listed in the 'Bibliography' at the end of this review.

A summary of the APA studies cannot do justice to the detailed nature of the investigations, and may erroneously convey the impression that the studies were macro in conception, and concerned with the flow of information in the general sense rather than in detail. Other studies on the scale of the APA study are inconceivable unless supported by large institutions and employing a large research staff. Few organisations could match the APA's potential for the design and operation of new information systems following the results of user studies.

The APA studies focused attention upon the information system in psychology that existed at the time the studies were begun, and evaluated the findings about the flow of information between scientists in terms of the existing system. The system was seen to be vast and rapidly changing. The system was expanding although some journals and meetings were disappearing. Central to the system were some 50 channels for the exchange of information, but a number of them seemed to compete with one another rather than fulfil any separate, special function with respect to the whole. Some of the earlier reports described the flow of information from the time it was generated by the researcher to the time when it could be retrieved from a secondary source. The public portion of such exchanges is small and the information it conveys is relatively old. Where no appropriate channel exists, the producers or the consumers of information create new channels or modify old ones. These occur much more frequently in the informal network than in the formal.

Contrary to the first impressions gained by some of the staff on the APA project, the results showed that the system exhibited impressive regularities. Information flows through the system in an orderly manner and, although there are various routes, specific kinds of information produced by specific types of researchers seek certain outlets on predictable occasions in predictable sequences and time patterns. The outlets chosen by the researcher are very often associated with the specific needs of the user, and the information is shaped and reshaped to fit the characteristics of the channels and the needs of the users. The ultimate form for the dissemination of the information produced within the field of psychology is publication in an archival journal. The limitations of this channel give constant impetus to the creation and maintenance of the best features of the informal network (Garvey and Griffith, 1964a).

One of the advantages of an investigation on the scale of the APA studies is that the results can be set in a wide context, and the behaviour of individual users can be evaluated in terms of the total system. Observing the user in the context of the information system that exists in psychology the APA studies were able to show that the user constructs his own system, and takes from the total system only a small part. For the individual user some order exists: he may suspect that the total system is vast and chaotic, but the part of the system to which he is frequently exposed is structured by him. When the information scientist observes usage habits of a few users he may see no pattern at all, because each user, associated with but a fraction of the total system, will exhibit idiosyncracies in the gathering and retrieving of information. As Garvey and Griffith (1967) point out, the change of role from a researcher within the system to a researcher upon the system, led to an initial impression that communication in psychology was both complex and chaotic. It was only after large scale enquiries that regularities in the system could be seen.

As the studies have progressed, the initial appearance of complexity and chaos has to some extent been resolved. The dissemination system was seen to be constrained by factors relating to the social context, economic factors, and the functional characteristics of the system itself. These factors imparted to the system a degree of orderliness.

The design and testing of innovations by the APA stemmed directly from the conceptualisation of the system as a social one. The information system in psychology which existed at the beginning of the APA project had three features which seemed to call for modification: (1) the long time lag between submission of a manuscript and journal publication; (2) the fifteen-month lag between publication of an article in a journal and its appearance as an abstract in *Psychological Abstracts;* and (3) the annual national scientific meeting of psychologists. The APA has been able to effect a considerable improvement in the first two features and has successfully altered the publication format of its annual meeting to provide a pre-convention publication of a portion of contributed papers. In this manner it has been possible to establish an early and widely accessible means of disseminating current research reports in psychology. Also, this innovation offers an alternative to journal publication, relieves some of the pressure on archival journals, and provides for a more effective and formal exchange of information during the convention session. Details of these changes were given in Report Number 16.

5.7.2 Other disciplines and fields of study

A survey by Carter (1968) of sociological research in Britain, while not a user study as such, gives a good deal of data about the information resources that are required and used by researchers in sociology. A questionnaire was distributed to 744 full members of the British Sociological Association. There were 416 respondents and they came from university teachers/researchers, researchers at non-university institutes (including national and local government research departments), teachers/researchers in colleges of technology and commerce, and other active sociologists including school teachers, housewives, and people working in industry. Data was obtained about area of research, status, experience, and demographic variables of location and age.

Sociology of education was given most often (102 of the 416 respondents) as the main area of interest. It was also judged to be a very important growth point. Only 'theory' was judged to be a growth point by more respondents, and this may be because it included many subsections of which 'organisation theory' was mentioned the most. Other areas frequently mentioned as 'main interest' included basic theory, social stratification, industrial sociology, and sociology of work. The growth in organisation theory was particularly prominent and it tended to be associated with an interest in industrial sociology. An area hitherto neglected, mathematical sociology, was given as another possible future point of growth. As a more general comment, a large number of respondents predicted growth in those areas where sociology can be seen to be, or thought to be, making a useful contribution to practical problems because large amounts of money are potentially available for research.

From such a wide-ranging enquiry many useful findings about information requirements emerged. Many respondents in universities, old and new alike, referred to a lack of adequate library facilities, but little detail was given about the facilities that were required.

Informal and interpersonal contacts were judged to be adequate and in the main satisfactory by respondents in universities, but much more of a problem for the remainder of the respondents. Lack of contact, it was pointed out, makes for wasted and duplicated research effort. Suggestions for overcoming this problem included more conferences, more summer schools, more journals, and registers of research activities.

The information requirements of those (including social scientists) attending the Congress of the International Union for the Scientific Study of the Population, held in Belgrade, September 1965, were studied by Groenman and Riesthuis (1967) who circulated a questionnaire to 600 participants. They obtained a response rate of 20 per cent (representing 135 respondents). 75 per cent of the respondents said they always explored the availability of relevant literature when starting a new project: no respondent indicated that he never tried to collect literature on his subject. There was a relationship between information seeking activity and correspondence with colleagues. Those who attempted retrospective searches utilised abstract journals, indexes, and unpublished material more often than those who stated that they did not regularly precede their work with retrospective searches of the literature. Those who always explored the literature were differentiated from those who infrequently explored the literature by a number of characteristics. For the former, conversations with colleagues, keeping abreast of current literature, the use of indexes to journals (including abstract journals), the use of subject indexes in the libraries, and the following up of cited references were the methods used most often in their exploration of the literature. Less use was made of reports circulating in the organisation to which the researcher belonged, personal records, and information gained from librarians. Although those who explored the literature irregularly used all these methods to a far less extent, when the methods were ordered according to the frequency of use, the hierarchy was the same for both the regular and irregular users. The irregular users (that is the ones that did not always try to find the literature relevant to a new topic of research) enumerated a number of reasons for their behaviour. They mentioned that consulting the literature can hamper their own creativity, that a literature search can have little meaning either because the library does not have the literature or because of the language barrier (where no translation is available), and a good many said that they had no time for such activity. Surprisingly, there were some respondents who stated that they knew all the relevant literature!

The language sciences are interdisciplinary in nature and overlap at a number of points with the social sciences. The report of a conference on 'Information in the language sciences' edited by Freeman, Pietrzyk and Roberts (1968) contains a number of papers on information needs, but it is noted that no empirical studies of information needs and requirements were reported.

.8 Practitioners[39] using social science information

n this section mention will be made of the information needs and equirements of those social scientists who can be called practitioners ecause they are concerned with the application of the results of social cience research and thinking rather than with the creation of more naterial (e.g. social workers, clinical psychologists, some university and ollege of education lecturers), and also with practitioners outside the ocial sciences who require and make use of social science information .g. architects, non-social science educationalists, administrators, rban and regional planners). It will be seen that there are at least as nany studies of the information requirements of practitioners (including he use made of social science information outside the social science lisciplines) as of pure researchers.

.8.1 *Social and community work*

There is some work completed and some in progress on the information equirements of social workers, although few studies have attempted nything more than an assessment of current reading habits.

The field of social work is characterised by a number of features that nake the assessment (and satisfaction) of information requirements articularly difficult. The field is very heterogeneous, recruiting ersonnel from many different disciplines and drawing upon nearly all he social sciences (and medicine) for information, and it lacks an cceptable and stable terminology. Hoffer (1969, p. 201), for example, ointed out that 'The problem of creating improved methods and echniques for searching and retrieving social welfare data is made more lifficult because of the nature and complexity of social welfare. The JCSW[40] projects and the workshops have demonstrated one fact—

---

[39]The distinction between practitioner and researcher is not entirely satis-actory. (See article by Lundberg, 1966, for definitions of the terms 'scientist' nd 'practitioner'). Some social scientists may of course be both researchers nd practitioners: e.g. clinical psychologists may spend considerable time in the pplication of techniques for the treatment of mental illness that have been leveloped by others over a long period of time, but may also be concerned with heir own research from time-to-time. Many users outside the field of social cience require social science information and they are properly classified as ractitioners, although many users of social science information will also be esearchers (e.g. medical scientists, physiologists, etc.). The distinction etween practitioner and researcher finds a parallel in the sciences where pure nd applied science is differentiated. There does not exist such agreement about his distinction in the social sciences, but there is obviously a great difference etween the work of (say) social workers and researchers pursuing full-time esearch in universities.

that an attempt to classify the services and activities of the soci welfare field under any of the existing conventional classificatio schemes (Dewey, LC, and UDC) using a hierarchical structure i impractical and ineffective'. Hoffer discussed the need for a social wor thesaurus in the context of the experimental KWIC index of publication produced by the NCSW.

Up-to-date methods of information retrieval, information specialists and information services are rarely to be found in the social work field Hoffer suggests that there is a great need for a national and internation network of co-operating information centres and for informatio specialists who should, as one of their first tasks, assist researchers i compiling state-of-the-art papers on selected social problems. Som idea of the present gaps in social work information can be gained b reference to the model (reported by Cohen 1964) developed by th National Association of Social Workers where the ideal objectives fo social workers were contrasted with current practices, facilities, an resources.

However, there is some doubt about the value of large-scale, new information resources and services—even if they could be financed an staffed. The uncontrolled expansion of such services would be inadvis able without more consideration of the current use of existing service and the nature of social work and its information requirements. B university standards the extent and standard of information services fo social work are meagre, but the few studies of information requirement that have been completed report that little use is made of existing ser vices. Perhaps they are not the ones that are required, but new service should not be introduced before potential needs have been estimated From the Brown and McCulloch studies, reported below, it is apparen that social workers have little exposure to published material and mak little use of the existing bibliographical aids[42] in their field. Hoffer' suggestion for information specialists can hardly be questioned. Ther can be no doubt that such a specialist could supply social workers with

---

[40]National Conference on Social Welfare.

[41]See collection of readings edited by Hoffer and Price (1967) for a discussio of the application of computer processing for social work data.

[42]These include *Abstracts for Social Workers* and *Poverty and Huma Resources Abstracts* published by the National Association of Social Workers the Data Institute of Social Sciences *Abstract Journal*, and the National Con ference on Social Welfare manuscript abstracts. See Crossley (1969) for comprehensive list of sources of information in applied social studies.

information and that social workers could be persuaded to use such a service. But the provision of more remote centres can be questioned in the light of the results of existing studies. It is tempting to suggest that a systematic programme for the education of social workers in the area of bibliography is required before sophisticated retrieval systems and information services are provided.

Brown and McCulloch looked, in some detail, at the formal information uses of social workers. The populations sampled were psychiatric social workers (McCulloch and Brown, 1969), education welfare officers (McCulloch and Brown, 1968b), child care officers (Brown and McCulloch, 1968a), medical social workers (Brown and McCulloch, 1968b), probation officers (Brown and McCulloch, 1969a), and mental welfare officers (Brown and McCulloch, 1969b). A summary of all the findings was reported in a short article by McCulloch and Brown (1968a). The study concentrated upon the printed material that social workers read. The results showed that social workers tended to read their own professional literature and publish in their own professional journals, although there were great variations between the different types of social workers. For example, 93 per cent of medical social workers read the journals related to their own discipline (*British Hospital Journal* and *Medical Social Work*) whereas only 38 per cent of child care officers read *Child Care News* and *Child Care*. In all the groups less than half the workers in the sample read journals related to social work (e.g. *Nursing Mirror, Social Service Quarterly, British Journal of Criminology*). There were age differences in reading habits, with the younger workers tending to pay more attention to publications outside their field. In the main, the material used was of a secondary nature, often written for their own discipline by their colleagues and drawing upon source material in the social sciences. Their exposure to primary sources of material from the social sciences was very small.

There have been few published studies of the information requirements of social workers, and if not carefully interpreted the McCulloch and Brown studies are likely to give a misleading picture. It should be emphasised that their study was concerned with journal reading only, and although social workers do not appear to be avid readers on this front, a more detailed investigation would perhaps show them to be active in the use of other channels of communication. Certainly a corrective to the McCulloch and Brown study has been seen in another investigation,[43] where it was noted that social workers were often very conscious of material outside the confines of the journals specifically related to their own disciplines, and that medical social worker especially were active in a large number of communication channels.

The question of the application and utilisation of research data is c paramount importance to all the social services, and certainly to socia and community work. Some fundamental questions are outstanding and it has yet to be established if the results of so-called 'pure' researcl in the social sciences do have immediate and practical application.[44]

In the United States, where social and community work tends to b more eclectic than in Britain 'practical' research is occasioned by socia and community problems.[45] This 'practical' research takes the result of existing research and attempts to apply them. For example, a projec underway at American University (reported by Lake, Ritvo and O'Brien, 1969) is working on attitudinal and institutional change regarding racism with the aim of increasing the understanding and skill of social workers in dealing with racism. Existing information abou attitudes (e.g. theories of attitudes, techniques of measurements, the relation between attitudes and actions, attitude change) is taken fron existing sources in psychology and sociology and supplemented with new data from the immediate area of concern. But in many areas o social and community work existing data is meagre (or irrelevant) and much new material must be collected. Although such work often requires direction and supervision by professional social scientists, the information requirements are very different from those of professiona sociologists or psychologists pursuing 'pure' research. An example o very special information requirements can be found in the community development effort at Redondo Beach, reported by Glaser (1968) where citizens' committees were formed to study problems of the need: of youth, transportation, recreation, crime prevention, and control etc. Obviously the information requirements of these groups were loca and specialised, and could not be served by the bibliographic system to which professionals are accustomed.

The results of the Redondo Beach projects are impressive: the

[43]'Investigation into the information requirements of the social sciences (INFROSS) in progress at Bath University of Technology. See Line (1968a 1969a) for outlines of the research. Details of the results of the main part of the study, a survey by questionnaire, and of the interviews of social science prac- titioners (which included social workers) will be presented in a report to the Office for Scientific and Technical Information.

[44]See 3.1.3. for a discussion of the application of basic research, where it is seen that even in science immediate and/or direct application is questioned.

[45]See Havighurst and Jansen (1967) for a trend report and bibliography or community research.

community, as a result of research discussion, established a youth aptitude, assessment, and job-finding centre, sent a monthly newsletter and calendar of events to all citizens, established a crime prevention bureau in the police department (which in turn has instituted a comprehensive operation Crime Stop), established and publicised the availability of the neighbourhood information centre, set up a youth counselling centre, and provided many other services and facilities. Each part of the programme had its own information problems. Such programmes obviously involve the recruitment of teams with wide ranging skills, drawing upon the expertise of sociologists, psychologists, social workers and administrators as well as on the non-expert members of the community whose enthusiasm and spontaneity, as well as complaints, provide the occasion for activity.

The study of information needs and requirements is particularly difficult in areas that have no accepted standard of terminology, and where boundaries have not been established. In the field of social work, some coherence is found in the professional associations (e.g. Probation Officers, Welfare Officers), in the distinctive services separately administered (e.g. probation, psychiatric social work), and in standardised, accepted, and approved courses of training. But in the more diffuse area of community work the boundaries are hard to draw, personnel may come from very many backgrounds and trainings, and little cohesion is brought about by professional contacts and associations. In the long term, the investigation of information requirements of community work may be no more difficult than in other (less diffuse) areas. When dealing with community work it will be necessary to give much thought to problem-centred rather than discipline-centred research; and although the information requirements of problem-centred activities may in theory be easier to define, in practice they may be more difficult to satisfy.

3.8.2 *Urban and regional planning*

This is another very heterogeneous area for the information scientist to attack, with respect to the disciplines involved, the training and background of personnel, and the type of problem encountered. The 1947 Town and Country Planning Act was seminal in the development of local authority planning departments and subsequent acts have encouraged this development. The two main functions of local authority planning departments are development planning and development control. Planning research is also incorporated in some local authority planning departments, although 'research' may be misleading here because very often this activity consists of data[46] collection and collation only.

There are now specialised courses of instruction in planning, and some of the personnel to be found in planning departments have qualifications obtained in such courses. Additionally these departments employ architects, economists, sociologists, and other social scientists.

Until very recently no empirical studies of the use of, or demand for, information by planners were in existence. It could be argued, in the absence of empirical confirmation, that planning was an obvious area where the results of social science research would be relevant, and therefore required. But there is not unanimous agreement that the results of existing social science research are required, or of value, in regional and urban planning. For example, Cullingworth and Orr (1969) dismiss much of the current work in sociology and politics; they treat sociology lightly since it has 'as yet had little to offer to the larger issues of modern urban and regional policy' and politics is dismissed because it is 'still scarcely involved in planning in this country'. Another expression of doubt about the use of the results of social science research in planning comes from Reade (1969), who is sceptical of present contributions of sociology. Reade maintains that the contribution of sociology to planning is commonly seen as helping planners to discover human needs and preferences, particularly by means of social surveys. He argues that the sociologist is far less able to do this than most planners suppose. He suggests that sociologists might more usefully direct at least some of their attention away from such planning surveys and instead study planning itself, for example, the role of planning in British society as an activity of government, as a profession, and as a movement for social reform. Reade (1969, pp. 1181–1182) suggests that in future the applied social scientist may have more to contribute than the basic researcher. 'Real dialogue between "applied" social scientists (social administrators and social workers) and "applied" environmental scientists (physical planners) has been almost entirely absent. Where a dialogue does exist (and this is comparatively recent),

---

[46]This data may be geographical (e.g. road networks), demographical (e.g. age structure of population, mobility), economical, or statistical. White and Willis (1969) draw attention to the fact that much of the data required in urban development is already collected in one form or another. The form in which the data is to be collected, collated and stored, and also the likely pattern of future demands are the main questions.

it has been between academic rather than "applied" social scientists and planners. Insofar as there is a need to discover the role of planning in society, this is an advantage. But planning is, after all, an instrumental activity, and it could probably have been more effectively instrumental if its contacts with these "applied" social scientists had been closer and if the social ideology of these "applied" social scientists had been less conservative.'

Another point of view comes from White and Willis (1969). They draw attention to an interesting development in the information requirements of urban planners, and like Cullingworth and Orr, and Reade, maintain that the established social science disciplines have little to offer in the way of research results ready made for application. White and Willis argue that as a result of the growing understanding of the complex inter-relationship of the various components involved in urban planning, there has been a convergence of the kinds of information different decision makers require. For example, health officials, educators, and employment analysts may all be interested in household-mobility, though for different reasons. The need for similar types of data by such different professions provides a clear opportunity for shared collection and storage.

White and Willis also raise the question of a possible relationship between the quantity of information available and the quality of the resulting decisions made in the light of the information. In the research laboratory information is typically required in order to make decisions regarding the acceptance, modification, or rejection of hypotheses. The procedure for the use of information in this way is clearly specified by the methods of science. Where information is used to make decisions outside the laboratory the procedures for use are not nearly so well established or accepted. Outside the laboratory the user plays a much greater role in the acceptance or the rejection of information. This point is discussed by Levin (1967) in the context of planning. He introduces the interesting idea of a 'discretion level' associated with each piece of information. In planning many pieces of information will be taken into account and will be reflected in the decisions made, but to different degrees. 'The reason for this is that with every piece of information is associated a certain "level" of discretion for the planner, and that while site conditions, like physical and chemical laws, give the planner no option (i.e. no discretion) to do other than accept them, the experience of others allows him a good deal of discretion in drawing inferences about the user requirements for which he must provide and the demands that they make upon a plan. Thus the information fed into the planning process influences not only the design decisions reached but also the planner's area of discretion and thus . . . his decision-making behaviour' (Levin, 1967, p. 439).

Before any conclusions can be drawn and decisions made about the provision of information for planners, and about the relevance of the results of social science research, a series of well designed empirical studies of the information requirements of planners is required. A start has been made, and the study by White, reported below, goes a long way to clarifying some of the issues in this field. But necessarily, in line with good research methodology, other confirmatory studies are now required.

The study by White was an empirical investigation of the information requirements of planners. In a published paper White (1969a) reviewed the sources from which planners get information. In a paper read to the 1969 London Conference[47] of the Centre for Environmental Studies, White (1969b) presented some of the results of the investigation based upon a preliminary analysis of the data. A final report, containing full details of the findings, has been submitted to OSTI by White (1969c). An edited version of this report will be published by the Library Association.

As user studies go White's investigation is unusual: it is one of the few studies to include a survey of library resources available to the target population. As a result of this survey White (1969a) concludes that in relation to other subjects, planning is fairly well served in city and county public libraries as regards special services and bibliographical materials, but that organised libraries are virtually nonexistent in local authority planning departments.

In a survey of user requirements (confined to published material) White (1969c) sent a questionnaire to a sample of 450 planners. There was a response rate of 63 per cent. From an analysis of the questionnaire data it was possible to list fourteen sources (e.g. maps and plans, data from own survey, office records) of information in order of importance, and to break down this list separately for usage of planners in practice, teaching, and research. There were differences in the usage of the

---

47Other papers read at the 1969 London Conference of the Centre for Environmental Studies were by White and Willis (1969), Laver (1969) on 'The future of national information systems' and Salomonsson (1969) on 'Data banking systems for urban planning'. Other papers presented were less relevant to social science information.

fourteen sources between the three types of activity. For example, in teaching planners used, in order of importance, monographs, journals, and corporate texts; in practice they used maps and plans, data from own survey, and office records; and in research they used data from own survey, journals, and data from other surveys.

The sources of information were broken down into three categories: printed sources, libraries, and personal sources. When information was required about the main areas of planning these sources were used equally often. But when information was required about related subjects library and personal sources were preferred to printed sources. Of library sources, roughly equal use was made of librarians, library catalogues, and browsing along library shelves. Of the personal sources, discussion with colleagues within the department was the most used, and subject experts came a close second. Discussions with colleagues in other departments, and with contacts outside the organisation, were judged to be quite useful. Of the printed sources, abstracts and bibliographies were little used, but references in books and journals were found to be useful by more than half the sample. The planner in the lower age groups (45 and under) was more likely to use printed sources than the planner in the age groups over 45. Having determined that relevant information exists, 39 per cent of the sample regularly obtained it through the librarian of their own organisation and 17 per cent went to the public library to obtain it. Other means of obtaining information were little used. Two thirds of the sample considered that it was very important to keep up to date with developments in planning, and this was usually done by reading journals. In peripheral areas, planners were seen to be interested in a wide range of subjects: less than half consistently attempted to keep up to date in subjects of peripheral interest.

White notes that there is no shortage of articles on planning, but in order to cover them all, it is necessary to cast the net fairly widely—how widely is not accurately known. From the questionnaire it was found that the majority of planners regularly scanned six or fewer journals, and only a very small percentage regularly followed up references at the end of an article as a matter of course. But 61 per cent of the sample kept a personal index of articles which may be of interest in the future. On the question of the use of foreign material this investigation produced similar conclusions to other studies in this area. There was a great interest in American literature and techniques in the field of planning. There was interest in material published in languages other than English, but only half the sample were proficient in any one foreign language, and about half had no translation facilities available locally.

The opinions of planners regarding the usefulness of reference sources were procured. The majority opinion was that an encyclopaedia or compendium of quick-reference information would be useful. Opinion was equally divided on the need for textbooks on planning. There was a clear demand for a national standardisation of planning terms, dictionary or glossary containing them, and for basic planning information issued in the form of data sheets, regularly revised and brought up to date and issued from a central authoritative source. In general, planners did not make much use of the bibliographies, abstracting and indexing services which *are* available, and indeed a proportion of them were not aware of what services were available. For example, The Town Planning Institute's *Planning research* was not widely used. Many commented that it quickly became out of date. The abstracting and indexing services which cover subjects relevant to planning (e.g. in psychology, sociology, economics) were little used by planners.

Planners used considerable quantities of statistical information and this was often self-generated. More than half the users of statistics said they would make use of wider resources if available. The main difficulty experienced in the use of statistics was the incompatibility of statistics from different sources.

Planners do not use to any great extent unpublished sources of information. Less than half of the sample usually tried to locate unpublished information; and for those who established its existence, less than half usually tried to obtain it. Of those who tried to obtain unpublished information, at least 40 per cent experienced difficulty, mainly with central government departments, often for reasons of confidentiality.

Mention has been made of the requirements of architects for social science information (see, for example, Allen in the 1969 *Annual Review of Science and Technology*). Allen maintained that architects have largely ignored the social sciences and noted that there are no empirical studies of the social science information requirements of architects.

A research group at The Institute of Advanced Architectural Studies, University of York, continues to work[48] on the communication of the results of research (from all disciplines) to architects. The group is

---

[48]Personal communication from K. A. Matthew, The Institute of Advanced Architectural Studies, University of York.

attempting to discover the extent to which information contained in the literature produced by The Building Research Station is used by architects. Research is also in progress to assess the value of abstracting some of the literature contained in the BRS publications, and circulating it to architects who for one reason or another have not received the BRS publications.

3.8.3   *Teachers*

One of the few[49] studies to report on the information requirements of university teachers can be found in the APA Report Number 17 'The use of scientific information in the undergraduate teaching of psychology'. A total of 1,123 questionnaires were mailed to psychologists from the faculties of 246 universities and colleges, representing a cross-section of American institutions of higher learning with a four-year course in psychology. There was a response rate of 63 per cent and a follow-up of the nonrespondents indicated that 44 per cent of those who replied to the follow-up were not teaching any course in psychology at the time of the survey. Teaching was regarded as a very time-consuming activity, and teaching was seen by slightly less than half of the respondents as their most information-demanding activity.

Two thirds of the respondents sought and used current information for teaching purposes and this information went beyond that needed for their research activities. Two thirds of them maintained files related to their undergraduate teaching and these files contained both archival and informally circulated, relatively current, materials—preprints, reprints and convention papers especially were required for filing. At least one third of the teachers used all four major archival sources[50] and, with the exception of *Contemporary Psychology*, all types of information were used more often for research purposes than for undergraduate teaching.

Almost half the teachers were conducting or had conducted research related to their most recent lecture, and about a third of them incorporated information from their research into their lectures. 14 per cent of the sample were conducting applied or clinical work relevant to their last lecture and 13 per cent included such information therein. One

---

[49]A study, by questionnaire, of the need for documentation and information on educational research, included university teachers/researchers, as well as teachers in schools of education. The survey was undertaken by the Swedish Educational Research Office of the Board of Education.

[50]Identified, in this study, as *Annual Review of Psychology, Psychological Bulletin, Psychological Abstracts,* and *Contemporary Psychology.*

third of the respondents indicated they had sought no information for their most recent lecture. Among those who did seek informatiom the reason given most frequently was to up-date lecture material. Textbooks and other books were sources from which information was sought most frequently for lectures. One quarter of the respondents had incorporated information received at a professional meeting, and one eighth of the teachers had used material from foreign sources. Three quarters of the teachers expressed special interest in the topic of their last lecture and such interests most often resulted from the research implications of the material. Two thirds considered the lecture preparation they had described as typical. The main information problem mentioned was insufficient time to locate and assimilate all relevant materials.

The courses in which teachers reported the least need for current information were in statistics and experimental design, and the history of psychology. Those who reported the greatest requirements for current information taught courses in physiological psychology, learning theory, developmental and industrial psychology, and courses outside psychology. The teachers who used files least in their undergraduate teaching gave lectures in statistics and experimental design, systems and contemporary theories, and the history of psychology. The heaviest dependence upon the *Annual Review of Psychology* occurred among teachers of physiological psychology; the greatest use of *Psychological Bulletin* among teachers of learning; and the greatest use of *Psychological Abstracts* among teachers of clinical, industrial, adolescent, and child psychology. Teachers of statistics and experimental design made relatively little use of these sources. Regardless of their degree-granting institutions, respondents used the same archival source for undergraduate teaching, but for research purposes fewer graduates of 'distinguished' schools used *Psychological Abstracts*. Technical institution teachers made greater use of the *Annual Review of Psychology* and *Psychological Abstracts* than teachers in other institutions. About half the teachers at Liberal Arts Colleges and Teachers' Colleges used archival sources for purposes of undergraduate teaching but for no other activity. University teachers tended to use all sources more frequently than non-university teachers.

The report concludes that university teachers consult a great diversity of formal and informal media in the course of their work; seek and are eager to use information on current research; use and rely upon their own experiences as researchers and clinicians in preparing lectures;

ind encounter a paucity of material appropriately selected and processed for their own and their students' needs. In aggregate these findings suggest several areas in which there are poor matches between the tasks of teachers and the information sources available to them.

As part of a study of *Sociology of Education Abstracts* (SEA) and its users Winn (1969b) reported the results of a group discussion amongst one section of SEA users—college of education lecturers. In an attempt to promote discussion about information needs (as opposed to current demands) a paper about information services and problems was presented before the discussion. This helped to make participants familiar with the range of services that can be made available, and to free them from expectations based upon past experiences. From the discussion it was seen that the single most important information problem was physical access to books and serials. Library stocks at colleges of education were seen to be inadequate and access to other stocks difficult. However, there was little support for a massive expansion of local bookstocks; but there was support for an information service of restricted scope. In this service the emphasis would be upon easy access to a rather limited range of materials, and some evaluation of the material. This evaluation, perhaps supplied by information scientists, could act as a filtering device between the users and the mass of published material (only a very small proportion of which was wanted or could be assimilated). There was agreement that evaluation should not be included in abstracts. The participants also mentioned that abstracts were more valuable than titles. Present facilities for browsing were adequate: the retrospective search for a particular item was a far greater problem and it suggested that an information service should be designed as a 'finding tool'.

College of education lecturers were also included in the INFROSS investigation, where data was obtained by interview and questionnaire. A picture similar to the one gained from the SEA study emerged. Again physical accessibility to material was the single most important factor. Inter-library loan services, however good, did not compensate for poor local stocks, because in the absence of a good stock the user was unable to specify exactly the nature of his information requirements—a prerequisite for a good inter-library loan service. Many interviewees mentioned the need for easy and quick retrieval of items of knowledge (rather than documents), although there were no suggestions how this could be effected. In practice this requirement is fairly easy to specify (e.g. a good review article) but very difficult to satisfy. The user cannot give the reference, although he could recognise a relevant text (and perhaps reference) if he saw it. The use of the library catalogue, the librarian, and scanning library shelves would often produce a suitable reference, and an increase in the range of material in the library would ensure that more information requirements of this type were met. The solution, as also mentioned by the SEA discussants, would be an information service that was geared to finding specific pieces of information. Not, it must be noted, any single article or book—the demand for information in colleges of education is not usually of this nature. There is a large element of substitutability in the information required.

The INFROSS study departs in its findings from the SEA study on the issue of abstracts. The SEA discussants were primed by a preliminary paper on possible information services and discussed the use and possible use of abstracts. The college of education lecturers interviewed in the INFROSS study never mentioned abstracts, or even the possible use of them. They were extremely ignorant about this bibliographical tool. Even when questioned about the possible use of abstracts the lecturers had little to say—no doubt because they had never used an abstract and were not familiar with its possibilities. In fact, abstract journals could be very useful for college of education lecturers. In the absence of large library stocks (including a wide range of journals) abstracts could be used for scanning and the identification of sufficient detail for an inter-library loan.

University lecturers were included in the sampling frame of an investigation by Dews[51] and Pout at the Manchester Business School into the information requirements of business studies. The lecturers in the sample had qualifications in management (e.g. accounting/finance, production, marketing and personnel), management services (e.g. research and development, operational research, organisation and methods, computing), and social sciences (economics, sociology, psychology, law and political science). In the main these lecturers were active in the field in which they were qualified.

Business studies is a field apart from the main body of the social sciences in terms of its personnel, its professional associations, its goals and objectives, and its literature;[52] but it does draw fairly heavily upon social science material.[53] The field of business studies, with its

---

[51]As part of this investigation a report (by Dews and Ford) of *An investigation into existing documentation services in business studies* was submitted to OSTI in January 1969. The report of the enquiry by questionnaire into information uses of those engaged in business studies will be submitted to OSTI in the near future (personal communication with Mr. Dews).

diverse range of interests and personnel, presents a very heterogeneous field. Enquiries about the flow of information are perhaps best attacked from the standpoint (as in the Dews study) of business studies itself—rather than from the standpoint of the social sciences. Although much of the material required falls just within the borders of social science it is doubtful if social scientists outside business studies make much use of it. For example such journals as *Occupational Psychology*, *Journal of Marketing*, and *Personnel and Training Management* have a superficial affiliation with psychology but their usage is restricted in the main to those (psychologists and others) actively engaged in business, marketing, training and personnel management, or the teaching of these subjects. Neither researchers or teachers in main-stream psychology, nor social science practitioners, call upon these specialised serials. However, it could be argued, for example, that psychologists working in the field of perception rarely call upon the literature of animal experimentation, and that a citation analysis of the literature of perception and animal studies would show as little bibliographic coupling as would a citation analysis of the literature of personnel management and perception. The issue here concerns the place of business studies (defined widely as in the Dews investigation) in the social sciences. There is obviously a great deal of information required in business studies that is not remotely connected to the social sciences, although there is no doubt that business studies require and use social science information. It is the place of the fringe material that is in doubt, and it is open to question whether this material is integrated with mainstream disciplines.

When available the study by Dews will be the first[54] detailed and

---

[52]A number of journals are very specific to business studies (e.g. *Journal of Management Studies*, *Management Studies*, *Business Management*, *Journal of Business*, *Business Horizons*, *Business News*).

[53]For example, in the Dews investigation non-social scientists mentioned that they used economic journals (e.g. *Economist*, *Economic Journal*, *Ministry of Labour Gazette*, *American Economic Review*) sociology and psychology journals (e.g. *British Journal of Sociology*, *American Journal of Sociology*, *Occupational Psychology*) and statistics journals (e.g. *Royal Statistical Society Journal*).

[54]A good deal has been written about business studies and management education. See, for example, the 1968, volume 20(1), issue of the *International Social Science Journal* which contains a collection of papers on theory, training, and practice in management. The relationship between social science and business studies is discussed in a monograph by Leeds and Smith (1963), and the contribution of the behavioural sciences to business is mentioned by Newman (1958). More recently there have been a few conceptual analyses of the information needs of management (e.g. Dantine, 1966; Murphy, 1969; Stern, 1969). Murphy suggests that the question of relevance is much more closely related to timing than in some other fields. He draws a distinction between 'data systems'

empirically determined account of the information demands and uses of business studies. In the meantime the first part of this investigation (Dews and Ford, 1969) into the nature of management literature is available, and as the authors note: ' . . . no previous research had been traced which was concerned exclusively with management literature' They point to a single exception, a short article by Penny (1966), on the documentation of management literature. Penny comments on the dichotomy in management between 'business' and 'technological' literature. This presents an obstacle for studies of information flow Dews and Ford (1969, p. 5) comment that the combination of these two aspects presents a subject field too vast and cumbersome to be covered by one study—and in their study the 'technology' literature was neglected in favour of the 'business' and 'social' literature.

The investigation by Dews and his colleague is relevant to this section on teachers because it was confined to lecturers in business and management studies, although as Dews points out,[55] an investigation into the information requirements of those engaged in management functions and management services, rather than teaching, is very necessary.

Schoolteachers have rarely figured in user studies, although there has been comment (usually not backed-up by empirical data) about their information requirements (see, for example, Eastern Regional Institute for Education, 1967, and Washington Joint Board of County School Directories, 1967). There have been one or two studies of marginal interest to information scientists (e.g. the purchasing and use of school textbooks; see Mayer, 1962).

An account of the gap that exists between the work of social psychologists and the practice of classroom teaching is given by Schmuck (1968) who was interested in the factors that inhibit communication between behavioural scientists and educators. Schmuck's analysis is not based upon a user study, but the result of direct contact with many school principals, curriculum consultants, school counsellors, and classroom teachers. Schmuck discusses the absence of professional research

---

and 'information systems'. According to Murphy (1969, p. 77) 'Data is a loose collection of facts about a situation. In relation to management information systems, information is the collection and processing of these facts in such a form that they can be used for decision-making purposes. The need is still for a well disciplined data base, and its end product should always be *useful* information'. Murphy also discusses such topical concepts as random access, multiprogramming, and time-sharing.

[55]Personal communication.

journals for teachers, difficulties of language in communicating the results of basic research, the nature of journals that are directly relevant to practitioners,[56] and the employment of outside consultants. He suggests, along with Watson (1967), that the most successful innovations result from the development of research knowledge from within the school system.

A detailed study of the flow of information about curriculum materials to schoolteachers was reported in 1967 by the Eastern Regional Institute for Education (ERIE). The institute is concerned with helping schools adapt to new ideas and procedures in instructional methods, materials for teaching and learning, and curriculum developments. The specific aim of the Curriculum Materials Information Program (CMIP) is to provide significant and useful information on instruction material to educators within the ERIE region.

The ERIE survey noted that although the newer instructional materials (often referred to as 'software') had become a major topic of discussion in educational circles, there was little evidence that this discussion was making an impact in the classroom. Most teachers still depended on printed matter—textbooks and supplementary reading materials—as the backbone of classroom activity, although most teachers were aware (albeit in very vague terms) of the technological revolution in education. The ERIE report suggested that inertia, lack of motivation, and fear[57] may have been some of the causes for the lack of innovation in the classroom.

According to the ERIE survey teachers did not seek information about new materials; expressed need for information was not proportional to the lack of knowledge nor to the lack of use of new educational materials; and even among the minority of teachers who were using the newer instructional materials (e.g. programmed instruction, packaged kits, simulation, film loops) usage was minimal and marginal compared with the usage of traditional materials. Only 5 per cent of teachers made regular and intensive use of more recent educational materials. Also the survey reported that schoolteachers had little information about the buying and use of new materials; that elementary schoolteachers used, and were more familiar with, a wider array of curriculum materials

---

[56]For example *Trans-action, Psychology Today, Theory into Practice, Journal of Applied Behavioural Science.*

[57]See studies by Tobias (1966) about the fear that schoolteachers have of automation, by Haughton and Ericson (1965) on the use of programmed instruction in schools, and by Becker (1969) on educational technology and the software gap.

than were secondary teachers; that teachers had insufficient time to se
information about instructional materials; that school administrato
felt they had inadequate information about newer materials; and th
major differences existed between subject areas with regard to inform
tion about curriculum materials.

3.8.4 *Educational administrators*

A distinction must be made between education as a discipline (whic
includes researchers), education as a practice (i.e. teaching, which ma
involve any subject), and educational administration. Investigatio
directed towards the first two categories of educationalists have be
considered (3.8.3). Little is known about the information requiremen
of educational administrators. One of the few studies to inclu
educational administrators was undertaken by Informatics Incorporate

The study by Informatics Incorporated,[58] for the United Stat
Office of Education, was an extensive study of educational informati
designed to provide guidance in the development of the Education
Research Information Center (ERIC). The study was directed to fo
questions in particular: (1) What kinds of information do education
researchers and educators need? (2) How do they now obtain t
information? (3) How can advanced technology improve the flow
research information? (4) How should ERIC evolve in order to u
technology effectively and economically?

The study used semi-structured interviews—and deliberate
avoided questionnaires which it was maintained would have answer
only those questions that the investigators had the foresight to pose
and interviewed 154 people from universities, state departments
education, USOE staff, and information scientists and informatic
system operators in government and private research organisations.

Three types of users of educational research materials were identifi
—administrators, teachers, and researchers; although it was noted th
a person may combine all these activities and their characterist
information use patterns. From the interviews it was concluded th
the administrator required 'packets' of accurate, timely information
specific subjects, in good journalistic style, easily assimilated. T
teacher required operational-type information of a professional rath
than technical nature, including information that would satisfy a ne
to be generally aware of developments in educational research (a ne

---

[58]Mersel, Donohue and Morris (1966).

est served by adequate and critical state-of-the-art reviews). In ddition the teacher may, from time to time, be involved in experinental programmes and will need the full literature available to him. The researcher—the most demanding in terms of range of material and he least tolerant of delay—required detailed research reports and data n his main area of interest, and general information in other, peripheral ields of interest.

Many interviewees mentioned the impractical size and format of esearch reports. There was seen to be a need for short reports (for xample, a 20-page reduction of a 250-page document), and for highevel journalism which brings together the most significant facts of esearch, presenting them in non-technical forms. One of the most requently mentioned demands on the part of the research community vas for a thinning of the literature: suggestions included a suppression f some literature before publication, a review score, literature 'birth ontrol', and literature 'euthanasia'; and a plea for greater attention to he evaluation of research results rather than to their dissemination.

Information did not flow among the educationalists as had been redicted. It was initially expected that the universities would be reators of research products and that the state departments of education vould be concerned with the consumption of this product. There was a remendous scepticism in most of the state departments as to whether he universities were concerned with the problems that the state department people knew to be the problems of education, and a similar ntipathy existed in the universities where there was often a doubt as to vhether there really was a research group in any state department of ducation. Perhaps as a result of these antipathies the principal lines f communication for the university researcher were with his fellow esearchers, and the major communication for the state departments vas the flow of statistical data from schools. In its way this study by nformatics Incorporated is valuable, but the use of the semi-structured nterview did impede the quantification and statistical analysis of the lata.

The report contains no bibliography, and makes no reference to other ser studies. It seems strange that such a large undertaking was not receded (at least no mention is made of this) by a search of the literature for relevant reports and researches into the information requirements of educationalists. The investigation does not do justice to the readth and variety of material used by educationalists, nor to the nterdisciplinary nature of many educational pursuits.

The field of education has been very inadequately covered by user studies, although education is perhaps better covered by bibliographical tools and information services than any other social science.

3.8.5   Some omissions

Finally, brief mention must be made of the needs of government and industry for social science information. They require the results of social science research, the services of social scientists, and new research. Very often the information is required as a background to policy making.

One of the most extensive accounts of the use of the social sciences in government domestic policy is given in the five-part report[59] of the United States House of Representatives Committee on Government Operations (1967) on *The use of social research in federal domestic programs*. The social sciences[60] attracted much attention during World War II in the United States, and government interest and finance[61] of the social sciences on any large scale dates from that period. Since that time the United States Government has financed numerous social science projects and recruited many thousands of social scientists. On all levels there has been an involvement of social science in government. This trend is apparent during the last decade in the United Kingdom. Armstrong (1969) estimates the amount of money spent by (UK) government departments (excluding the SSRC) on research in the social sciences has increased over the three-year period 1965/6 to 1968/9 from about £1m. to about £1.7m. Most of this money went to research commissioned by departments and undertaken by researchers outside government service. Commissioned research doubled in this three-year period, whereas the amount of money going into social science research conducted by civil servants themselves remained roughly the same.

A clear distinction must be made between the requirements of governments for social science information, and the requirements of individual

---

[59]A useful and short observation on the report, especially the sections dealing with the adequacy and usefulness of government-financed research in six major domestic social areas, is made by Orlans (1968) who directed the House of Representatives Committee on Government Operations investigation.

[60]Accounts of the mobilisation of social scientists and the use of social science research during World War II are given by McDiarmid (1945), and Nichol (1944). The contribution of specific disciplines has also been documented: in particular Embree (1946) mentions the contribution of applied anthropology, Lanier (1949) psychiatry and anthropology, Cartwright (1948) psychology, and Stouffer (1948) the application of survey results to policy during the war.

researchers and administrators within government departments. The information requirements of governments tend to be stated in very general terms and do not usually involve the day-to-day interactions with sources of information that characterise the information seeking activities of individual researchers. For example, government departments may commission research, support individual research projects, and set up departments to deal with the administration of research. These activities may be occasioned by an expressed need for information, but such needs cannot be investigated by the methods found in user studies. It is the needs and requirements of the researchers undertaking government-sponsored research or the social scientists working in government departments that have to be investigated.

Little is known about the information requirements of social scientists employed in government departments, and few investigators have recognised this numerically formidable group of users of social scientist information. A notable exception is Line (1969a) who, in planning for user studies in the social sciences, pointed to this important group of users. Line's INFROSS study will provide much needed detail about the information requirements of social scientists in government employment.

A little is known about the information requirements of MPs. A forthcoming publication by Barker and Rush (1970) will contain the details of an investigation into MPs' sources of information; and no doubt many sources will fall in the social science disciplines. Further light is thrown upon the usage of information by MPs from an experimental current awareness service in the social sciences made available to MPs (through the House of Commons Library) between August 1968 and February 1969. The service was supported by OSTI and undertaken jointly by the House of Commons Library and the UK Atomic Energy Authority Culham Laboratory Library.[62] It was hoped[63] that user response to the experiment would be useful in planning future developments in social science information services.

---

[61]Wilson (1952) traces the evolution of research in psychology supported by the United States Government. Darley (1957) notes the financial support given to psychology by the United States Office of Naval Research. A recent article by David (1969) traces the history of the relationship between the behavioural sciences and the United States Federal Government. This relationship is very extensively documented. Recent references include Lyons (1969), Orlans (1968), and Lompe (1968).

[62]See Hall (1969) for a technical report and Poole (1969) and Hall, Palmer and Poole (1970) for more general discussion of the project.

[63]*OSTI Newsletter*, 1968, No. 4, p. 5.

There is one other aspect of government operations that has a bearing upon information requirements. During the last decade changes have come about in the internal organisation of government departments which, as Armstrong (1969, p. 2) points out, 'have been made with a view to organising research more systematically and bringing it into closer contact with policy. In most cases this has meant linking up departments' planning branches with the statistical services. Most departments have had a statistical unit (or branch, or division) for some time, but the connection between the work of those units and policy-making has often in the past been rather sketchy. Some departments have regarded statistical work mainly as means of recording the progress of their various activities; they have not regarded it has having very much connection with policy-making. Since the war this linking of statistical branches has been going on steadily—and increasingly in the last few years with the growth of specific planning units in departments. All this means that departments are now better equipped than they were to think about the problems that require research, to provide themselves slowly with an apparatus that will enable them to have a research programme, to make intelligent choices between subjects for research, and to discuss their problems with the researchers outside the government'. This reorganisation of government departments, together with the changes in attitude that it reflects, will no doubt determine to some extent the expressed information requirements of individual researchers within government departments.

Many other omissions could be noted, but perhaps the most outstanding case is the requirements of industry for social science information.

3.8.6 *The poverty of usable material*

In the applied field a good many of the present information requirements and needs cannot be met by the present state of social science knowledge: the information required, and the type of research that would produce it, do not exist. Although one of the needs is for more research, it is for research that is guided and occasioned by practical problems; and in some cases for more research into the application of existing basic research. This type of application would perhaps involve the creation of a new breed of social scientist—a social science technician. Comment from practitioners about existing basic research is often unfavourable. There is an impatience with research that is highly theory-orientated and at the best many practitioners regard basic research with ndifference. And yet there is a need. In a discussion of the research and nformation needed to guide new policies and practices in education, Schwarz (1969, p. 344) is in no doubt that there 'are daily needs for evaluative research to assess the increasing flow of new concepts, gadgets, and approaches' and that there are hundreds of specific questions only research can answer. 'Yet the outcomes of research undertaken to date have in fact had little impact on international education. The effectiveness of educational practices has not been demonstrably upgraded.'

The information scientist looking at information needs of practitioners is presented with a dilemma. In some areas the information scientist may identify information needs and requirements that cannot be fulfilled at present. And with this knowledge in hand it would be foolish to perpetuate information systems (and services) that are not meeting these requirements.

It is known that social science information does not flow freely from basic research to the practitioner—the Mersel, Donohue, and Morris (1966) study shows how crude is the model that identifies universities with creators of research products, and practitioners with consumers of the products. This leaves practitioners very ignorant about the mass of basic research and basic researchers very often ignorant (and/or indifferent) of the needs of practitioners.

Why, it might be asked, if there is so much information, and if practitioners express interest and maintain that they ought to know about it, does the information not flow? One possible reason may be that practitioners have neither the time nor the facilities for participation in the flow. There is a similar situation in science and technology where applied scientists and technicians do not have the time or the facilities to participate in the information that could be made available to them from basic research. In practice applied scientists and technicians receive, with the assistance of professional communicators, information officers, and 'gatekeepers', information relevant to their activities. Until very recently, there have been few information specialists, professional communicators, or information officers in the social sciences. There is now an information officer in the social sciences at Bath University of Technology, supported for an experimental period by OSTI. And a group of researchers at The Institute of Advanced Architectural Studies, University of York, is looking at the possibility of communicating the results of social science research (along with other information) to architects.

Even where social science information does flow, and is used (or made note of) by practitioners, it is difficult to determine the effect it has upon policy-making decision, case-work behaviour, clinical practice, government policy, teaching practice, etc. In the applied field the criterion must be *does it work*: that is, are the decisions made, and the practices initiated, improved in the light of the information, or would they have been much the same in the absence of the information? In many areas of science and technology the effects of information are palpable, and therefore relatively easy to assess. In the social sciences the effects are less demonstrable. At the present time the information resources, services, and facilities that exist for the basic researcher and the practitioner do not have much overlap. The basic researcher is essentially close to, although he may very often be ignorant of, and not use, the traditional bibliographical tools of his discipline. Practitioners often do not know, and when they do they seldom make use of, such bibliographical aids. In certain applied fields information services and bibliographical aids have evolved spontaneously to meet local and specific needs, but a good many social science practitioners have no such services. The non-social science user of the products of social science research is even less well placed to obtain relevant information.

CHAPTER FOUR

The Systemic[1] Approach: Studies of Communication Artifacts

4.1 General

In the typical user study individual researchers/teachers/practitioners are the units of analysis, and they are questioned about their information requirements, needs, and uses. At the systemic level of analysis it is the artifacts of communication created by researchers/teachers that are the units of analysis. These artifacts of communication include citations, articles, monographs, and prepublication papers. The systemic approach is particularly suited to the study of changing patterns of communication over time, and it is in this sense that it is used here. The systemic approach can give data about information use patterns, and information demands, but cannot give data about information needs. Unsatisfied information needs are not associated with communication artifacts, and hence cannot be identified by systemic approaches.

Included in this chapter are studies of the growth, size, and obsolescence rate of social science literature, reference scattering and bibliographic coupling. Studies of the circulation and pattern of use of monographs and periodicals in libraries are not included in this chapter, although they do provide additional data about information requirements. Often they are undertaken to provide material to guide policy decisions about book and journal purchase and storage. Studies of book and journal circulations have a fairly long history—going back, as is the case with library surveys (see 3.2), at least as far as the 1930s—

---

[1]There is no accepted name for the studies covered in this chapter. The term 'systemic approach' is used by Paisley (1965, chapter 4) to cover, among other topics, studies of the growth and obsolescence rates of literature. The term 'statistical bibliography', perhaps first used by Hulme (1923), is ambiguous and Pritchard (1969) suggests 'bibliometrics', which he defines as 'the application of mathematics and statistical methods to books and other media of communication'. Fairthorne (1969a, p. 319) approves of the term, and defines bibliometrics as the 'quantitative treatment of the properties of recorded discourse and behaviour appertaining to it'.

although they continue to attract interest. An example of an account of the pattern of use of books in a large library is Fussler and Simon (1969).

Although many of the studies included in this chapter provide valuable details about the parameters of the literature in the social sciences, few have set out to be comprehensive in their treatment of the subject.

4.2   Growth of social science literature

Although a good deal has been written about the growth of literature in science,[2] there is surprisingly little agreement about the exact rate of growth. No attempt will be made here to cover studies of the growth of literature in science and technology, except to point out the difficulties they have faced. For some time it was assumed (largely as a result of misreading and out-of-context quotation of Price's 1956 article) that the growth rate of scientific literature followed an exponential curve. More recently it has been assumed (after further statements by Price, 1963 and Orr and Leeds, 1964) that the growth rate of scientific literature is exponential with saturation. And this produces the logistic S-shaped curve. Estimates continue to appear that show growth rate to be exponential, and although such results do not necessarily conflict with the suggestion that the rate is exponential with saturation—the point of saturation could be some distance ahead—they do add to the confusion in this area. It is now agreed that many estimates of growth rate are inflated. For example, Bryan (1968) suggests that growth rates may be inflated because in the counts of published materials, second and subsequent editions and translations are often included. Most estimates of growth have been based upon abstracting journals, and in the absence of data about the coverage of the primary by the secondary literature the data base cannot be relied upon.

A study of the growth of the professional literature in economics and psychology, and a comparison with growth rates in biology, electrical engineering, and physics, was made by Holt and Schrank (1968), who used the *Index of Economic Journals* for a data base. They showed that the growth of the periodical literature in economics from 1886 to 1965 followed an exponential curve and estimated that about 49,500 articles

---

[2]For estimates of growth rates in various parts of the scientific literature see Mantell (1966), Kent (1962), Schmookler (1962), Selye (1966), Lynn (1966), Gottschalk and Desmond (1963), Barr (1967), Vickery (1968), Bourne (1962b), Carter *et al.* (1967), Bryan (1968), Orr and Leeds (1964), and further papers by Price (1963, 1965a, 1966b, 1967).

had been published in economics by the end of 1963, with an output of 9,642 in the 1960–1963 period. An approximate measure of the size of psychology literature was gained from a count of the number of abstracts contained in *Psychological Abstracts*. When the number of articles per year was plotted against time another exponential growth curve appeared, although the fluctuations over the last decade made it difficult to see the recent trend. The long term growth rates of psychology (2.90 per cent per annum, 1927–1964) and economics (5.50 per cent per annum, 1886–1959) were compared with biology (4.39 per cent per annum, 1927–1964), electrical engineering (3.50 per cent per annum, 1903–1962), and physics (3.73 per cent per annum, 1903–1964). It was seen that economic literature has a very high growth rate, but a comparatively small absolute size. However, Holt and Schrank (1968) were cautious in their interpretation of the results; they took the advice of Gottschalk and Desmond (1963), about the dangers of premature extrapolations, and noted the inaccuracies involved in using *Psychological Abstracts* (the suggestion of the Executive Editor) as a measure of psychological literature. There was no way of knowing the percentage of the literature covered by the two abstracting journals, or if the coverage varied from one year to another.

There is obviously a great deal more work to be done before an accurate picture of the growth of literature in the social sciences is established. A detailed analysis is required of the growth (and, in some areas, decay) of the literature in all the social sciences.

An interesting lead has been given by Louttit (1957a) in a study of the publication trends in psychology. From *Psychological Index* (1864–1929) and *Psychological Abstracts* (1934–1954) Louttit took a random sample of 200 entries from each of 13 volumes (representing every fifth year for the period 1894 to 1954). For each entry data were recorded about subject classification, method of publication, language, and, for entries that were journal articles, the subject field of the journal in which it appeared. The sample size permitted the breakdown of the items into the twelve major categories that were in current use in *Psychological Abstracts*. These categories, representing the major fields of psychology, were: general, physiological, receptor, response, higher, developmental, social, clinical, abnormal, educational, personnel, and applied. The number of items found in each of these categories was plotted as a function of time. In the subject fields of general, physiological, receptor, and abnormal, there was a decline throughout the 61-year period. In the subject fields of developmental, clinical, educational, personnel, and applied, there was a continuous increase in the total number of items, although the absolute number of items in developmental, personnel, and applied was small. The field of clinical and educational showed the steepest gradients. In the subject fields of social and higher the fluctuations were great and precluded the identification of trends.

Louttit went on to record the disciplines from which the items in the sample were drawn. The ten major disciplines were psychology, psychiatry, biological science, medicine, general science, education (educational research, but not educational psychology), social science (sociology, anthropology, social welfare), general (nonscientific journals and reviews), philosophy, and finally a group of miscellaneous journals. Journals in psychology showed the largest trend increase. The three-fold increase between 1894 and 1954 was attributed, in part, to the increasing number of journals in psychology.[3] In contrast to psychology journals those in philosophy were less frequently a source for titles to be indexed. The other areas to show a decrease were medicine, general science, and general. Education journals showed a significant increasing usage, and the last group of miscellaneous journals showed a very significant increasing trend. Thus, in the main, citations from psychological and educational journals increased; and from other disciplines citations remained steady, or in some instances actually decreased.

This type of study, if replicated and extended (especially to the other social science disciplines), would provide invaluable data for those concerned with the assessment of information requirements and needs and the provision of information. The Louttit study provides a good example of the way in which work in bibliometrics might proceed, although as a guide to the parameters of published literature it represents only a beginning, and it has many limitations. The data base was represented by only *Psychological Abstracts* and *Psychological Index,* neither of which gives total coverage of psychology literature, and the number of items in the sample did not prove to be large enough to produce smooth curves, from which trends could be identified and future growth rates predicted. The study used the main subject headings from *Psychological Abstracts,* but this classificatory system has undergone considerable modification since 1954—the date of the last issue used in Louttit's study.

---

[3]Daniel and Louttit (1953) reported a sixfold increase in the number of psychology journals between 1894 and 1949. During a decade ending in 1894 there had been 22 psychology journals in existence, whereas during the same length of period ending in 1949 there had been 131 journals.

4.3   Citation[4, 5] studies of social science literature

Citation analyses can be used to investigate: (1) the obsolescence rate of journals, journal articles, and monographs; (2) the characteristics of citation practices; (3) author and journal hierarchies; and (4) the scattering of literature across time and journals.

As already seen, there are few user studies in the social sciences compared with the large number in science and technology; but in the case of citation studies this is not so. There are quite a number that deal exclusively with the social sciences. In sociology there are studies by Bain (1962), Broadus (1952, 1967), Hobbs (1951), Lin and Nelson (1969), MacRae (1969), and Oromaner (1968); in psychology by Daniel (1967), Lawler (1963), and Xhignesse and Osgood (1967); and also studies covering the whole field of social science by Parker, Paisley and Garrett (1967), Earle and Vickery (1969a), and a study of lending by Wood and Bower (1969).

---

[4]Lin and Nelson (1969) have pointed out that some confusion may arise from the indiscriminate use of the terms 'citation' and 'reference'. If 'citation' is read literally, it refers to each occasion upon which a reference is cited in the text. Thus, a single work may be cited many times in a publication, although it will appear only once in the bibliography (i.e. as a reference). Most citation studies have not made clear this distinction and it is possible that some error has been introduced into citation studies by the different usages of 'citation'. Lin and Nelson (1969) compared the data that they obtained using 'reference' as the unit of count with the data that Broadus (1967) obtained using 'citation'. The different methods produced very similar results. For example, Broadus found that 38.5 per cent of all citations were to serials and Lin and Nelson reported a figure of 38.8 per cent. But this degree of agreement may not always be the case.

[5]An interesting aspect of the study of citations, not covered here, is their function in the development of science. It is known that journal articles in science make, on average, ten citations. Cawkell (1968), for example, has suggested that the building blocks of an article can on average be adequately specified, regardless of the volume of published information, by reference to about eleven items in the past. No research takes place in complete isolation and most research activities (the type of research that Kuhn finds characteristic of consolidation, rather than exploratory, periods of science) are facilitated by reference to, and knowledge of, similar activities. Progress in science and technology is cumulative, and a new piece of research usually relies heavily upon the reliable and valid findings of previous research: this fact alone makes the role of citations very important, and there exist one or two examples in the history of science where the course of discovery has temporarily gone astray because of a false or unreliable publication. Citations also fulfil other functions. These include: recognition, patents, and establishment of personal ownership. Status and prestige of individuals and institutions are enhanced by citations. It can be shown that independent measures of status and prestige agree with the patterns that emerge from citation studies, so that the most famous scientists and the high prestige institutions tend to get cited more often than their less famous colleagues. Citations can also be used, as Westbrook (1960) suggested, in the identification of significant research.

4.3.1 *Obsolescence rate of literature*[6]

A measure of the obsolescence rate of literature, which can be assessed by citation analysis, can give an indication of how far a search must go back to obtain a representative sample of the published literature in a given field.

In science it has been estimated (see Price, 1965a) that as many as three quarters of all references are to publications less than ten years old. In the social sciences the obsolescence rate depends, to a large extent, upon the nature of the research. In some areas of sociology, economic history, and political science, social scientists make greater use of the older literature than do natural scientists (Guttsman, 1966), but in the experimental areas of social science the obsolescence rate is closer to that in the natural sciences.

A survey by Wood and Bower (1969) at the National Lending Library for Science and Technology (NLL) of requests received for serials in social science showed that more than 93 per cent of the journals requested were published after 1950, and that the half-life[7] of social science journals was $3\frac{1}{2}$ years. It could be objected, as Wood and Bower pointed out, that in the early stages of the development of the NLL's social science service, only requests for recent literature were attracted to the library, and that the results do not present a true picture of the date distribution of the literature used by social scientists. They did find

---

[6]There are many studies of the obsolescence rate of scientific and technical literature. It is generally agreed that the scientist requires a large amount of material that is of recent date and a very small amount that is more than ten years old. Price (1965a), for example, has estimated that in any year, half of all the references in journal articles are to half the entire prior art, and the other half form a tightly knit pattern with recent papers. In a small scale study Cawkell (1968) extracted, at random, 60 articles from the 1964 *SCI Source Index*, and calculated the citations to them in the 1965, 1966, and 1967 *Science Citation Index*. In any one year 64 per cent of the articles were not cited, and the average number of citations per year was seen to be between 0.6 and 1.1 for all the articles. When this parameter was estimated from computer generated statistics about the 1964–1967 *Science Citation Index*, it remained steady at around a mean of 1.65 citations per authored item cited. In science it is estimated (Price, 1965a; Cawkell, 1968) that on average each article is cited five to six times before it is forgotten. But there are large variations in the number of citations per article, number of received citings, and total number of citations during the life of an article. Some may never be cited and some, perhaps as many as 25 per cent of all articles, may be cited at least ten times. From the curves produced by Cawkell (1968) it can be seen that the mean number of citations per year increases during the first three-year period after publication, reaches a peak during the third year and thereafter follows a negatively accelerated trend.

[7]Line (1970) argues that the common meaning of 'half-life', as used in most studies, is inaccurate and of limited value. He suggests the use of *median citation age* for 'half-life' in its customary usage. *Median citation age* is defined by Line as the time within which half the citations in a citation study occur.

some differences in the date distributions of requests for literature in different disciplines. More than average use was made of recent literature in management, where 66.8 per cent of the requests were for literature published in the last $3\frac{1}{2}$ years, and 86.5 per cent for items published over the last $8\frac{1}{2}$ years. Of the items that educationalists requested 57.5 per cent were published in the last $3\frac{1}{2}$ years. At the other extreme, there was relatively heavy use of the older literature in geography, psychology, statistics, and sociology, in which fields 52.0, 44.8, 44.8, and 37.5 per cent respectively of the literature requested was published before 1960, compared with 26.1 per cent for the whole sample.

A study of citations in psychology periodicals by Xhignesse and Osgood (1967) showed that only 35 per cent of the citations in 21 psychology journals published in 1960 were to material more than 10 years old. The 1901 to 1940 period accounted for 38 per cent of the citations in 1950, and this figure fell to 12 per cent in 1960. The comparable figure from the NLL survey was 8 per cent.

Another citation study of social science literature, by Earle and Vickery (1969a), overlaps to some extent with the NLL study (Wood and Bower, 1969) of social science serials. These two studies, therefore, provide an opportunity for the comparison of two methods to assess the use made of material (Earle and Vickery specifically mention this point). The NLL study was a study of use as indicated by demand on the NLL service, whereas the Earle and Vickery study was a study of use as indicated by citation.[8]

Earle and Vickery limited their material to Dewey classes 300 (excluding 340, law and public administration), 500 and 600 (excluding 640, domestic science). The sources of items were the 1965 volume of the *British National Bibliography* and titles in the 1965 edition of Toase's *Guide to current British periodicals*. Citations in all types of social science publications (including books, periodicals, government publications, etc.) had a mean citation age of 9 years, and citations in social science periodicals a mean citation age of 6 years. Some discipline differences were apparent. In the literature of social welfare, economics, and education mean citation ages were lower than the average

---

[8]See Vickery (1969) for a discussion and study of the various methods for assessing use. Vickery points out that the 'citation' indicator of use disregards the fact that much that is read is not cited. A 'holdings' indicator does not take into account that some titles are more intensively used than others, and the 'loan' indicator assumes that patterns of recorded loans run parallel to the total usage pattern.

for all social science literature, and in the literature of economics of commerce and social customs mean citation ages were above the average (weighted, no doubt, by historical studies in these fields).

The Earle and Vickery figure for literature in science and technology is very close to the NLL figure for the same type of literature—even though the former was a citation study and the latter a measure of loan demand—but the two surveys give slightly different figures for social science literature. The mean citation age (periodicals) was 6 years (Earle and Vickery), and the mean half-life measured by loan demand was 7 years (NLL study).

Daniel (1967) plotted the citation age in years against the percentage of all citations in the 1950 volumes of 20 journals considered to be a definitive list of psychological journals in the United States at the time. He compared the resulting distribution with that obtained from Lawler's (1963) data gathered from 6 journals in psychology in the 1958 literature. Daniel produced another count on the 1965 volumes corresponding to the 6 used by Lawler. Thus Daniel was able to present age distributions for psychological literature of 1950, 1958, and 1965. The median age of the citations was 9.0 years in 1950; 6.11 in the 1958 sample of journals; and 5.75 for the same sample in 1965. Daniel noted that the distribution demonstrated signs of asymptoting, and suggested that the asymptote for the function may be a minimum median of 5.5 years, at least under current distribution systems. Lawler (1963) gathered data from 6 major psychology journals and found that 43 per cent of all articles cited were less than 6 years old, and that 70 per cent were less than 11 years old. The modal age of the articles cited was 3 years and the median age 7 years. Over the past 20 years there was a general trend for the number of single author articles to decrease in favour of an increase in multi-author articles.

MacRae (1969) compared the age distributions of citations in the 1965 issue of the *American Sociological Review*, the 1957 issue of *Physical Review*, and journals in biomedical sciences. He found that citations in sociology referred to older articles than those in the natural sciences.[9] For example, nearly 30 per cent of the citations in *American Sociological Review* were to articles older than 10 years, whereas only

---

[9] In an analysis of loans from a medical library Wender (1969) found that behavioural science literature showed a much less rapid decay rate than medical science literature.

about 11 per cent of citations in the natural science journals were as old.

4.3.2 *Characteristics of the literature used by researchers*

Few studies have looked at the type of material cited in publications—as opposed to the more common type of citation study which reports on date and/or scatter of citations.

Lin and Nelson (1969) showed that in sociology a large number of citations are to books rather than to serials. They compared the pattern of citation in three sociology journals (*American Sociological Review, American Journal of Sociology,* and *Social Forces*) with a science journal (*Journal of the Optical Society of America*) for the years 1965 and 1966. In the three sociology journals about half of all citations were to books and a third of all citations to journals. In the JOSA three quarters of all citations were to serials and only 16 per cent to books. Lin and Nelson offered two explanations for this large difference. They suggested that the finding gives some support to Kuhn's hypothesis that disciplines without paradigms tend to publish in books. Alternatively, the finding can be explained in terms of the different rejection rates of articles submitted to journals in optics and sociology. If rejection rates are higher in sociological journals than in optical journals, book publication may very well be used because it is an alternative outlet, rather than because it is the preferred channel of communication. There is some data (Johns Hopkins University Center for Research in Scientific Communication, 1968b) to show that the rejection rate of articles submitted in sociology is high. This study reported that 45 per cent of sociologists in a sample drawn from participants in the 1966 Annual Meetings of the American Sociological Association had their manuscripts rejected by at least one journal within the year following the meeting, whereas only 6 per cent of the optical scientists had had their manuscripts rejected in the same period.

A much earlier study, by Hobbs (1951), of citations in sociological textbooks[10] gives a great deal of data about the sources of material used by writers. The study is now obviously out of date, but some of the trends (e.g. a decreasing use of biology and psychology material) during the period 1926 to 1945 are of interest. Hobbs was concerned with the claims of sociology textbooks—primarily claims to be representative. On the basis of sources listed three or more times in the index (this

---

[10]For a study of sociology texts up to 1949 see Odum (1951).

restriction was imposed because sources referred to only once or twice in the index may have involved irrelevant factors) 25,828 sources were obtained. This number may seem very large until it is realised that the same source was cited many times in a single textbook, and that a few sources sometimes received hundreds of citations. For example, four anthropologists (Benedict, Mead, Lowie and Boas) were cited 250 times in only nine textbooks. There was a good deal of citing of other introductory texts: 21 per cent of the references in the introductory sociology texts were to other introductory texts and this practice was seen to be increasing. Cultural anthropology was second to sociology in frequency of citation. These sources were cited 2,000 times in the introductory texts published during the period 1926 to 1945. In the early part of this period (1926 to 1930) this source constituted 13 per cent of the total. Social theory was seen to decrease as a source of data, and this was followed by government with 5 per cent of the citations. Psychology and biology followed with 4 per cent each, and both declined during the period studied. Economics accounted for only 4 per cent of the total citations, and the majority of these were to references relating to the extent of poverty and to inequalities in the distribution of wealth and income. Very few were to economic theory. Only 2 per cent of the references were devoted to each of the major disciplines—history, philosophy, religion, law, and geography—and less than 1 per cent each to scientific method, education, war, eugenics, physical science, and medicine.

A decade later, Bain (1962), in a study of the most cited sociologists in textbooks used in introductory sociology courses and published between 1958 and 1962, noted that social anthropology was a rapidly increasing source of citation. Bain raised the question of future trends. Another study by Oromaner (1968), using the same method as Bain, covered the period 1963 to 1967. In comparing the 1958–1962 period with the 1963–1967 period Oromaner noted that sociologists continued to cite non-sociologists a good deal, and that the influence upon sociology, from other social sciences, had shifted from anthropology to psychology. One-third of the list of most cited names had changed within this short period, and Oromaner suggested that this trend may reflect either the rapid growth of sociology, or the fact that the citations were from introductory texts where authors made an effort to indicate that sociology is a dynamic discipline. Oromaner suggested that a comparative study was required of the rate at which contemporary scientists find their way into introductory texts.

There are a number of studies, in the main student MA theses, that have used citation analyses to detail the characteristics (e.g. age, serial or monograph) of literature used by authors. These studies stand apart from the citation analyses included in the rest of this chapter because they are concerned with the characteristics of the literature in specific disciplines. The number of citations analysed is relatively small, and the results do not have general applicability to the parameters of social science literature. The majority of these studies were conducted in the 1950s and came from the Graduate Library School, University of Chicago. They included studies of the characteristics of material used by authors on economics (Mark, 1956; Livesay, 1953), education (Albert, 1939; Cox, 1936), geography (Payne, 1954), business adminis-tration (Sarle, 1958), sociology (Meier, 1951; Quinn, 1951), and politics (Martin, 1952). Stevens (1953b) compared the citations in doctoral dissertations using historical and experimental methods.

Another type of investigation, particularly popular some twenty or so years ago, was the readership[11] study, which involved questioning users of libraries about the nature of the literature they read. Most of the earlier work in this area is of historical interest only, although a few studies have continued to use this method. In a recent survey by Hoban (1967) a questionnaire was sent to subscribers to four journals in the field of public communications. Data was collected about the professional qualifications of subscribers, professional involvement, work, and response to journals. It was found that respondents had a long-term main interest in communications, and worked mainly in universities. Journals were read for keeping up-to-date, and for confirming the stability and normality of readers' thoughts about their subjects. Journal reading also provided a stimulus for thought, and sometimes assisted in the redirection of patterns of thought and action. Some criticism was made about journals: in particular, respondents stated that there were too many articles and research reports dealing with trivial and insignificant problems, and too much technical jargon.

4.3.3 *Author and journal hierarchies*

In any discipline some journals will be cited more frequently than

---

[11]Marquardt (1955) reviewed readership studies, Kirkpatrick (1946) reported a readership study of psychologists, Roberts and Davis (1929) looked at teachers, and Elliott (1933) surveyed business personnel. A more general study was reported by Strang (1942).

others, and some journals will have a higher status than others. The same is true of authors: some will receive many citations and be rated as key or important contributors to the discipline, others will not. These aspects of authors and literature can be investigated by citation analyses.

From the user's standpoint at least two aspects of this hierarchy of journals and authors are important: (1) when a discipline is entered and authors and journals are taken at random from a large number of listings it is obvious that the journals and authors with the highest number of citations (other conditions—e.g. acquisition policies—given as controlled and unrelated to frequency of citation) will appear more often than the least cited journals and authors; (2) a case can be made for the identification of important or key articles/authors in a field by frequency of citation.

To deal first with studies of the citation patterns of journals. In a citation study Xhignesse and Osgood (1967) counted the number of citations to other journals that occurred in a sample of psychology journals. The *Journal of Experimental Psychology* (JEP) headed the list: it received more citations than any of the other journals. But, on the other hand, the JEP contained fewer citations to other journals than most of the other journals in the sample. Xhignesse and Osgood went on to compute the ratios between citations received and citations made. They found that this ratio was related, to some extent, to judgements about the status of journals. In another report (Jakobovits and Osgood, 1967) it was seen that the JEP was regarded, by psychologists, as a high status journal.

Another method of establishing a hierarchy of journals consists of a straightforward count of the most cited references. For example, Gerould and Warman (1954) compiled a list of the most cited periodicals in geography. They broke down the total field of geography into the five main areas—general, geology, meteorology, political, and other. Within each area the frequency with which journals were cited was given. The list was based upon a count of the entries in the 1948 *Current Geographical Publications*. In the area of political geography, for example, there were 12 citations to *World Today*, 9 citations to *Foreign Affairs*, and 4 citations to *Annals of the American Academy of Political and Social Science*.

Some idea of the structure of citations in periodicals, and the linkage between journals, can be gained from studies of self-citations. One such study, interesting but unpublished, was conducted by Boll (1952) on the pattern of self-citations in 22 psychology journals. The 1950 issue of 22 journals was scanned for bibliographical references and foot-notes. Boll found that the *Journal of Experimental Psychology* made more self-citations than any other journal. From a total of 952 references counted in the 1950 issue of the JEP, 26.6 per cent were to articles in the journal itself. *The Journal of Comparative and Physiological Psychology* also had a high self-citation rate: 25 per cent from a total of 520. Journals characterised by low self-citations included *Psychoanalytic Review* (3.9 per cent), *Journal of General Psychology* (4.2 per cent), *Journal of Personality* (5.2 per cent), and *Journal of Genetic Psychology* (5.3 per cent). Review-type journals were not characterised by similar self-citation figures: *Psychological Bulletin* had a low self-citation rate of 5.8 per cent, but *Psychological Review* was much higher with 15.2 per cent.

A very similar study was reported by Xhignesse and Osgood (1967). This study was based upon the 21 journals published in 1955 used by Osgood and Wilson (1961), which in turn had been based upon the 22 journals included in Boll's (1952) study. From the citations con-tained in 21 psychology journals published in 1960, Xhignesse and Osgood reported a self-citation rate for *Journal of Experimental Psycho-logy* of 35 per cent (containing 1,152 citations), *Psychological Review* 12 per cent (855 citations), *Psychological Bulletin* 3 per cent (1,892 citations), *Journal of Comparative and Physiological Psychology* 24 per cent, and *Journal of General Psychology* 2 per cent. Considering that the two studies were separated by ten years, and that the Boll study was an unpublished term paper for use in teaching,[12] there is remarkable agreement between them.

A second method of establishing journal and author hierarchies involves getting people to rate journals for status, image, etc., and authors for importance of contributions, etc. Jakobovits and Osgood (1967) had psychologists rate twenty journals on twenty semantic differential scales. A factor analysis of the scales yielded four factors accounting for 74 per cent of the total variance. The factors in order of importance were: valuableness, scientific rigour, interestingness, and orientation (i.e. theoretical-empirical or basic-applied). This finding suggests that psychologists are reliable judges of the valuable-ness and the interestingness of journals, that they assess the rigour of the reported experiments, and note the orientation of the journal. When the journals were grouped according to their loadings on the rating scales it was found that those journals with a tradition of high

---

[12]Personal communication from Boll in 1969.

K

scientific rigour (e.g. *Journal of Experimental Psychology*, *Psychometrika*, *Psychological Review*, *Behavioral Science*, *Journal of Comparative and Physiological Psychology*) formed the first factor, those journals orientated towards the applied aspect of information in the psychological network (e.g. *Journal of Applied Psychology*, *Journal of Consulting Psychology*, *Educational and Psychological Measurement*) formed the second factor, those journals that could be termed the service (or interest) journals (e.g. *American Psychologist*, *Contemporary Psychology*) formed the third factor, and those journals reflecting the clinical aspect of psychology (e.g. *Journal of Clinical Psychology*, *Journal of Personality*) the fourth factor.

Interpoint distances from each journal to every other were computed by Shepard's (1962) procedure. Using distances of less than unity as the criterion for clustering it was found that the *Journal of Experimental Psychology*, *Psychometrika*, and *Journal of Comparative and Physiological Psychology* formed one tight cluster; they were simultaneously considered the most rigorous and the least interesting or personal. *Psychological Bulletin* and *Psychological Review* formed another cluster: they were seen to have value and to be theoretically orientated. *American Psychologist* and *Contemporary Psychology* formed a third cluster, judged as valued, highly interesting, and personal. These 'images' were reliable and constant, regardless of the personal preference of the raters, as determined by divisional, occupational, educational, or other differences.

This type of study serves to identify the structure and order in a given field of study. Although the communication networks may appear chaotic from the outside, to the experienced researcher there are a number of structures in the system that guide his research activities. To the outsider the problem of retrieving and collecting information about a particular topic may appear bewildering: faced with hundreds of journals, all of which could, with varying degrees of probability, contain the desired information, the problem of obtaining knowledge looks formidable indeed. To the researcher well versed in his field a number of sources appear as obvious first choices. For example, the strictly experimental psychologist has a number of 'core' journals which include those regarded as methodologically sound: he will turn to the *Journal of Experimental Psychology* or to the *Journal of Comparative and Physiological Psychology* (depending upon interest) for details of experimental work, and to *Psychological Review* and *Psychological Bulletin* for state-of-the-art surveys on given topics.

Another indication of journal hierarchies can be gained from a knowledge of rejection rates of articles offered for publication. It is often assumed (perhaps quite wrongly) that journal status and rejection rate go hand in hand. An example of this approach can be seen in a study by Lin and Nelson (1969) who asked authors about the journals to which they first submitted their manuscripts, and which journals, subsequent to rejection by the first, they chose. Of the manuscripts derived from the 1966 American Sociological Association Meeting, and subsequently submitted, but rejected, by *American Sociological Review* (ASA), six were then submitted to the *American Journal of Sociology* (AJS) and three to *Social Forces* (SF). But none of the manuscripts rejected by AJS or SF were submitted to ASR. Four of the manuscripts rejected by the AJS were next submitted to SF, but none of those rejected by SF were submitted to AJS. Furthermore, 28 per cent of the authors at the ASA meeting submitted their manuscripts to ASR for publication, whereas 16 per cent submitted to ASJ, and 7 per cent to SF. A similar finding was reported by Lin and Nelson (1969) who recorded the frequency with which three sociological journals (ASR, AJS, and SF) were cited, the institutional affiliation of the authors, the age of the references, and the number of self-references. It was seen that the ASR attracted a greater number of citations, more authors from prestige institutions, and more self-references than AJS or SF. Also ASR contained citations to more recent material than the other two journals.

4.3.4 *Scattering of references across journals*

It is interesting to know, especially when initiating a bibliographical search, the number of journals that must be covered in order to give a certain coverage of the field of interest and also how far back the search must go. In general the scattering of references tends to follow a pattern such that the great majority of references in any one area are

---

[13]This phenomenon is known as Bradford's Law of Scattering. An exposition of the law can be found in Bradford (1948). There are now many studies of reference scattering in the sciences. See, for example, Bernal (1948b), Vickery (1961), Cole (1958, 1962), Boig and Luftman (1949), Orr and Leeds (1964), and Martyn and Gilchrist (1968) for studies in science and engineering. A very extensive citation study, covering material from science, technology, and social science, undertaken at Aslib by Earle and Vickery (1969a, 1969b), reports on the distribution of citations across subject fields. The law has now been refined and is becoming known as the Bradford-Zipf distribution [see Brookes (1968); Buckland and Hindle (1969); Fairthorne (1958, 1969a); Mandelbrot (1953); Kendall (1961)].

to be found in a comparatively small number of journals.[13] In some established areas in science good coverage can be obtained by searching relatively few journals. In some new fields, where several disciplines converge and where the literature is not yet channelled into relatively few core journals, high degrees of scatter are sometimes found. For example, Orr and Leeds (1964) have shown that biomedical scientists operate under a greater scattering handicap than chemists or physicists. They also report a high degree of scatter in the relatively new area of psychopharmacology. It is not always the case that the scatter of literatures in newer disciplines is greater than in established disciplines. In situations, for example, where a very specialised group breaks away from a main discipline, one or two new journals may contain, at least for a time, most of the documents of interest to the new group of specialists.

There are one or two empirical studies of reference scattering in social science disciplines. One study, by Daniel (1967), looked at the scatter of psychology material, and the coverage of psychology literature by *Psychological Abstracts*, the chief abstracting tool in psychology. Daniel (1967, p. 675) found that psychology needs access to literature in many other subject fields. 'Psychological materials are to be found in each of the basic Dewey Decimal categories, whether one selects by title or by content, and the scattering is only a little less in the Library of Congress system.' Other evidence for the high degree of scatter in citations in psychology literature comes from one of the APA projects[14] which encountered nearly 1,000 journals which were outside mainstream psychology. And Daniel (1967) showed that the 1965 issue of *Psychological Abstracts* covered 637 periodicals, not more than 29 per cent of which could be considered psychology journals. In another study of the coverage of *Psychological Abstracts*, Louttit (1955a) showed that only 30 to 35 per cent of the journals searched were clearly psychology journals; and that this percentage had been fairly constant throughout the life of the *Abstracts*. Other fields covered by *Psychological Abstracts* include psychiatry, medicine, education, and biological science, in decreasing proportions.

A citation analysis proper, as opposed to the counting of journals included in abstracts in *Psychological Abstracts*, was performed by Daniel (1967) with the help of graduate students who determined the number of authors cited in a given psychology journal who could be

---

[14]Report No. 9 'The use of scientific journals by psychologists and the readership of current journal articles'.

located in *Psychological Abstracts*. Daniel concluded that, at the very best, *Psychological Abstracts* can supply only 85 per cent of the citations in mainstream psychology journals. And this figure was appreciably less for many of the journals covered by Daniel and his graduate students. Other data about the coverage of *Psychological Abstracts* comes from Adams (1959) who showed that only 30 per cent of German and Austrian psychological literatures reaches American psychologists through the *Abstracts;* and from Louttit (1955a), who calculated that the coverage of *Psychological Abstracts* ranged from 29 per cent for an interdisciplinary area to 100 per cent for a tightly knit field like 'learning'.

Psychological Abstracts may leave something to be desired with respect to the coverage of primary sources and the subject distribution of abstracts and delay in including original sources—at least in certain areas of psychology and especially in interdisciplinary areas. Elliott (1969), however, has shown that it is superior in all these respects to the only other major abstracting service in psychology, *Bulletin Signalétique: Section 20*.

An indication of scatter was obtained in a study by Daniel (1967) by taking the 375 papers read at the 1957 National Convention of the American Psychological Association and tracing the journals and disciplines in which the papers eventually appeared. 63 per cent of the original reports appeared in psychological journals, 15 per cent in inter-disciplinary (psychology-related) journals, and the remaining 22 per cent in 9 different disciplines clearly not psychology.

The problem of scatter facing the researcher in psychology is not unlike the problem facing other scientists. Daniel (1967), using some of the data reported by Daniel and Louttit (1953) and by Fussler (1949), compared the scattering in psychology with that in physics and chemistry. In all three fields the use of endogenous citations was similar: 70.4 per cent in psychology, 72.7 per cent in physics, and 72.8 per cent in chemistry. But whereas the remaining citations spread over four fields in physics and five in chemistry, the psychologist required eight other fields to account for the total number of citations in the literature sampled. However, the degree of scatter in psychology was not increasing. Daniel (1967), using his own data and that of Schauber (1952), reported an increase in scatter for physics citations but a slight decrease in scatter for psychology citations, during the period 1950 to 1965. In a further citation study Daniel (1967, pp. 679–681) concluded that there was no evidence that psychology was characterised by a unique or special scattering of literature. Taking 20 journals published in 1950

Daniel found that 7,381 citations to journal articles were cited and these could be found in 660 different journals: only 2 per cent of these journals were required to account for 50 per cent of the citations whereas 310 (47 per cent of the 660 journals covered in the study) were required to account for the last 4 per cent of the cumulative curve of citations.

Daniel constructed Bradford curves (showing percentage of citations as a function of percentage of journals) for citations from:

> *Physical Review*, 1965 (one quarter)
> *Journal of Experimental Psychology*, 1965
> *American Journal of Sociology*, 1964–65
> *American Journal of Psychology*, 1965 (one quarter)
> *American Anthropologist*, 1965
> *Journal of Applied Psychology*, 1965
> *Journal of Clinical Psychology*, 1965
> *Journal of Experimental Zoology*, 1965 (one quarter)
> *Journal of Education Research*, 1965.

From the Bradford curves it can be seen that the serial literatures of zoology and anthropology are the most scattered, and of physics the least. The serial literature needed by authors in the *Journal of Experimental Psychology* closely approximates in terms of scatter to the serial literature needed by authors in the *Physical Review:* in both there is a low level of scattering. The literature in education (represented by the *Journal of Educational Research*), in zoology (represented by the *Journal of Experimental Zoology*), and in anthropology (represented by the *American Anthropologist*) is widely scattered. In other areas of psychology (*Journal of Applied Psychology* and *Journal of Clinical Psychology*) the pattern of scatter falls midway between these extremes. From his data Daniel (1967, p. 680) was able to calculate what proportion of the citations in a given journal are found in journals in the same discipline, and thus capable of retrieval by the use of secondary bibliographic tools in that field. For physics, 94 per cent of the references are to physics journals; for experimental psychology, 86 per cent are to psychology journals; for clinical psychology, 69 per cent are to psychology journals; for applied psychology, 79 per cent are to psychology journals; for anthropology, 56 per cent are to anthropology journals; and for education, 41 per cent are to education journals.

In this context it is interesting to note that although psychology draws heavily upon other disciplines for its literature, *Psychological Abstracts* is not widely used by clinicians or medical researchers for current awareness; although, in 1965 for example, *Psychological Abstracts* covered 600 journals, of which 26 were in the field of neurology (Brosin, 1965).

4.4 The relationship between primary and secondary literature

There has been very little evaluation of secondary literature in the social sciences. Evaluation involves measures of the coverage of primary literature and the delay between the appearance of an item in the primary literature and its reappearance in the secondary literature. During the past two years there have been two studies directed towards this aspect of the literature: one by Herner, Griffith and Herner (1968) on the literature relevant to education, and one by Roberts (1970), not yet published, on abstracting and indexing tools in economics.

Herner, Griffith and Herner (1968) identified English language periodicals relating to education, analysed the coverage and treatment of the primary periodical literature by abstracting and indexing publications, and attempted to identify deficiencies in the bibliographical system. A list of 357 periodicals (approximately 55 per cent were within the field of education) was compiled through the use of a questionnaire survey. Ten secondary publications (*Education Index, Educational Administration Abstracts, College Student Personnel Abstracts, Sociology of Education Abstracts, Psychological Abstracts, Sociological Abstracts, Child Development Abstracts and Bibliography, Mental Retardation Abstracts, Deafness, Speech and Hearing Abstracts,* and *Language and Language Behavior Abstracts*) concerned directly and peripherally with the published literature relating to education were selected for intensive study. Details about the coverage of the primary literature, and delay between appearance in primary literature and its appearance in secondary literature were obtained. The periodicals selected for study were the 83 periodicals read by 10 or more of the survey respondents and an additional group of 13 journals from areas less heavily represented in the survey sample. A sample of articles was selected for study. The only purely indexing publication (i.e. *Education Index*) covered the largest number of periodicals in education, and cited all articles in the journals it covered. The 9 abstracting publications covered a wider range of journals outside education, but were selective in their treatment of articles in the journals they covered. The report listed a number of features which respondents to the questionnaire gave as desirable features for secondary coverage of primary literature.

In the study by Roberts (1970) of the coverage of British journals in economics by six abstracting and indexing journals[15] both title and content coverage were investigated. None of the six indexing and abstracting journals gave particularly good coverage: for example, the *Journal of Economic Literature* gave a 57 per cent coverage and the *British Humanities Index* a 60 per cent coverage. Of the individual services the most extensive listing of titles was provided by the *Economic Journal*, with a coverage of 79 per cent of the titles. Roberts summarised the findings from this part of the study by listing journals according to their range of coverage. The first group, including *Economic Journal*, *Public Affairs Information Service Bulletin*, and *Bulletin Analytique*, gave a 70 to 79 per cent coverage; the second group, including *Journal of Economic Literature*, *Economic Abstracts*, and *British Humanities Index*, gave a 57 to 63 per cent coverage; and the third group, which included only *Documentation Economique*, gave a 22 per cent coverage.

Further data were obtained about the coverage of articles within given titles. This measure of coverage ranged from 8 to 57 per cent and as Roberts pointed out it was far too low to enable a useful level of control to be established by secondary bibliographical tools. There were three exceptions, which gave 100 per cent issue coverage—the *British Humanities Index*, *Journal of Economic Literature*, and the *Economic Journal*.

Further data were obtained about the time which elapsed between the first appearance of an article in the primary literature and its reappearance in the secondary literature.

Roberts provided a useful summary table in which the seven abstracting and indexing journals were ranked according to title coverage, issue coverage, literature coverage, and time lapse. *Economic Journal* headed the list on all criteria except that of time lapse. Roberts points out that the success of the *Economic Journal* is based upon the simplicity of the service which it offers. This involves a listing of

---

[15]*Documentation Economique, Journal of Economic Literature,* and *Economic Abstracts* for the abstracting journals; and *Bulletin Analytique, Public Affairs Information Service Bulletin,* and *British Humanities Index* for indexing journals. In addition the *Economic Journal* was included because of its regular listing of the contents of periodicals. *Social Science and Humanities Index* and *Business Periodicals Index* were excluded as marginal and the *International Bibliography of Economics* was excluded because of its belated appearance.

ontents and although this method has a part to play in secondary
ibliographic literature there is also a need for indexing and abstracting
ervices providing systematic subject control which the *Economic
ournal* does not attempt to do.

Studies similar to those by Herner, Griffith and Herner (1968), and
Roberts (1970) are required in all the social sciences, although it is
questionable if the method (i.e. questionnaire survey) used by Herner,
Griffith and Herner to establish a basic list of periodicals relevant to
education is the best and most accurate method.

4.5 Summary

The social sciences are fairly well provided with secondary bibliographical tools, but until such time as details are known about the
parameters of the literature (the coverage of the primary literature by the
secondary literature, the absolute growth, growth points, etc.) it is
impossible to evaluate secondary sources.

Bibliometrical work is unevenly distributed across the social sciences:
more is known about the parameters of psychology literature than the
literature of any of the other social sciences, but even in psychology
there is no authoritative account, based upon empirical studies, of the
structure of the literature. Lancaster (1970) has given a very comprehensive outline of the literature in statistics. He does not base his paper
on bibliometrical studies—there are in any case few bibliometrical
studies to draw upon—but an outline of the structure of the literature
of a discipline such as this provides a very helpful model for future
bibliometrical work. On the question of the growth of literature a
recent analysis by Anthony, East and Slater (1969) on the growth of
the literature of physics provides a good example of the sort of study
that is very much needed in the social sciences.

CHAPTER FIVE

Overview

5.1 The number of social science user studies

This monograph set out, as did Paisley's (1965), to review social science user studies. Five years ago Paisley concluded that there were none to review and suggested that extrapolations could be drawn from user studies in science and technology. There are still very few user studies in the social sciences compared with the number in science and technology, and the present review gives little support to Allen's (1969) conclusion, made after reviewing the 1968 literature, that the number of user studies in the social and behavioural sciences had become quite large during the 1965–1968 period and was growing at a prodigious rate.

In point of fact there are no more than 18 user studies in the social sciences that have used empirical methods, and not all of these could be called user studies in terms of strict definitions (chapter 3). Of these 18 empirical studies, 3 have dealt with the use of foreign language material by psychologists, 2 with the informal communication system in psychology, 4 have focused attention upon the relationship between productivity and availability of information and one was concerned with the relationship between status and communication (these last 5 studies are of marginal interest only to students of information needs and requirements). One study in sociology dealt with user interests and areas of research, rather than with information requirements. There has been one study of the reading habits of social workers, 2 studies of the information requirements of teachers, and one study of the information used by educationalists. The only really comprehensive investigation of the information requirements of the social sciences is the INFROSS investigation under way at Bath University and due for completion by the end of 1970.

The number of user studies in the social sciences is not very great and Allen certainly overstates his case. Moreover, coverage of social science disciplines is erratic: psychology and education have received more ttention than other disciplines. Political science, anthropology, and conomics have received very little attention.

The methodology of social science user studies

Unlike Paisley's review this monograph has not been concerned with he extrapolation of the results from science user studies to the social sciences, but with the methodological issues of science user studies that are relevant to social science user studies.

The main methods of enquiry found in science user studies were reviewed in chapter 2. User studies in the social sciences are of relatively recent origin, and necessarily they have looked to user studies in science and technology for guidance on methodological issues. There has been little attempt to introduce new methods into social science user studies, or to modify existing methods taken from science user studies in the light of the special problems that confront investigations into information requirements of the social sciences.

This is an unsatisfactory state of affairs, and more so because of the uncertainties that exist about the validity of the results of science user studies. Even after a long run of studies in science and technology there is little agreement about the possibility of establishing information needs (as opposed to demands or requirements). There has been adverse comment upon the large number of methods that have featured in user studies, the absence of a standardisation of methods, and the difficulty of amassing a body of knowledge about user information needs and requirements in the absence of such a standardisation. More fundamental questions have been raised, for example by Menzel (1967) and Bernal (1959), about the possibility of establishing information needs by questioning users.

Uncertainties about appropriate methods, about the application of the methods of science user studies to social science studies (1.3), and about the feasibility of establishing information needs (1.1.2) reflect an absence of theory. As the science of information becomes established (1.2) it is to be hoped that these uncertainties will be resolved.

5.3 Neglected aspects of users and their information requirements

Many user studies have attempted little more than a determination of the demand for documents. The problem of information requirements, as opposed to document accessibility and retrieval, has not been successfully investigated. Fairthorne's (1969b) suggestion that information scientists and librarians should, until such time as their art is more developed, refer only to document retrieval and not information retrieval, is as appropriate in the field of user studies as in information retrieval.

The problem of information needs has been much discussed but not satisfactorily dealt with. It is an oustanding problem in science user studies. The remarks below are directed primarily to social science user studies, although some of the areas mentioned as having been neglected apply to science user studies as well as to those in the social sciences.

5.3.1 *Aspects of use*

User studies have typically concentrated upon information demands and requirements at a stage before the information is made use of by the researcher/teacher. Very little is known about the uses that a researcher makes of information once he obtains it in the form of a document, a conversation, etc. For example, does the researcher store information on cards, in his own filing system, does he carry about some information in his head, does he use information as a stimulus for thought, for filling in time between experiments, or for its factual content? These, and many other questions about the uses of information, have rarely been asked. User studies have typically neglected the user as the ultimate processor of information.

It is hardly surprising that user studies have avoided these difficult questions: they include fundamental questions about the nature of social science research and about the psychology of users. It would be pertinent to enquire about the stimulus value of information, user assimilation capacity and overload, redundancy in information systems, optimisation of information intake, preferred signal/noise ratio, and relationship between information and action, and many other topics. Other aspects of use about which little is known include the effect of informal contacts on use of information, the function of seemingly casual conversations, the nature of scientific writing, the way in which information is abstracted and used in the creation of new material, and the sociological aspects of users and patterns of use. There are also the more obviously psychological aspects of user behaviour: the relationship between motivation and information seeking and information usage, and the relationship between personality factors and creativity and productivity.

In a few cases information scientists have turned to psychology in an ttempt to answer some of these questions. Rees and Schultz (1967), or example, suggest that it is reasonable for information scientists to sk psychologists about the types of information services most appropriate for specific cognitive processes, the differences in information equirements between hypothesis formation and hypothesis testing, and he nature of problem solving and the way in which it can be facilitated. Rees and Schultz come to the depressing conclusion that it is unlikely, t the present time, that psychology can provide short term definitive answers to problems relating to user motivation, to the cognitive processes of scientists, or to the relationship between information inputs nd intellectual creativity. Rather, they suggest, the contribution from sychology would seem to lie in the area of experimental methodology. Rees and Schultz note that extraordinary attention has been paid by psychologists to the formulation of problems, the design and execution f experiments, and the analysis and interpretation of data. It is in his area, they suggest, in which psychology could make great contributions, because information science has had no research methodology of ts own. At the present time the formulation and execution of empirical esearch in information science contrasts markedly, and unfavourably, with experimental psychology.

A knowledge of the way in which information is used would perhaps go a long way to solving the pressing problem, almost completely unolved, of information needs.

Very little is known about the amount of information that is required or a particular task. There is some evidence to suggest that too much nformation may be disruptive to research, teaching, and intellectual creative processes, and also to goal setting and decision-making. For example, Porat and Haas (1969) found that the provision of information or decision-making activities followed the law of diminishing returns. In the applied field it may be possible, and sensible, to attempt a measure of the minimum amount of information that is required to complete a ask: not only may too much information be disruptive to the task, or he research, but the retrieval and supply of information is costly, and he filtering, assimilation and processing is costly in terms of users' ime and energy. In pure research it may never be possible, or sensible, to work along these lines. In research the serendipity value of nformation is often high, and the attempt to provide just enough nformation to complete some a priori established goal would certainly meet with strong disapproval from researchers.

Little is known about long term effects upon research activities of exposure to information (and also nonexposure). It may be the case that information requirements change with research experience, or during the progress of a particular project. If user studies are to include these aspects of use then existing methods and studies will be inadequate.

5.3.2 *Costing information services*

The economic aspects of information systems are not well understood and especially is this so in the social sciences. For a good many years some attention has been paid to the economics of conventional library services, but in the main cost alone, rather than cost in relation to benefit or performance, has been assessed. Traditionally costing is required to answer questions about (1) allocation of scarce resources; (2) budgeting; (3) long-range planning; (4) profit or loss; (5) capital v operating costs; (6) unit cost computations; and (7) depreciation. With the advent of computer-based information services (and the national directives and support they often require) and the systems approach that such services attract, the cost of providing services, in relationship to performance and benefit, has attracted a good deal more attention. However, much more needs to be known in this area. Unplanned information services and systems, perhaps constructed as a result of local or idiosyncratic requirements, can be unnecessarily costly.

The typical user study, whether by questionnaire or interview, does not confront the user with the question of cost. When cost considerations are included priorities for information materials and services may be altered, and some may be excluded altogether on the basis that effectiveness is minimal compared with the cost. Information services cannot be provided irrespective of the cost involved, and it is unwise of user studies to proceed as if the user was in an ideal world in which every information requirement (no matter how unimportant or whimsical) could be met with the minimum of effort and cost.

Users can often outline their ideal information system, in which most information requirements are met by pressing a button (involving no programming), close at hand, where the goods are delivered, in the right form, and with the minimum of delay—and also with no cost to the user. This picture is naïve. The cost required to provide such a system on any large scale would be enormous. To the individual user his own information requirements usually appear very reasonable, but a service that functioned at this level would require an information system with a etrieval potential far more sophisticated than anything existing at the present time, or likely to exist in the near future.

It is a common experience of those with experience of information centres and libraries that users say 'yes' to any new service offered. If a university library, for example, enquires of academic staff about the desirability of receiving (say) a current awareness service, most users will reply in the affirmative. In industry, where the costing of information services attracts a good deal more attention, and where the cost has to be accounted for, there is a tendency to supply only those services that can be shown to be effective. It would be an instructive exercise for designers of social science information systems to have a look at the way in which information services in science and technology have been developed and the source of financial support. Page (1967) made the interesting observation that only in atomic energy and space research have there been international policies for information systems. These disciplines have in common heavy expenditure and a subject content which is widely dispersed.

As users come to know more about information technology and its potential applications to facilitate information transfer, there is reason to believe that greater demands will be made for information services. At some point in the design of information systems constraints must be applied. There is a growing awareness that information services and systems will have to be costed, and that economic factors will play a large part in the design of systems and provide a constraint upon uninhibited expansion (see, for example, Judge, 1967).

Although it will be very expensive to provide more and better information services, there is also a cost (to individual researchers, to institutions and to society) when services are inefficient, inadequate, or nonexistent. There is also the question of the cost of duplicated research, which may occur because of imperfect information systems when a researcher is not in possession of the relevant information at the time his research begins, or because information is available late in a programme of research which would have been of use, and have modified the programme, if it had been available at the beginning of the project.

In science and technology something is known about the cost of duplicated research. For example, Martyn (1964b) estimated that £40 million pounds per year was wasted in research activity because of research duplication alone. Furthermore, if other defects in the system are counted (e.g. the revision of research plans because of the late arrival of relevant information) as well, then wastage would be appreciably greater. It would be much more difficult to estimate the cost of duplicated research in the social sciences, where it is more difficult to say that one piece of research exactly duplicates another, due partly to the soft terminology of a good deal of social science research.

However the solution does not lie in supplying a researcher with all available information, even if judged by an information scientist or a librarian to be relevant. It is a common finding of information retrieval services that as the recall ratio increases the relevance ratio decreases. There comes a point at which computer-assisted recall of information is so inclusive (i.e. when the recall ratio approaches unity) that the material recalled approximates, in coverage, to the primary sources of information available in books, periodicals, indexes and abstracts. Such an information service becomes rather wasteful. It is also wasteful of an information service to supply the user with more material than he can assimilate. In an age of computerised retrieval it is easy to supply the researcher with very large amounts of information, which can appear very indigestible and may even, on occasions, be disruptive to research. Wallace (1964), for example, has suggested that in the field of mechanical engineering, information coming too early in a project can be disruptive and time wasting.

In science there is evidence to suggest that the duplication of research is most likely to occur during the first few years of a new discovery. For example, Neelameghan (1968) noted that duplication of research in the field of antibiotics was the highest in the same year as the publication of the original report. The curve representing duplication with time had alternate peaks and troughs for the first ten years of the discovery after which duplication fell to a negligible amount. There have been no similar studies in the social sciences. It may not be possible, because of the different nature of social science research, the soft terminology and the nonaccumulating nature of much of the data, to point to cases of exact, and therefore wasteful, duplicated work.

The amount of money invested in research programmes in the social sciences continues to rise and a large proportion of this money comes from governments. It is not surprising that governments are increasingly taking an interest in the effectiveness of social science research and in the uses to which it is put. In the United States, for example, during the 1960 fiscal year, expenditure on social and psychological research totalled 73 million dollars and in the 1967 fiscal year expenditure was estimated to rise to 380 million dollars or more.[1, 2]

As social science research comes to form an appreciable amount of a nation's expenditure there is likely to be growing concern that the most efficient methods of research are operative and that social scientists are supplied with the information that their research demands. In science and technology these factors have played a part in directing attention to user information requirements. It can readily be argued that only by providing scientists and engineers with pertinent services can high quality goods be produced, in the most efficient way. Of course, even in science, where many may keep an eye upon the potential commercial value of basic research the relationship between information flow and productivity and creativity has not been established.

In the social sciences the link between pure research and the commercial, or social, value of its products is more complex and less well established. There is now a much greater emphasis upon action research, upon practical research, and upon the utilisation of the results of research than in the past. Future user studies in the social sciences will not be unaffected by this emphasis upon the practical value of research.

One of the reasons for the comparatively late arrival of the social science user study may be related to the way in which social science research is financed, and to the absence of obvious economic rewards of basic social research. In science and technology individual industries and research laboratories are responsible for a good many user studies, and economic criteria may be a strong justification for spending money on this type of enquiry. In the social sciences, addressing themselves very often to social problems, where financial gain is not the aim, and indeed where financial gain is unlikely to be forthcoming (at least in the near future) user studies must be justified on other grounds. There would undoubtedly be economic advantages accompanying a reduction in crime rate, more efficient methods of teaching, improved industrial relations, reducing the incidence of mental illness, and many other social ills that social scientists have traditionally been concerned with. But these are not economically viable projects to support (at least at the present time) because social scientists have given little indication that they can effect practical solutions.

---

[1]United States House of Representatives Committee on Government Operations (1967), Vol. 2.
[2]See Armstrong (1969) for an estimate of the United Kingdom Government expenditure on social research.

L

5.3.3   *The formal system*

The formal system refers to the complex of primary and secondary, and sometimes tertiary, materials that form the bulk of printed materials. These include periodicals, monographs, collections of papers, conference proceedings, research reports, and unpublished formal communications. In chapter 4 the formal system was dealt with insofar as details about this system can throw light upon information requirements; following Paisley's suggestion that the artifacts of communication, including citations, articles, monographs, and prepublication papers, can give valuable data about information use patterns, and information demands. In this sense a study of the formal system can provide additional data to that obtained from questioning users.

In fact very little is known about the formal system in the social sciences. When assessing information requirements it is important to have at hand details of the formal system to show how far these requirements are met by existing formal systems.

In chapter 4 studies that have looked at the structure of social science literature and its statistical regularities were reviewed. A little is known about the literature of psychology and, to a lesser extent, the literature of economics. But even in these two disciplines the coverage of the literature is erratic, depending very much upon local conditions of availability and interest, and there have been no comprehensive studies. One or two citation studies involving sociological literature exist, but these apart, very little is known about the statistical parameters of the literature of the other social sciences.

As a beginning it is necessary to know about (1) growth rates; (2) growth points; (3) the scatter of literature across secondary tools; (4) the structure of primary literature; (5) the extent and nature of review literature; (6) the geographical origin of the literature; and (7) language of origin.

The situation in science and technology is certainly not ideal, but a good deal more is known about the statistical parameters of science literature than of social science literature. A recent publication by Anthony, East, and Slater (1969) on the nature of the literature of physics provides a good example of the sort of material that needs bringing together under one cover for each of the social science disciplines. This study includes, for example, a review of the growth of the literature, its size, and an account of the evolution of information services in physics.

Few user studies have paid much attention to the statistical parameters of the formal communication system. Paisley (1965) suggested that literature is an artifact of communication between scientists, and that these artifacts give valuable supplementary data to studies of information demands and requirements. Few studies have followed Paisley's suggestion. Paisley's review looked at the communication artifacts in science but paid little attention (in spite of the aim of the review) to the social sciences. Where the aim of a user study is to provide data for the design and provision of information services, it is very necessary to know how far existing services meet both existing and potential demands for information, and what modifications to formal communication systems must be made before these requirements can be met.

Those responsible for the design and development of new information services and the modification of existing ones are now under a good deal of pressure to look to user requirements and the results of user studies. In fact, such bodies often initiate user studies. It is now realised that information system design cannot be left to the computer expert or the librarian or to management. On the other hand those conducting user studies have a responsibility to ensure that enquiries are related to what is technically and financially possible. Dialogue between those interested in user requirements and those interested in the technical and physical aspects of information system design has not been forthcoming. As Bergen (1968) has pointed out, a relatively unexplored problem in information science is the nature of the relationship between the structure and transmission of knowledge, on the one hand, and the array of bibliographic devices which have been developed to facilitate access to that knowledge, on the other. Bergen may have simplified the problem: it is doubtful if bibliographic devices have always been developed with the idea of facilitating access to knowledge, or that knowledge comes first and bibliographic devices develop later, or that knowledge production takes place independently of bibliographic devices. In principle there is general agreement that bibliographic devices should facilitate access to knowledge but in practice many bibliographic devices have appeared as a result of commercial interests. Still, Bergen raises a very important issue. User studies should be concerned with the growth and structure of knowledge, with the creative process, with the way in which knowledge accumulates, its transmission, as well as with the psychological aspects of information flow.

5.4   Future trends in the study of information requirements

Because there have been so few user studies in the social sciences it is difficult to see a pattern emerging and to predict future developments. Science user studies have exerted, and will no doubt continue to do so, a major influence on social science user studies—but even in science and technology there is a good deal of dissatisfaction with the progress in studying information requirements, and it would be difficult to predict the future of science user studies.

The first fully-fledged user studies in science and technology appeared in the late 1940s—before the extensive use of computers, before the upsurge of interest, in post-war society, of consumer research, before systems approaches, and before the national and international coordination of economies, monetary policies, research policies, and more recently, information policies. Also, before the advent of the science of information. It is fairly certain that the same approach that characterised the early, pioneering user studies in science and technology will not be followed in the social sciences. But one can be less certain of the positive direction that will be taken.

Social science user studies came on to the scene in the mid-1960s and were superimposed upon a body of empirical data and knowledge about information needs and requirements in science and technology. By this time a good many problems of user studies (including research design, methodology, method of enquiry, interpretation, needs versus demands, etc.) had been discussed, and there existed the rudiments of a theory of information science (Kochen, 1969).

It is suggested that (1) factors internal to social science disciplines; (2) general attitudes to the organisation and support of research and (3) technical aspects of information transfer including mechanisation will influence the pattern of future user studies.

There is growing awareness that the fundamental differences which exist between science and social science may play a large part in the determination of information requirements, and that the methods found in science user investigations may be inappropriate for social science user studies.

It is likely that user studies will be affected by changing attitudes towards research, the research process, the organisation and financial support of research, and the coordination of effect that is now taking place on an international level to coordinate information systems. It is unlikely that user studies will proceed in isolation from external factors related to coordinating policies, cost, and technical and social feasibility, to produce, for example, plans for information systems that have no chance, because of cost or many other factors, of implementation.

The cost conscious approach to information services has been super-imposed upon an earlier upsurge of interest in user requirements which had occurred concomitantly with a change of attitude towards consumers in general. The post-war economic scene saw the advent of consumer research and mass advertising. It is to be expected that consumer research will continue to play a large part in market economies, and there is no reason to suppose that information systems will be exempted from this interest. However, the attention that is now paid to user orientated systems presents a paradoxical situation. As information systems become more complex the user finds himself at the end of an increasingly long chain of components making up the total information system, of which he knows less and less. As information networks develop and become more complex the fears expressed over twenty-five years by Bernal, and subsequently by others (for example, Taube, 1959), are still relevant today.

It is most unlikely that users have nothing to contribute to information systems. Rather, the results of user studies will form one of the ingredients of information systems, although by no means the most important. From the results of existing user studies it can be seen that users are depressingly unsophisticated in the use of existing bibliographical tools and information services, and especially is this the case in the social sciences. The recent interest in user education suggests that a more optimistic view can be taken of the future. If user education is acceptable, and possible, on a fairly wide front, then users may be in a better position than they have been in the past to specify their information requirements. On a fairly small scale, but representing a beginning, the area of reader instruction in the university libraries has recently been discussed by Mackenzie (1969). And already there exists a list of user education courses in the United Kingdom for scientists and engineers (see Wood, 1969). It is to be hoped that this new role for the information scientist and librarian will not be used as a power-house in which instruction is geared to the interests and skills of instructors instead of user requirements. In the past there have been attempts to instruct users, especially in the use of card catalogues and bibliographical tools. As long ago as 1934 the University of California, as a result of recommendations made by Hurt (1934) following a user study of students, offered a course in library use and general bibliography. This type of instruction has continued, although usually at a local level. A much more extensive, perhaps nationally organised, policy of instruction of users in the sophisticated methods of information retrieval, their potentialities, and their use, is now required.

General attitudes to research, and to information problems in general, both amongst professional information scientists and administrators, will play a part in the future in directing attention to the user. These effects are less tangible than the forces due to economic and technological factors, but their effect may be felt just the same. It is suggested that the following have contributed to the upsurge of interest in the user during the last twenty years: (1) a growth in marketing and consumer studies in general; (2) the great cost of computer systems and the risk involved in bringing into being very expensive systems without first studying consumers and potential demand; (3) a renewed interest in the human as an individual, which may partly be due to a reaction against the 'inhuman' planning systems that have developed in post-war society, for example, high blocks of flats, complex welfare states; (4) the realisation that a number of non-academic factors may influence research and planning for research; (5) a coordination at a national level, concerned with the finance of research, its ancillary services, and more recently national and international coordination and direction of policies on the study of information problems.

User enquiries that have looked at informal communication, including telephone calls, correspondences with colleagues, informal contacts at conferences have made a start in the investigation of the numerous factors that play a part in research. Some studies also have had a look at the less immediate work environment. In a previous age in which scientists were expected always to be rational and systematic in their work environment extra curricula activities could not be discussed. There is good evidence to show (for example, Watson's, 1968, account of the discovery of DNA molecule) that in science irrational behaviours, contacts outside immediate work environment, and many non-academic influences all play a part in scientific discovery. In the social sciences the influence of non-academic factors, for example from the mass media, are probably much more significant than in the sciences because of the nature of the subject matter of the social sciences. To the extent that this is the case the problem of identifying the important and relevant factors in social science research are increased. User studies have typically concentrated upon the demand for the palpable components of communication networks (the formal bibliographical system, communications from professional societies, apparatus information) but have typically neglected the less palpable influences upon research. Apart from extremely idiosyncratic influences upon research, of a very personal nature (and it would not seem sensible to attempt to identify and investigate these) there is a large grey area of influence, including the mass media, political pressures, ideals, climates of opinion, and statements of national directive, all of which may play, to a greater or lesser degree, a part in research.

Changing attitudes to the research process and to the 'scientific paper' may influence information requirements. There is growing impatience and dissatisfaction with pure research, removed from practical and social problems. There is impatience with some types of laboratory research in psychology, and the complex and unrealistic theories of nearly all the social sciences.

The third set of factors, at a technological level, relates to recent developments in information transfer technology which are proceeding at a very fast rate. At this level information networks may be identified in terms of: (1) the class of equipment used, for example, telephone network, computer network; (2) the form of data in the network, for example, digital network, audio-network, film network; or (3) their function, for example, financial network, library network, education network. Information networks include some combination of all the above three elements, which, when combined to form a communication system provide the desired pattern of information exchange. Some idea of technological developments in information networks is given in reviews by Hammer (1967) and by Becker and Olsen (1968) who suggest that the expensive equipment required in information networks is forcing organisations to share rather than duplicate technical resources. At the same time advances in communications technology, including a rapidly increasing stockpile of machine-readable information, makes it possible to use multi-media communications channels, makes for easy distribution of information, and the possibility of sharing resources. Becker and Olsen suggest that information networks are propagated largely by economic and technological forces.

It is always possible that these forces will become overriding factors in the determination of information networks and that the direction dictated by such forces will on many occasions be incompatible with user orientated information services and subsystems.

In the past user studies have usually set out to investigate information requirements or demands, and the more ambitious have attempted to investigate information needs. But very often these investigations have done no more than find out the documents a researcher uses, or would like to use if he knew about them and obtain them. In the future it is likely that greater attention will be paid to information. Those responsible for user studies should be encouraged to be more accurate in their use of terminology.

The concept of information, like that of need, has been most unsatisfactorily dealt with by information scientists and librarians. The heart of the problem may not lie in the youthfulness of this type of enquiry or a lack of data about needs or information, but in the conceptualisation of the problems. Some of the confusion and uncertainty that now surround investigations of user needs, and of information transfer in general, could be avoided by the use of controlled vocabulary. The use of the term 'information' is responsible for a good deal of the misunderstanding and confusion. It is used by librarians and information scientists as an abstract term, and like 'needs', is difficult to define operationally and therefore measure.

It can be agreed that users would like to have information (rather than documents) retrieved and supplied to them and, along with Fairthorne, that at present documents rather than information are retrieved. Information can be thought of as a relational concept. A document, in isolation, and unused, may contain data, theory, and references perhaps, but these contents do not constitute information until they are read and assimilated, thereby placing them in context. There is also information in the fact that one document is cited much more frequently than another, that a library has a copy of a given document rather than another, and that one document can be retrieved easily but another only with difficulty. This tells us something about a library, an information system, and the structure of a discipline, and it also gives us information about the document, the state of a discipline and users.

There is a similar problem when defining 'needs'. Information scientists and librarians continue to talk about information needs, and there is agreement that it is an important topic in research and teaching. But little progress has been made in defining or measuring information needs.

Because 'information' and 'needs' are general and abstract terms it is difficult to provide satisfactory operational definitions. Investigations that set out to determine information needs as such place themselves at a tremendous disadvantage from the start compared with investigations that attempt to measure the more tangible aspects of information and user requirements. If, instead of attempting to measure needs outright, information scientists investigated aspects of use, the cost of information services, the structure of the literature, the research process, the nature of scientific writing, citation patterns, and so forth—aspects of information systems and user behaviour that can be operationally defined—more progress might be made. It has to be admitted that the body of knowledge resulting from such studies would not in itself be data on information needs. Before needs can be satisfactorily investigated a theory of information science must exist: it may then be that information needs will be incorporated into such a theory. But until such time the concepts of 'need' and 'information' present very difficult problems. The methods of user studies have only a limited relevance to these problems. Information needs are so much more interesting than demands; and the problem presents a very real challenge. In the social sciences, where information requirements cannot be so clearly stated as in many cases in science, where it is more difficult to predict the economic and commercial value of information, and where existing bibliographical and other information services are underutilised, information needs rather than demands are especially interesting and important.

One final point must be made on the question of the relevance of user studies to users, to suppliers of information, and ultimately to social science problems. No matter how good from a methodological and technical point of view, the contribution user studies make to research and teaching will be judged in terms of the importance of the problem that has been investigated. User studies by definition are orientated towards the clients of information services, but this is perhaps not enough. User studies could so easily be concentrated upon problems of marginal relevance, or upon only one part of the information system. For example, studies that looked only at formal communication would misrepresent the true state of the flow of information, because there is now ample evidence to show that the informal network (3.4) may carry as much as 80 per cent of all communications in the dialogue of researchers with one another.

5.5 Conclusions

(1) User studies in the social sciences have a very short history. It is only during the last four or five years that empirical studies of the information requirements of social scientists have appeared.

(2) User studies in the physical sciences have a relatively long history —some twenty-five years—and studies in the social sciences have

drawn heavily upon user studies in science for guidance on methodological issues.

(3) User studies have been conducted, both in the physical and social
sciences, in the absence of strong theoretical or conceptual frameworks. In the absence of good theory, developments in methodology have not made much progress. User studies have not
always taken as an example the best of past work.

(4) Because there are so few user studies in the social sciences it is
difficult to see a trend developing; but there is no indication that
user studies will proliferate in the social sciences as they have
done in science and technology.

(5) The few user studies that have appeared in the social sciences—
and only one has covered all the major disciplines—have made
little attempt to tackle the special problems found in the study
of social science information requirements. The existing methods
of enquiry found in science user studies have been applied without much modification to the social sciences. There is reason to
suppose that the differences between the sciences and the social
sciences make the methods of user studies in the one inappropriate in the other.

(6) Developing trends in the social sciences, including the use of
data archives, the emphasis upon the usability of the results of
research, and the realisation of the importance of social science
information in policy making, taken together with developments
in the emerging discipline of information science, including an
emphasis on bibliographical control and the effects of new technologies on the writing, storage, retrieval, and dissemination of
information, are likely to influence future research into information needs and requirements, and the subsequent design of
information systems followed by a provision of information
services.

References

ADAMS, J. F. (1959). 'Towards better communication of psychological research between countries.' *Journal of General Psychology*, 60, 1959, 289–290.

ADVISORY COMMITTEE ON SCIENTIFIC POLICY (U.K.) (1965). 'Survey of information needs of physicists and chemists.' *Journal of Documentation*, 21 (2), 1965, 83–112.

ALBERT, R. W. (1939). *Evaluation of educational journals from the standpoint of research*. (Master's dissertation, University of Chicago, 1939.) [*unpublished*]

ALBRIGHT, L. E. and GLENNON, J. R. (1963). 'Journal tables of contents.' *American Psychologist*, 18, 1963, 109–110.

ALLEN, T. J. (1964). *The utilization of information sources during R and D proposal preparation*. (Report no. 97–64, Research program on the organization and management of R and D.) Cambridge, Mass.: M.I.T., 1964.

ALLEN, T. J. (1965). *Sources of ideas and their effectiveness in parallel R and D projects*. (Alfred P. Sloan School of Management. Report no. 130–65) Cambridge, Mass.: M.I.T., 1965.

ALLEN, T. J. (1966a). 'Studies of the problem-solving process in engineering design.' *IEEE Transactions on Engineering Management*, 13 (2), 1966, 72–83.

ALLEN, T. J. (1966b). *Managing the flow of scientific and technological information*. (Doctoral thesis, Massachusetts Institute of Technology, Alfred P. Sloan School of Management, 1966.) [*unpublished*]

ALLEN, T. J. (1967). 'Communications in the research and development laboratory.' *Technology Review*, 70 (1), 1967, 2–8.

ALLEN, T. J. (1968). 'Organizational aspects of information flow in technology.' *Aslib Proceedings*, 20 (11), 1968, 433–454.

ALLEN, T. J. (1969). 'Information needs and uses.' *Annual Review of Information Science and Technology*, 4, 1969, 3–29.

ALLEN, T. J., ANDRIEN, M. and GERSTENFELD, A. (1966). *Time allocation among three technical information channels by R and D engineers*. (Alfred P. Sloan School of Management. Working paper no. 184–66.) Cambridge, Mass.: M.I.T., 1966.

ALLEN, T. J. and COHEN, S. I. (1969). 'Information flow in research and development laboratories.' *Administrative Science Quarterly*, 14 (1), 1969, 12–19.

ALLEN, T. J. and GERSTBERGER, P. G. (1967). *Criteria for selection of an information source*. Cambridge, Mass.: M.I.T., 1967.

ALLEN, T. J., GERSTENFELD, A. and GERSTBERGER, P. G. (1968). *The problem of internal consulting in an R and D laboratory.* (Alfred P. Sloan School of Management. Working paper no. 319–68.) Cambridge, Mass.: M.I.T., 1968.

ALPERT, H. (1958). Congressmen, social scientists, and attitudes toward Federal support of social science research. *American Sociological Review*, 23, 1958, 682–686.

ALPERT, H. (1960). The Government's growing recognition of social science. *Annals of the American Academy of Political and Social Science*, 327, 1960, 327.

ALTMAN, I. (1968). 'Choicepoints in the classification of scientific knowledge', *in* B. P. Indik and F. K. Berrien (*eds.*) *People, groups, and organisations.* New York: Columbia University, Teachers College Press, 1968, 47–69.

AMERICAN BEHAVIORAL SCIENTIST (1966–). *The ABS Guide to recent publications in the social and behavioral sciences.* Supplements, 1966–. New York: A.B.S. *and* Oxford: Pergamon, 1966–.

AMERICAN PSYCHOLOGICAL ASSOCIATION (1963–). *Reports of the Project on Scientific Information Exchange in Psychology.* Vols. 1–3. Washington, D.C.: American Psychological Association, 1963–69.
Vol. 1 (1963):
> Report B. An overview of the structure, objectives, and findings of the American Psychological Association's Project on Scientific Information Exchange in Psychology. December, 1963.
> No. 1. Scientific activity and information problems of selected psychologists: a preliminary survey. August, 1963.
> No. 2. An informal study of the preparation of chapters for the *Annual Review of Psychology*. August, 1963.
> No. 3. A general study of the Annual Convention of the American Psychological Association. August, 1963.
> No. 4. Convention attendants and their use of the Convention as a source of scientific information. August, 1963.
> No. 5. Convention participants and the dissemination of information at scientific meetings. August, 1963.
> No. 6. Publication fate of formal presentations at the 1957 Convention of the American Psychological Association. August, 1963.
> No. 7. Archival journal articles: their authors and the processes involved in their production. August, 1963. (Revised December, 1963.)
> No. 8. A comparison of scientific information-exchange activities at three levels of psychological meetings. December, 1963.
> No. 9. The use of scientific journals by psychologists and the readership of current journal articles. December, 1963.

Vol. 2 (1965):

No. 10. A preliminary study of information exchange activities of foreign psychologists and a comparison of such activities with those occurring in the United States. May, 1964.

No. 11. The discovery and dissemination of scientific information among psychologists in two research environments. September, 1964.

No. 12. Theoretical and methodological considerations in undertaking innovations in scientific information exchange. January, 1965.

No. 13. The role of the technical report in the dissemination of scientific information. April, 1965.

No. 14. The use of books as a medium for the dissemination of scientific information. November, 1966.

No. 15. A study of *Psychological Abstracts*: some findings on its current functions and operation and a proposed plan for innovation. December, 1965.

Vol. 3 (1969):

No. 16. Innovation in scientific communication in psychology. December, 1966.

No. 17. The use of scientific information in the undergraduate teaching of psychology. March, 1967.

No. 18. Information exchange at the American Psychological Association Annual Convention and the function of the Convention *Proceedings* in such exchange. April, 1968.

No. 19. Information exchange activities involved in psychological work. March, 1968.

No. 20. Scientific communication at the XVIII International Congress of Psychology, Moscow, 1966, and some implications for the design and operation of international meetings. (Supplement to vol. 2.) April, 1968.

No. 21. Networks of informal communication among scientifically productive psychologists: an exploratory study. December, 1968.

ANDRY, R. G. (1965). 'Existing documentation services in criminology —and future needs.' *Aslib Proceedings*, 17 (2), 1965, 50–59.

ANTHONY, L. J., EAST, H. and SLATER, M. J. (1969). 'The growth of the literature in physics.' *Report on Progress in Physics*, 32, 1969, 709–767.

APPEL, J. S. and GURR, T. (1964). 'Bibliographic needs of social and behavioral scientists: report of a pilot survey.' *American Behavioral Scientist*, 7 (10), 1964, 51–54.

ARIES CORPORATION (1969). *Interferon scientific memoranda: a report on the feasibility of increasing the efficiency and effectiveness of scientific research through the use of new communications media.* McLean, Va., Aries Corp., 1969.

ARMSTRONG, Sir W. (1969). 'Research and government: the view from the government'. *SSRC Newsletter*, no. 7, 1969, 1–4.

AUERBACH CORPORATION (1965). *Review of methodologies for studying user needs for scientific and technical information.* Philadelphia, Pa. Auerbach Corp., 1965. [*includes 676 item bibliography*]

BAIN, R. (1962). 'The most important sociologists?' (Letter.) *American Sociological Review*, 27 (5), 1962, 746–748.

BARBER, A. S. (1966). 'A critical review of the surveys of scientists use of libraries', *in* W. L. Saunders (*ed.*) *The provision and use of library and documentation services.* London: Pergamon, 1966, 145–179.

BARBER, B. and FOX, R. C. (1958). 'The case of the floppy-eared rabbits: an instance of serendipity gained and serendipity lost.' *Amercian Journal of Sociology*, 64 (2), 1958, 128–136.

BARINOVA, Z. B. *and others* (1968). *Investigation of scientific journals as communication channels. Appraising the contribution of individual countries to the world scientific information flow.* Washington, D.C.: Joint Publications Research Service, 1968.

BARKER, A. and RUSH, M. (1970). *The Member of Parliament and his information.* London: Allen & Unwin, 1970.

BARNES, R. C. M. (1964). 'Some recent investigations into information use at A.E.R.E.' *in* Aslib Annual Conference Proceedings *Looking forward in documentation.* London: Aslib, 1964, 4.1–4.5.

BARNES, R. C. M. (1965). 'Information use studies, Part 2—Comparison of some recent surveys.' *Journal of Documentation*, 21 (3), 1965, 169–176.

BARR, K. P. (1967). 'Estimates of the number of currently available scientific and technical periodicals.' *Journal of Documentation*, 23 (2), 1967, 110–116.

BATH UNIVERSITY OF TECHNOLOGY (1968). Investigation into information requirements of the social sciences: report on the preliminary stage. Bath University of Technology Library, April, 1968.

BATH UNIVERSITY OF TECHNOLOGY (1970). Experimental information officer in the social sciences: report to OSTI on work carried out in 1969. Bath University of Technology Library, February, 1970. [Mimeographed report.]

BECK, C. and MCKECHNIE, J. (1968). *Political elites: a select computerized bibliography.* Cambridge, Mass.: M.I.T., 1968.

BECKER, H. A. (1969). 'Educational technology and the software gap.' *Automated Education Letter*, 4 (10), 1969, 7–8.

BECKER, J. and OLSEN, W. C. (1968). 'Information networks.' *Annual Review of Information Science and Technology*, 3, 1968, 289–327.

BERGEN, D. P. (1968). 'Foreword' *in* E. B. Montgomery (*ed.*). *The foundations of access to knowledge: a symposium.* Syracuse: Syracuse University Press, 1968.

BERNAL, J. D. (1948a). 'Preliminary analysis of pilot questionnaire on the use of scientific literature,' in Royal Society *Report on the Royal Society Scientific Information Conference, 1948.* London: Royal Society, 1948, 589–637.

BERNAL, J. D. (1948b). 'Provisional scheme for central distribution of scientific publications,' in Royal Society *Report on the Royal Society Scientific Information Conference, 1948.* London: Royal Society, 1948, 253–258.

BERNAL, J. D. (1957). 'The supply of information to the scientist: some problems of the present day.' *Journal of Documentation,* 13 (4), 1957, 195–208.

BERNAL, J. D. (1959). 'The transmission of scientific information: a user's analysis,' in International Conference on Scientific Information, Washington, 1958, *Proceedings,* vol. I. Washington, D.C.: National Academy of Sciences, National Research Council, 1959, 77–95.

BEVIS, J. C. (1948). 'Economic incentives used for mail questionnaires.' *Public Opinion Quarterly,* 12, 1948, 492–493.

BISCO, R. L. (1964). 'Information retrieval from data archives: the ICPR system.' *American Behavioral Scientist,* 7 (10), 1964, 45–48.

BISCO, R. L. (1966). 'Social science data archives: a review of development.' *American Political Science Review,* 40 (1), 1966, 93–109.

BISCO, R. L. (1967a). *On the development of social science information and documentation services in the university library (interim report).* (California University—Institute of Library Research. *Final report on mechanized information services in the university library, Phase 1—Planning,* part II.) Los Angeles: University of California, Institute of Library Research, 1967.

BISCO, R. L. (1967b). 'Social science data archives: progress and prospects.' *Social Science Information,* 6, February, 1967, 39–74.

BIVONA, W. A. and GOLDBLUM, E. J. (1966). *Selective dissemination of information: review of selected systems and a design for army technical libraries.* Information Dynamics Corporation, Reading, Mass., 1966 (AD 636 916).

BLOOM, M. (1969). 'The selection of knowledge from the behavioral sciences and its integration into social work curricula.' *Journal of Education for Social Work,* 5 (1), 1969, 15–28.

BOEHM, E. H. (1963). 'Dissemination of knowledge in the humanities and social sciences.' *ACLS Newsletter,* 14 (5), 1963, 3–12.

BOEHM, E. H. (1965). *Blueprint for bibliography: a system for the social sciences and humanities.* Santa Barbara, Cal.: Clio Press, 1965.

BOIG, F. S. and LOFTMAN, K. A. (1949). 'Domestic and foreign periodicals in the field of petroleum chemistry: a statistical analysis.' *Oil and Gas Journal,* 47 (51), 1949, 199, 200, 204, 207–208.

BOLL, J. J. (1952). *The input and output of 22 psychological periodicals: a study of bibliographic coverage.* Urbana, Ill.: University of Illinois, 1952. [*unpublished*]

BORKO, H. (1962). 'Determining user requirements for an information storage and retrieval system: a systems approach', *in* C. P. Bourne (*ed.*) *Information systems workshop.* Washington, D.C.: Spartan Books, 1962, 37–60.

BORKO, H. (1968). 'The conceptual foundations of information systems', *in* E. B. Montgomery (*ed.*) *The foundations of access to knowledge: a symposium.* Syracuse, N.Y.: Syracuse University Press, 1968, 67–99.

BOTTOMORE, T. B. (1962). *Sociology: a guide to problems and literature.* London: Allen & Unwin, 1962.

BOURNE, C. P. (1962a). 'A review of the methodology of information system design', *in* C. P. Bourne (*ed.*) *Information systems workshop.* Washington, D.C.: Spartan Books, 1962, 11–35.

BOURNE, C. P. (1962b). 'The world's technical journal literature.' *American Documentation,* 13 (2), 1962, 159–168.

BRADFORD, S. C. (1948). *Documentation.* London: Crosby Lockwood, 1948.

BROADUS, R. N. (1952). 'An analysis of literature cited in the American Sociological Review.' *American Sociological Review,* 17 (3), 1952, 355–357.

BROADUS, R. N. (1967). 'A citation study for sociology.' *American Sociologist,* 1, 1967, 19–20.

BROOKES, B. C. (1968). 'The derivation and application of the Bradford-Zipf distribution.' *Journal of Documentation,* 24 (4), 1968, 247–265.

BROSIN, H. W. (1965). 'Information explosion—information retrieval.' *American Journal of Psychiatry,* 122 (4), 1965, 453–454.

BROWN, M. J. and McCULLOCH, J. W. (1968a). 'Some characteristics and continuity of learning in child care practice.' *Child Care News,* no. 79, 1968, 2–4.

BROWN, M. J. and McCULLOCH, J. W. (1968b). 'Research findings relevant to some characteristics of the medical social worker.' *Medical Social Worker,* 21 (7), 1968, 200–204.

BROWN, M. J. and McCULLOCH, J. W. (1969b). 'Mental welfare officers in practice: some associated variables.' *Case Conference,* 15 (10), 1969, 399–400.

BROWN, M. J. and McCULLOCH, J. W. (1969a). 'Reading habits of probation officers: a comparative study by age and training.' *Probation,* 15 (1), 1969, 13–17.

BRYAN, H. (1968). 'The explosion in published information—myth or reality. *Australian Library Journal,* 17 (11), 1968, 389–401.

BUCKLAND, M. K. and HINDLE, A. (1969). 'Documentation notes: library Zipf.' *Journal of Documentation,* 25, 1969, 52–57.

BURCHINAL, L. G. (1967a). 'ERIC and dissemination of research findings.' *Theory into Practice*, 6, 1967, 77–84.

BURCHINAL, L. G., (1967b). 'ERIC and the need to know.' *NEA Journal*, 56, 1967, 65–72.

BURCHINAL, L. G. (1967c). 'Needed: local, one-stop information centers.' *Educational Researcher*, special supplement, 1967, 8–9.

CAHALAN, D. (1951). 'Effectiveness of a mail questionnaire technique in the army.' *Public Opinion Quarterly*, 15, 1951, 575–578.

CAMP, W. L. (1968). Guide to periodicals in education. Metuchen, N.J.: Scarecrow Press, 1968.

CARTER, C. F. and WILLIAMS, B. R. (1967). *Industry and technical progress*, London: O.U.P., 1967.

CARTER, L. F. and others (1967). *National document-handling systems for science and technology*. London: Wiley, 1967.

CARTER, L. J. (1966). 'Social sciences: problems examined by Senate panel.' *Science*, 153 (3732), 1966, 154–156.

CARTER, L. J. (1967). 'Social sciences: where do they fit in the politics of science?' *American Sociologist*, 2 (1), 1967, 9–11.

CARTER, M. P. (1968). 'Report on a survey of sociological research in Britain.' *Sociological Review*, 16 (1), 1968, 5–40.

CARTWRIGHT, D. (1948). 'Social psychology, in the United States during the Second World War.' *Human Relations*, 1, 1948, 333–352.

CARTWRIGHT, D. (1949). 'Basic and applied social psychology.' *Philosophy of Science*, 16, 1949, 198–208.

CAVANAGH, J. M. A. (1967). 'Some considerations relating to user-system interaction in information retrieval systems', *in* A. B. Tonik (*ed.*) *Fourth Annual National Colloquium on Information Retrieval*. Philadelphia, Pa.: International Information Inc., 1967.

CAWKELL, A. E. (1968). 'Documentation notes. Citation practices.' *Journal of Documentation*, 24 (4), 1968, 299–303.

CENTRAL STATISTICAL OFFICE (1965). *List of principal statistical series available*. (Studies in Official Statistics, no. 11.) London: H.M.S.O. 1965.

CHALL, L. P. (1966). *Documenting sociology*. (Paper read at the 6th World Congress of Sociology, Evian, September, 1966.) [*unpublished*]

CHAMPION, D. R. and SEAR, A. M. (1969). 'Questionnaire response rate: a methodological analysis.' *Social Forces*, 47 (3), 1969, 335–339.

CHERNS, A. (1969). 'Social research and diffusion.' *Human Relations*, 22 (3), 1969, 209–218.

CLEVERDON, C. W. (1962). *Aslib-Cranfield Research Project: report on the testing and analysis of an investigation into the comparative efficiency of indexing systems*. Cranfield College of Aeronautics, 1962.

COHEN, N. E. (1964). 'A social work approach', *in* N. E. Cohen (*ed.*) *Social work and social problems*. New York: National Association of Social Workers, 1964, pp. 362–391.

COLE, P. F. (1958). 'Analysis of reference question records as a guide to the information requirements of scientists.' *Journal of Documentation*, 14 (4), 1958, 197–207.

COLE, P. F. (1962). 'A new look at reference scattering.' *Journal of Documentation*, 18 (2), 1961, 58–64.

COLE, S. and COLE, J. R. (1967). 'Scientific output and recognition: a study in the operation of the reward system in science.' *American Sociological Review*, 32, 1967, 377–390.

CONNOR, J. H. (1967). 'Selective dissemination of information: a review of the literature and the issues.' *Library Quarterly*, 37 (4), 1967, 373–391.

COOPER, M. (1968). 'Current information dissemination: ideas and practices.' *Journal of Chemical Documentation*, 8 (5), 1968, 207–218.

COOVER, R. W. (1969). 'User needs and their effects on information center administration.' *Special Libraries*, 60 (7), 1969, 446–456.

COX, F. L. (1936). *What are the basic education periodicals for a teachers' college library?* (Master's dissertation, Columbia University, 1936.) [*unpublished*]

CRANE, D. (1965). 'Scientists at major and minor universities: a study of productivity and recognition.' *American Sociological Review*, 30 (5), 1965, 699–714.

CRANE, D. (1969). 'Social structure in a group of scientists: test of the "invisible college" hypothesis.' *American Sociological Review*, 34 (3), 1969, 335–352.

CRAWFORD, E. T. and BIDERMAN, A. D. (*eds.*) (1969). *Social scientists and international affairs*. London: Wiley, 1969.

CROS, R. C., GARDIN, J. C. and LEVY, F. (1964). *L'automatisation des recherches documentaires: un modele général 'Le SYNTOL'*. Paris: Gauthier–Villars, 1964.

CROSSLEY, C. A. (1969). 'Sources of information in applied social studies.' *Applied Social Studies*, 1 (3), 1969, 137–149.

CUADRA, C. A. (1964). 'Identifying key contributions to information science.' *American Documentation*, 15 (4), 1964, 289–295.

CULLINGWORTH, J. B. and ORR, S. C. (1969). 'Participation of social scientists in planning—a background to the studies', *in* J. B. Cullingworth and S. C. Orr (*eds.*) *Regional and urban studies: a social science approach*. London: Allen & Unwin, 1969, 1–19.

CURNOW, R. C. (1968). Scientific and technical information systems in Europe, with particular reference to computerisation and possible ECE roles. Science Policy Research Unit, University of Sussex, 1968. [*unpublished*]

DANIEL, R. S. (1967). 'Psychology.' *Library Trends*, 15 (4), 1967, 670–684.

DANIEL, R. S. and LOUTTIT, C. M. (1953). 'A survey of psychological literature', *in* R. S. Daniel and C. M. Louttit *Professional problems in psychology*. New York: Prentice-Hall, 1953, 35–66.

DANNATT, R. J. (1967). 'Books, information and research: libraries for technological universities.' *Minerva*, 5 (2), 1967, 209–226.

DANTINE, D. J. (1966). 'Communications needs of the user for management information systems', *in* American Federation of Information Processing Sciences *Proceedings of the Joint Computer Conference, 1966*. Washington, D.C.: Spartan Books, 1966, 403–411.

DARLEY, J. C. (1957). 'Psychology and the Office of Naval Research: a decade of development.' *American Psychologist*, 12, 1957, 305–323.

DARLEY, J. C. (1966). 'Information exchange problems in psychology', *in* International Federation for Documentation *Proceedings of the 1965 Congress*, vol. 2. Washington, D.C.: Spartan Books, 1966, 179–183.

DAVID, H. (1969). 'Behavioral sciences and the Federal Government.' *American Psychologist*, 24 (10), 1969, 917–922.

DAVIS, R. A. and BAILEY, C. A. (1964). *Bibliography of use studies*. Philadelphia, Pa.: Drexel Institute of Technology, Graduate School of Library Science, 1964.

DAY, M. S. (1968). 'Selective dissemination of information', *in* AGARD *Storage and retrieval of information*. London: NATO, 1968, xiii/1–5.

DENUM, D. D. (1960). *A system of data banking and retrieval for educational research*. (Ph.D. dissertation, University of Texas, 1960.) [*unpublished*]

DEPARTMENT OF EDUCATION AND SCIENCE—COMMITTEE ON SOCIAL STUDIES (1965). *Report of the Committee on Social Studies*. (The Heyworth Report.) London: H.M.S.O., 1965. [Cmnd no. 2660]

DESROCHES, E. (1969). *Reference et bibliographie en sciences sociales*. 4 vols. Montreal: La Librairie des Presses de l'Universite de Montreal, 1969.

DESSAUER, F. E. (1949). *Stability*. New York: Macmillan, 1949.

DEWS, J. D. and FORD, M. M. (1969). *An investigation into existing documentation services in business studies*. Manchester: Manchester Business School, 1969.

DOWELL, L. J. (1969). 'The relationship between knowledge and practice.' *Journal of Educational Research*, 62 (5), 1969, 201–205.

DURHAM UNIVERSITY (1969). *Project for evaluating the benefits from university libraries: final report (PEBUL)*. (Mimeographed report to OSTI.) Durham University, 1969.

EARLE, P. and VICKERY, B. (1969a). 'Social science literature use in the U.K. as indicated by citations.' *Journal of Documentation*, 25 (2), 1969, 123–141.

EARLE, P. and VICKERY, B. (1969b). 'Subject relations in science/technology literature.' *Aslib Proceedings*, 21 (6), 1969, 237–243.

EASTERN REGIONAL INSTITUTE FOR EDUCATION (1967). *Curriculum materials information survey: a survey of school personnel in the ERIE region: their perceptions of the extent and dimensions of need for information on curriculum materials.* Syracuse, N.Y.: Eastern Regional Institute for Education, 1967.

EDGERTON, H. A., BRITT, S. H. and NORMAN, R. M. (1947). 'Objective differences among types of respondents to a mail questionnaire.' *American Sociological Review*, 12, 1947, 435–444.

EGAN, M. and HENKLE, H. H. (1956). 'Ways and means in which research workers, executives and others use information', *in* J. H. Shera, A. Kent and J. W. Perry (*eds.*) *Documentation in action.* New York: Reinhold, 1956, 137–159.

EIDELL, T. L. and KITCHEL, J. M. (*eds.*) (1968). *Knowledge production and utilization in educational administration.* Eugene, Oreg.: University of Oregon, Centre for the Advanced Study of Educational Administration, 1968.

ELLIOTT, C. K. (1969). 'Abstracting services in psychology: a comparison of "Psychological Abstracts" and "Bulletin Signalétique".' *Library Association Record*, 71 (9), 1969, 279–280.

ELLIOTT, C. K. (1970). 'The documentation of psychology.' *Bulletin of the British Psychological Society*, 23, 1970, 27–33.

ELLIOTT, G. H. (1933). 'The use of business periodicals.' *Special Libraries*, 24 (1), 1933, 9–11.

EMBREE, J. F. (1946). 'Anthropology and the war.' *Bulletin of the American Association of University Professors*, 32, 1946, 485–495.

ENGELBERT, H. (1968). 'Probleme der Erforschung des Informationsbedorfs der Gesellschftswissenschaften.' *ZIID Zeitschrift*, 15 (6), 1968, 243–248.

ETZIONI, A. (1968). 'Societal guidance: a key to macrosociology.' *Acta Sociologica*, 11, 1968, 197–206.

FAIRTHORNE, R. A. (1958). 'Algebraic representation of storage and retrieval languages', *in* International Conference on Scientific Information, Washington, 1958 *Proceedings*, vol. 2. Washington, D.C.: National Academy of Sciences, National Research Council, 1959, 1313–1326.

FAIRTHORNE, R. A. (1968). 'Response to H. Borko's paper "The conceptual foundations of information systems" ', *in* E. B. Montgomery (*ed.*) *The foundations of access to knowledge.* Syracuse, N.Y.: Syracuse University Press, 1968, 89–93.

FAIRTHORNE, R. A. (1969a). 'Empirical hyperbolic distributions (Brad-ford–Zipf–Mandelbrot) for bibliometric description and pre-diction.' *Journal of Documentation*, 25 (4), 1969, 319–343.

FAIRTHORNE, R. A. (1969b). 'The scope and aims of the information sciences and technologies', *in* International Federation for Documentation *On theoretical problems of informatics*. Moscow: All-Union Institute for Scientific and Technological Information, 1969, 25–31.

FAIRTHORNE, R. A. (1969c). 'Library Zipf.' (Letter.) *Journal of Documentation*, 25 (2), 1969, 152–153.

FELLOWS, E. W. (1957). 'Current bibliographical services in the social sciences.' *American Documentation*, 8, 1957, 153–167.

FISHENDEN, R. M. (1959). 'Methods by which research workers find information,' *in* International Conference on Scientific Information, Washington, 1958 *Proceedings*, vol. 1, Washington, D.C.: National Academy of Sciences, National Research Council, 1959, 163–179.

FISHENDEN, R. M. (1965). 'Information use studies: part I—past results and future needs.' *Journal of Documentation*, 21 (3), 1965, 163–168.

FLOWERS, B. H. (1965). 'Survey of information needs of physicists and chemists.' *Journal of Documentation*, 21 (2), 1965, 83–112.

FOSKETT, D. J. (1958). 'International control of documentation in the social sciences.' *Stechert–Hafner Book News*, 13 (2), 1958, 17–19.

FOSKETT, D. J. (1960). 'Documentation in the humanities.' *Library Association Record*, 62 (12), 1960, 391–396.

FOSKETT, D. J. (1963). *Classification and indexing in the social sciences*. Washington, D.C.: Butterworth, 1963.

FOSKETT, D. J. (1964). 'Classification in the social sciences.' *Library World*, 3, 1962, 161–166; *reprinted with title* 'Documentation in the social sciences', *in* D. J. Foskett *Science, humanism and libraries*, London: Crosby Lockwood, 1964, 68–77.

FOSKETT, D. J. (1965). 'Information problems in the social sciences, with special reference to mechanization.' *Aslib Proceedings*, 17 (12), 1965, 328–337.

FOSKETT, D. J. (1969a). 'Some fundamental aspects of classification as a tool in informatics', *in* International Federation for Documentation *On theoretical problems of informatics*. Moscow: All-Union Institute for Scientific and Technical Information, 1969, 64–79.

FOSKETT, D. J. (1969b). *Classification for a general index language: a review of recent research by the Classification Research Group*. London: Library Association, 1969.

FRANZEN, R. B. and LAZARSFELD, P. F. (1945). 'Mail questionnaires as a research problem.' *Journal of Psychology*, 20, 1945, 293–320.

FREEMAN, R. R., PIETRZYK, A. and ROBERTS, A. H. (*eds.*). *Information in the language sciences*. New York: Elsevier, 1968.

FRIEND, J. K. and JESSOP, W. N. (1969). *Local government and strategic choice: an operational research approach to the processes of public planning.* London: Tavistock Publications, 1969. [in particular pp. 69–97]

FUSSLER, H. H. (1949). 'Characteristics of the research literature used by chemists and physicists in the United States.' *Library Quarterly,* 19 (1), 1949, 19–35, 119–143.

FUSSLER, H. H. and SIMON, J. L. (1969). *Patterns in the use of books in large research libraries,* 2nd ed. Chicago: University of Chicago Press, 1969. [1st edition 1961]

GARDIN, J-C. (1964). 'A European research program in document retrieval.' *American Behavioral Scientist,* 7 (10), 1964, 12–16.

GARFIELD, E. (1963). 'Citation indexes in sociological and historical research.' *American Documentation,* 14 (4), 1963, 289–291.

GARFIELD, E. (1964). 'Citation indexing: a natural science literature retrieval system for the social sciences.' *American Behavioral Scientist,* 7 (10), 1964, 58–61.

GARFIELD, E. (1967). 'Primordial concepts, citation indexing, and historio-bibliography.' *Journal of Library History,* 2 (3), 1967, 235–249.

GARFIELD, E., SHER, I. H. and TORPIE, R. J. (1964). *The use of citation data in writing the history of science.* Philadelphia, Pa.: Institute for Scientific Information, 1964.

GARVEY, W. D. and GRIFFITH, B. C. (1963). 'Research frontier; APA Project on scientific information exchange in psychology.' *Journal of Counseling Psychology,* 10, 1963, 297–302.

GARVEY, W. D. and GRIFFITH, B. C. (1964a). 'Scientific information exchange in psychology.' *Science,* 146 (3651), 1964, 1655–1659.

GARVEY, W. D. and GRIFFITH, B. C. (1964b). 'The structure, objectives and findings of a study of scientific information exchange in psychology.' *American Documentation,* 15 (4), 1964, 258–267.

GARVEY, W. D. and GRIFFITH, B. C. (1966). 'Studies of social innovations in scientific communication in psychology.' *American Psychologist,* 21 (11), 1966, 1019–1036.

GARVEY, W. D. and GRIFFITH, B. C. (1967). 'Scientific communication as a social system.' *Science,* 157, 1967, 1011–1016.

GARVEY, W. D. and GRIFFITH, B. C. (1968). 'Informal channels of communication in the behavioral sciences: their relevance in the structuring of formal or bibliographic communication', *in* E. B. Montgomery *(ed.) The foundations of access to knowledge: a symposium.* Syracuse, N.Y.: Syracuse University Press, 1968, 129–147.

GARVIN, P. L. (1967). *Problems of processing information in the behavioral sciences.* (Paper read at the 29th Annual Convention of the American Documentation Institute, Santa Monica, California, October, 1967.) [*unpublished*]

GATES, J. L. and ALTMAN, J. W. (1968). *Handbook of information sources in education and the behavioral sciences.* Washington, D.C., Department of Health, Education and Welfare, Office of Education, 1968.

GEE, R. D. (1965). *Teaching machines and programmed learning: a guide to the literature and other sources of information.* Hertfordshire County Council, 1965.

GELLNER, E. A. and LUCAS, P. G. (1956). 'Explanations in history.' *Proceedings of the Aristolelian Society,* Supplementary vol. 30, 1956, 157–196.

GEROULD, A. C. and WARMAN, H. J. (1954). 'Most cited periodicals in geography.' *Professional Geographer,* 6 (2), 1954, 6–12.

GLASER, E. M. (1968). *Research findings utilized in the community.* Paper read at the American Psychological Association, California, San Francisco, 1968.

GLASS, B. (1965). *Science and ethical values.* Chapel Hill: University of North Carolina Press, 1965.

GOODE, W. J. and HATT, P. K. (1952). *Methods in social research.* New York: McGraw-Hill, 1952.

GORN, S. (1967). 'The computer and information sciences and the community of disciplines.' *Behavioral Sciences,* 12, 1967, 433–452.

GOTTLIEB, D. and REEVES, J. (1963). *Adolescent behavior in urban areas: a bibliographic review and discussion of the literature.* New York: Collier-Macmillan, 1963.

GOTTSCHALK, C. M. and DESMOND, W. F. (1963). 'Worldwide census of scientific and technical serials.' *American Documentation,* 14 (3), 1963, 188–194.

GOULDNER, A. W. (1957). 'Theoretical requirements of the applied social sciences.' *American Sociological Review,* 22 (1), 1957, 92–102.

GRAHAM, W. R. *and others* (1967). *Exploration of oral/informal technical communications behavior.* Washington, D.C.: American Institute for Research, 1967.

GREENBERG, A. and MANFIELD, M. (1957). 'On the reliability of mailed questionnaires in product tests.' *Journal of Marketing,* 21 (3), 1957, 342–345.

GRIFFITH, B. C. (1969). *Some conclusions and strategies for research into the study of scientific communication.* (Paper read at the 19th International Congress of Psychology, London, 1969.) [*unpublished*]

GRIFFITH, B. C. and GARVEY, W. D. (1964). 'Systems in scientific information exchange and the effects of innovation and change.' *Proceedings of the American Documentation Institute,* 1, 1964, 191–200.

GROENMAN, S. and RIESTHUIS, G. J. A. (1967). 'Documentary behavior of demographers.' *Social Science Information,* 6 (2/3), 1967, 239–245.

GROSE, D. (1967). 'A data bank: the Social and Economic Archive Centre. *Aslib Proceedings*, 19 (5), 1967, 126–128.

GUBA, E. G. (1968). 'Development, diffusion and evaluation,' *in* T. L. Eidell and J. M. Kitchel (*eds.*) *Knowledge production and utilization in educational administration.* University of Oregon, Center for the Advanced Study of Educational Administration, 1968.

GULLAHORN, J. T. and GULLAHORN, J. E. (1959). 'Increasing returns from non-respondents.' *Public Opinion Quarterly*, 23, 1959, 119–121.

GUSHEE, D. E. (1968). Reading behavior of chemists. *Journal of Chemical Documentation* 8 (4), 1968, 191–197.

GUTTSMAN, W. L. (1966). 'The literature of the social sciences and provision for research in them.' *Journal of Documentation*, 22 (3), 1966, 186–194.

GYŐRE, P. (1969). 'Informatika, kommunikáció, dialogus.' [Informatics, communication, dialogue.] *Tudom Musz, Tajek*, 16 (4), 1969, 245–255.

HALBERT, M. H. and ACKOFF, R. L. (1959). 'An operations research study of the dissemination of scientific information', *in* International Conference on Scientific Information, Washington, 1958, *Proceedings*, vol. I. Washington, D.C.: National Academy of Sciences, National Research Council, 1959, 97–130.

HALL, J. L. (1969). *Experimental current awareness service for the social sciences.* Culham, United Kingdom Atomic Energy Authority, Culham Laboratory, 1969.

HALL, J. L., PALMER, J. and POOLE, J. B. (1970). 'An experimental current awareness service in the social sciences: the House of Commons Library/Culham Laboratory project.' *Journal of Documentation*, 26 (1), 1970, 1–21.

HAMMER, D. P. (1967) 'National information issues and trends.' *Annual Review of Information Science and Technology*, 2, 1967, 385–417.

HANDY, R. and KURTZ, P. (1964). *A current appraisal of the behavioral sciences.* Great Barrington, Mass.: Behavioral Research Council, 1964.

HANSON, C. W. (1964). 'Research on users' needs: where is it getting us?' *Aslib Proceedings*, 16 (2), 1964, 64–78.

HARMON, R. B. (1965). *Political science: a bibliographical guide to the literature.* New York: Scarecrow Press, 1965.

HARRIS, M. H. (1967). 'Behavioralism in political science: a guide to reference materials. *American Legislative Research*, R Q, 7 (1), 1967, 30–35.

HARVARD UNIVERSITY (1967). *Harvard list of books in psychology.* 3rd ed. Cambridge, Mass.: Harvard University Press, 1967.

HARVEY, J. M. (1969). *Sources of statistics.* London: Clive Bingley, 1969.

HAUGHTON, R. and ERICSON, C. (1965). 'Why blame educators? or, How we learned to live with P.I. and still teach.' *Programmed Instruction,* 5 (2), 1965.

HAVIGHURST, R. J. and JANSEN, A. J. (1967). 'Community research: a trend report and bibliography. *Current Sociology,* 15 (2), 1967, 1-24.

HAYMES, M. F. (1951). *The dissemination of current technical information to the research personnel served by an industrial library.* (Master's dissertation, Carnegie Library School, 1951.) [*unpublished*]

HEILPRIN, L. B. and GOODMAN, F. L. (1965). 'Analogy between information retrieval and education.' *American Documentation,* 16 (3), 1965, 163-169.

HEISKANEN, V. S. (1969). 'Uses of sociology: a case study of commissioned research in Finland.' *Social Science Information,* 8 (3), 1969, 87-98.

HELMER, O. (1965). *Social technology.* Santa Monica, Cal.: Rand Corporation, 1965.

HERNER, S. (1954). 'Information-gathering habits of workers in pure and applied science.' *Industrial and Engineering Chemistry,* 46 (1), 1954, 228-236.

HERNER, S. (1958). *The relationship of information-use studies and the design of information storage and retrieval systems.* Prepared for Rome Air Development Centre, U.S. Air Force, by Herner & Co., Washington, D.C., 1958. (AD 213-781.)

HERNER, S. (1959). 'The information-gathering habits of American medical scientists', *in* International Conference on Scientific Information, Washington, 1958. *Proceedings,* vol. I. Washington, D.C.: National Academy of Sciences, National Research Council, 1959, 277-285.

HERNER, S. (1962). 'The determination of user needs for the design of information systems', *in* C. P. Bourne (*ed.*) *Information systems workshop.* Washington, D.C.: Spartan Books, 1962, 47-60.

HERNER, S., GRIFFITH, J. D. and HERNER, M. (1968). *Study of periodicals and serials in education.* Washington, D.C.: Department of Health, Education and Welfare, Office of Education, 1968.

HERNER, S. and HERNER, M. (1967). 'Information needs and uses in science and technology.' *Annual Review of Information Science and technology,* 2, 1967, 1-34.

HERRING, P. (1947). 'The social sciences in modern society.' *Items,* 1, 1947, 2-6.

HERTZ, D. B. and RUBENSTEIN, A. H. (1953). *Team research.* New York: Columbia University, Department of Industrial Engineering, 1953.

HOBAN, C. F. (1967). *Survey of professional journals in the field of public communication, including new media in education.* Washington, D.C.: Department of Health, Education and Welfare, Office of Education, 1967.

HOBBS, A. H. (1951). *The claims of sociology: critique of textbooks.* Harrisburg, Pa.: Stackpole Co., 1951.

HOFFER, J. R. (1960). 'Terminology means better communication', *in* National Conference on Social Welfare *Community organization, 1958–1959.* New York: Columbia University Press, 1960, 22–41.

HOFFER, J. R. (1967). 'The relationship of natural and social sciences to social problems and the contribution of the information scientist to their solution.' *American Documentation,* 18 (4), 1967, 228–234.

HOFFER, J. R. (1968). 'The communication of innovations in social welfare—the role of the specialized information centers', *in* American Society for Information Science *Proceedings of the Annual Meeting, 1968,* vol. 5. New York: Greenwood Publishing Corporation, 1968, 25–27.

HOFFER, J. R. (1969). Information exchange in social welfare: a myth or a reality? *Spec. Libr.,* 60 (4), 1969, 193–201.

HOFFER, J. R. and PRICE, E. (1967). *Readings on social welfare documentation.* Ohio, Columbus, National Conference on Social Welfare, 1967.

HOGEWEG-DE HAART, H. P. (1967). *Documentatie en uitwisseling van wetenschappelijke informatie in de sociaal wetenschappen; resultaten van een enquête.* (Handelingen van de Sociaal-Wetenschappelijke Raad, Nieuwe Reeks, no. 1.) Amsterdam: N.V. Noord-Hollandsche Uitgevers Maatschappij, 1967.

HOLT, C. C. and SCHRANK, W. E. (1968). 'Growth of the professional literature in economics and other fields and some implications.' *American Documentation,* 19 (1), 1968, 18–26.

HOROWITZ, I. L. (*ed.*) (1967). *The rise and fall of Project Camelot: studies in the relationship between social science and practical politics.* Cambridge, Mass.: M.I.T. Press, 1967.

HOROWITZ, I. L. (1968). *Professing sociology: studies in the life cycle of social science.* Chicago: Aldine, 1968.

HOSELITZ, B. F. (*ed.*) (1959). *A reader's guide to the social sciences.* Glencoe, Ill.: Free Press, 1959.

HOSHOVSKY, A. G. and MASSEY, R. J. (1968). 'Information science: its ends, means and opportunities', *in* American Society for Information Science *Proceedings of the Annual Meeting, 1968,* vol. 5. New York, Greenwood Publishing Corporation, 1968, 47–55.

HULME, E. W. (1923). *Statistical bibliography in relation to the growth of modern civilization: two lectures delivered in the University of Cambridge in May, 1922.* London: Grafton, 1923.

HURT, P. (1934). 'The need of college and university instruction in the use of the library.' *Library Quarterly*, 4 (3), 1934, 436–448.

HYSLOP, M. R. and CHAFE, D. H. (1967). 'User appraisal of an information system and services through a program of joint applied research', *in* G. Schecter (*ed.*) *Information retrieval—a critical review*. Washington, D.C.: Thompson, 1967, 151–176.

INTERNATIONAL INSTITUTE FOR EDUCATIONAL PLANNING (1964). *Educational planning: a bibliography*. Paris: I.I.E.P., 1964.

JAHODA, G. (1966). 'Information needs of science and technology—background review', *in* International Federation for Documentation *Proceedings of the 1965 Congress*, vol. 2. Washington, D.C.: Spartan Books, 1966, 137–142.

JAKOBOVITS, L. A. and OSGOOD, C. E. (1967). 'Connotations of twenty psychological journals to their professional readers.' *American Psychologist*, 22 (9), 1967, 792–800.

JANDA, K. (1968). *Information retrieval: applications to political science*. New York: Bobbs-Merrill, 1968.

JANDA, K. and RADER, G. (1967). 'Selective dissemination of information: a progress report from Northwestern University.' *American Behavioral Scientist*, 10 (1), 1967, 24–29.

JANIS, I. L. and FESHBACH, S. (1953). 'Effects of fear-arousing communications.' *Journal of Abnormal and Social Psychology*, 48, 1953, 78–92.

JOHNS HOPKINS UNIVERSITY–RESEARCH LIBRARY (1963). *Progress report on an operations research and systems engineering study of a university library*. Baltimore, Ind.: Johns Hopkins University, 1963. [5 parts published between 1963 and 1968]

JOHNS HOPKINS UNIVERSITY–CENTER FOR RESEARCH IN SCIENTIFIC COMMUNICATION (1967). *Scientific information-exchange behavior at the 1966 Annual Meeting of the American Sociological Association.* (Report 4.) Baltimore, Md.: Johns Hopkins University, 1967.

JOHNS HOPKINS UNIVERSITY–CENTER FOR RESEARCH IN SCIENTIFIC COMMUNICATION (1968a). *The publication fate of materials presented at the October, 1966, Annual Meeting of the Optical Society of America* (Technical note 1.) Baltimore, Md.: Johns Hopkins University, 1968.

JOHNS HOPKINS UNIVERSITY–CENTER FOR RESEARCH IN SCIENTIFIC COMMUNICATION (1968b). *The publication efforts of authors of presentations at the 1966 Annual Meeting of the American Sociological Association during the year following the meeting.* (Technical note 3.) Baltimore, Md.: Johns Hopkins University, 1968.

JUDGE, P. J. (1967). 'The user-system interface today', *in* A. de Reuck and J. Knight (*eds.*) *Communication in science: documentation and automation.* London: Churchill, 1967, 37–56.

KATZ, F. (1964). 'Analytic and applied sociologists: a sociological essay on a dilemma in sociology.' *Sociology and Social Research,* 48 (4), 1964, 440–448.

KENDALL, M. G. (1961). 'Natural law in the social sciences.' *Journal of the Royal Statistical Society,* 124 (Series A), 1961, 1–18.

KENDALL, M. G. and DOIG, A. G. (1962). *Bibliography of statistical literature, 1950–1958.* Edinburgh: Oliver Boyd, 1962.

KENDALL, M. G. and DOIG, A. G. (1965). *Bibliography of statistical literature, 1940–1949.* Edinburgh: Oliver & Boyd, 1965.

KENDALL, M. G. and DOIG, A. G. (1968). *Bibliography of statistical literature, pre-1940.* With supplements to the volumes for 1940–49 and 1950–58. Edinburgh: Oliver & Boyd, 1968.

KENT, A. (1962). 'Resolution of the literature crisis in the decade 1961–1970.' *Research Management,* 5 (1), 1962, 49–58.

KEPHART, W. M. and BRESSLER, M. (1958). 'Increasing response to mail questionnaires.' *Public Opinion Quarterly,* 22, 1958, 123–132.

KESSLER, M. M. (1963). 'Bibliographic coupling between scientific papers.' *American Documentation,* 14 (1), 1963, 10–25.

KING, M. (1969). *Report on the operation of the MEDLARS service in the Newcastle region from 1966 to 1968.* University of Newcastle-upon-Tyne, 1969. (Duplicated report.)

KIRKPATRICK, L. H. (1946). 'How narrow are the specialists?' *School and Society,* 64 (1656), 1946, 193–196.

KITTEL, D. A. (1955). *Bibliographic methods in the social sciences: a case study.* (Master's dissertation, Graduate Library School, University of Chicago, 1955.) [*unpublished*]

KOBLITZ, J. (1968). 'Information und Dokumentation—ein Teilgebiet der wissenschaftlichen Information.' *ZIID–Zeitschrift,* 15 (1), 1968, 36–43.

KOCHEN, M. (1969). 'Stability in the growth of knowledge.' *American Documentation,* 20 (3), 1969, 186–197.

KUHN, T. S. (1959). 'The essential tension: tradition and innovation in scientific research.' *Proceedings of the Research Conference on the Identification of Creative Scientific Talent,* University of Utah, 1959, 162–177.

KUHN, T. S. (1962). *The structure of scientific revolutions.* Chicago: University of Chicago Press, 1962.

KYLE, B. (1957). 'Current documentation topics and their relevance to social science literature.' *Review of Documentation,* 24 (3), 1957, 107–117.

KYLE, B. (1958a). 'Some further considerations on the application to social science material of up-to-date methods of bibliographical control and information retrieval.' *Journal of Documentation*, 14 (4), 1958, 190–196.

KYLE, B. (1958b). 'Towards a classification for social science literature.' *American Documentation*, 9 (3), 1958, 168–183.

KYLE, B. (1960a). 'Bibliographical control in the social sciences: some doubts and difficulties', *in* Library Association—Reference, Special and Information Section *Proceedings of the 7th Annual Conference, Leicester 1959*. London: Library Association, the Section, 1960, 15–21.

KYLE, B. (1960b). 'Merits and demerits of various classification schemes for the social sciences.' *Unesco Bulletin for Libraries*, 14 (2), 1960, 54–60.

LAKE, D. G., RITVO, M. R. and O'BRIEN, G. M. ST. L. (1969). 'Applying behavioral science: current projects.' *Journal of Applied Behavioral Science*, 5 (3), 1969, 367–392.

LANCASTER, F. W. (1968). *Evaluation of the MEDLARS demand search service*. Washington, D.C.: U.S. Department of Health, Education and Welfare, 1968.

LANCASTER, H. O. (1970). 'Problems in the bibliography of statistics.' Paper read to the Royal Statistical Society, 8th April, 1970.

LANIER, L. H. (1949). 'The psychological and social sciences in the National Military Establishment.' *American Psychologist*, 4, 1949, 127–147.

LASSWELL, H. D. (1960). 'The structure and function of communication in society', *in* W. Schramm (*ed.*) *Mass communications*. Urbana: University of Illinois Press, 1960, 117–130.

LAVER, F. J. M. (1969). 'The future of national information systems', *in* Centre for Environmental Studies *Proceedings of the Conference on Information and Urban Planning, London, 1969*, vol. 2. London: Centre for Environmental Studies, 1969, 93–98.

LAWLER, E. (1963). 'Psychology of the scientists: IX. Age and authorship of citations in selected psychological journals.' *Psychological Reports*, 13, 1963, 537.

LAZARSFELD, P. F. and LEEDS, R. (1962). 'International sociology as a sociological problem.' *American Sociological Review*, 27 (5), 1962, 732–741.

LAZARSFELD, P. F., SEWELL, W. H. and WILENSKY, H. (*eds.*) *The uses of sociology*. New York: Basic Books, 1967.

LEE, N. and SZRETER, R. (1966). *An annotated bibliography on the teaching of economics*. London: Economics Association, 1966.

LEEDS, R. and SMITH, T. (1963). *Using social science knowledge in business and industry: report of a seminar.* Homewood, Ill.: Irwin, 1963.

LEFTWICH, R. H. (1968). Report of the Committee on Classification. *American Economic Review,* 8 (2), 1968, 711–722.

LEGTERS, L. H. (1967). *Research in the social sciences and humanities.* Santa Barbara, Cal.: American Bibliographical Centre, Clio Press, 1967.

LEVIN, P. H. (1967). 'Toward decision-making roles for urban planners.' *Journal of the Town Planning Institute,* 53 (10), 1967, 437–442.

LEVINE, S. and GERALD, G. (1958). 'Maximizing returns on mail questionnaires.' *Public Opinion Quarterly,* 22, 1958, 568–575.

LEVY, F. (1966). 'Information storage and retrieval in the social sciences: an outline of two systems—Syntol and General Inquirer', *in* R. L. Merritt and S. Rokkan (*eds.*) *Comparing nations.* New Haven, Conn.: Yale University Press, 1966, 465–497.

LEVY, N. P. (1964). 'A survey of the information practices of engineers at Western Electric.' *American Documentation,* 15 (2), 1964, 86–88.

LEWIS, P. R. (1960). *The literature of the social sciences: an introductory survey and guide.* London: Library Association, 1960.

LEWIS, P. R. (1965). 'The present range of documentation services in the social sciences.' *Aslib Proceedings,* 17 (2), 1965, 40–49.

LIBAW, F. B. (1967). 'Information handling in the behavioral sciences: report of a first convocation of a conglomerate clean.' *American Behavioral Scientist,* 10 (7), 1968, 8–12.

LIBBEY, M. A. and ZALTMAN, G. (1967). *The role and distribution of written informal communication in theoretical high-energy physics.* New York: American Institute of Physics, 1967.

LIN, N. and NELSON, C. E. (1969). 'Bibliographic reference patterns in some sociological journals, 1965–1966.' *American Sociologist,* 4 (1), 1969, 47–50.

LINE, M. B. (1966). 'University libraries and the information needs of the researcher, 1: a provider's view.' *Aslib Proceedings* 18 (7), 1966, 178–184.

LINE, M. B. (1968a). 'Social scientists' information.' *SSRC Newsletter,* no. 3, May 1968, 2–5.

LINE, M. B. (1968b). 'The social scientist and his information needs', *in* Library Association—Reference, Special and Information Section, *Proceedings of the 16th Annual Conference, Durham, 1968.* London: The Section, 1968, 10–18.

LINE, M. B. (1969a). 'Information requirements in the social sciences: some preliminary considerations.' *Journal of Librarianship,* 1 (1), 1969, 1–19.

LINE, M. B. (1969b). 'Information services in university libraries.' *Journal of Librarianship,* 1 (4), 1969, 211–224.

LINE, M. B. (1969c). *Library surveys: an introduction to their use, planning, procedure and presentation.* Rev. ed. London: Clive Bingley, 1969.

LINE, M. B. (1970). 'The "half-life" of periodical literature: apparent and real obsolescence.' *Journal of Documentation*, 26 (1), 1970, 46–52.

LINSKY, A. (1965). 'A factorial experiment in inducing responses to a mail questionnaire. *Sociology and Social Research*, 49, 1965, 183–189.

LIVESAY, M. J. (1953). *Characteristics of the literature used by authors of books in the field of economics.* (Master's dissertation, University of Chicago, 1953.) [*unpublished*]

LOCK, C. B. M. (1968). *Geography: a reference handbook.* London: Clive Bingley, 1968.

LOMPE, K. (1968). 'The role of the social scientist in the processes of policy-making.' *Social Science Information*, 7 (6), 1968, 159–175.

LONGWORTH, D. S. (1953). 'Use of a mail questionnaire.' *American Sociological Review*, 18 (3), 1953, 310–313.

LOUTTIT, C. M. (1955a). 'Some problems of "Psychological Abstracts".' *Special Libraries*, 46, 1955, 456–460.

LOUTTIT, C. M. (1955b). 'The use of foreign languages by psychologists.' *American Journal of Psychology*, 68, 1955, 484–486.

LOUTTIT, C. M. (1957a). 'Publication trends in psychology.' *American Psychologist*, 12, 1957, 14–21.

LOUTTIT, C. M. (1957b). 'The use of foreign languages by psychologists, chemists and physicists.' *American Journal of Psychology*, 70, 1957, 314–316.

LUNDBERG, C. C. (1966). 'Middlemen in science utilization: some notes toward clarifying conversion roles. *American Behavioral Scientist*, 9, 1966, 11–14.

LUNDBERG, G. A. (1947). 'The Senate ponders social science.' *Scientific Monthly*, 64, 1947, 397–411.

LYNN, K. C. (1966). *The computerized analysis, storage and retrieval of dental literature.* (Paper read at the Joint Meeting of the Public Health Service, Clinical Society and Commissioned Officers' Association, Baltimore, 1966.) [*unpublished*]

LYONS, G. M. (1969). *An uneasy partnership: social science and the federal government in the twentieth century.* Washington, D.C.: Russell Sage Foundation, 1969.

McCULLOCH, J. W. and BROWN, M. J. (1968a). 'What do social workers read?' *New Society*, no. 316, 17th October, 1968, 570.

McCULLOCH, J. W. and BROWN, M. J. (1968b). 'Problems of development in education welfare: some research findings.' *Education Welfare Officer*, no. 131, 1968, 1–4.

McCulloch, J. W. and Brown, M. J. (1969). *Helpful factors in psychiatric social work practice: is there a place for research?* School of Applied Social Studies, University of Bradford, 1969. [*unpublished paper*]

McDiarmid, E. W. (1940). *The library survey: problems and methods.* Chicago: American Library Association, 1940.

McDiarmid, J. (1945). 'The mobilization of social scientists', *in* L. D. White (*ed.*) *Civil Service in wartime.* Chicago, Ill.: University of Chicago Press, 1945, 73–96.

Mackenzie, A. G. (1969). 'Reader instruction in modern universities.' *Aslib Proceedings,* 21 (7), 1969, 271–279.

Macrae, D. (1969). 'Growth and decay curves in scientific citations.' *American Sociological Review,* 34 (5), 1969, 631–635.

Madge, J. (1953). *The tools of social science.* London: Longmans, 1953.

Maltby, A. (1968). *Economics and commerce: the sources of information and their organisation.* London: Clive Bingley, 1968.

Mandelbaum, M. (1955). 'Societal facts.' *British Journal of Sociology,* 6 (4), 1955, 305–317.

Mandelbrot, B. (1953). 'An informational theory of the structure of language', *in* Symposium on Applications of Communication Theory, London, 1952 *Proceedings.* London: Butterworth, 1953.

Mantell, L. H. (1966). 'On laws of special abilities and the production of scientific literature.' *American Documentation,* 17 (1), 1966, 8–16.

Mark, F. M. (1956). *Characteristics of the literature used by contributors to American and English economic journals.* (Master's dissertation, Graduate Library School, University of Chicago, 1956.) [*unpublished*]

Marquardt, J. F. (1955). *Reading habits of 290 faculty members in Ohio State Universities.* (Master's dissertation Department of Library Science, Kent State University, 1955.) [*unpublished*]

Marron, H. and Burchinal, L. G. (1967). 'ERIC—a novel concept in information management.' *Proceedings of the American Documentation Institute,* 4, 1967, 268–272.

Martin, G. P. (1952). *Characteristics of the literature used by authors of books on political topics.* (Master's dissertation, University of Chicago, 1952.) [*unpublished*]

Martin, M. W. (1962). 'The use of random alarm devices in studying scientists' behaviour.' *IRE Transactions in Engineering Management,* EM–9 (2), 1962, 66–71.

Martin, M. W. and Ackoff, R. L. (1963). 'The dissemination and use of recorded scientific information.' *Management Science,* 9 (2), 1963, 322–336.

MARTYN, J. (1964a). *Report of an investigation of literature searching by research scientists.* London: Aslib, 1964.

MARTYN, J. (1964b). 'Unintentional duplication of research.' *New Scientist*, no. 377, 1964, 338.

MARTYN, J. and GILCHRIST, A. (1968). *An evaluation of British scientific journals.* (Aslib Occasional Publication no 1.) London: Aslib, 1968.

MARUYAMA, M. (1962). 'Philosophy as an open meta-science of inter-disciplinary cross-induction.' *Dialectics*, 16 (4), 1962, 361.

MASON, J. B. (1968). *Research resources: annotated guide to the social sciences, vol. 1: International relations and recent history indexes, abstracts and periodicals.* Santa Barbara, Cal.: Clio Press, 1968.

MAYER, M. (1962). 'The trouble with textbooks.' *Harpers*, 1962.

MEDAWAR, P. B. (1967). *The art of the soluble.* London: Methuen, 1967.

MEDAWAR, P. B. (1969). *Induction and intuition in scientific thought.* London: Methuen, 1969.

MEIER, E. L. (1951). *Characteristics of the literature used by contributors to American sociological journals.* (Master's dissertation, University of Chicago, 1951.) *[unpublished]*

MEISTER, D. and SULLIVAN, D. J. (1967). *Evaluation of user reactions to a prototype on-line information retrieval system.* Washington, D.C.: National Aeronautics and Space Administration, 1967.

MENZEL, H. (1957). 'Flow of information on current developments in three scientific disciplines.' *Federation Proceedings*, 16, 1957, 706–711.

MENZEL, H. (1958). *The flow of information among scientists—problems, opportunities and research questions.* New York: Columbia University Bureau of Applied Social Research, 1958. (Mimeo.)

MENZEL, H. (1959). 'Planned and unplanned scientific communication,' in *Proceedings of the International Conference on Scientific Information, 1958*, vol. 1. Washington, D.C.: National Academy of Sciences, National Research Council, 1959, 199–243.

MENZEL, H. (1960). *Review of studies in the flow of information among scientists*, 2 vols. New York: Columbia University, Bureau of Applied Social Research, 1960. (Mimeo)

MENZEL, H. (1964). 'The information needs of current scientific research.' *Library Quarterly*, 34 (1), 1964, 4–19.

MENZEL, H. (1966a). 'Behavioral studies of science information needs', in International Symposium on the Information Sciences, Excelsior Springs, 1966 *Proceedings*.

MENZEL, H. (1966b). 'Information needs and uses in science and technology.' *Annual Review of Information Science and Technology*, 1, 1966, 41–69.

MENZEL, H. (1966c). 'Scientific communication: five themes from social science research.' *American Psychologist*, 21 (11), 1966, 999–1004.

MENZEL, H. (1967). 'Can science information needs be ascertained empirically?' *in* L. Thayer (*ed.*) *Communications: concepts and perspectives.* Washington, D.C.: Spartan Books, 1967, 279–295.

MENZEL, H. (1968). 'Informal communication in science: its advantages and its formal analogues', *in* E. B. Montgomery (*ed.*) *The foundations of access to knowledge.* Syracuse, N.Y.: Syracuse University Press, 1968, 153–163.

MERSEL, J., DONOHUE, J. C. and MORRIS, W. A. (1966). *Information transfer in educational research.* Sherman Oaks, Cal.: Informatics Inc., 1966.

MERTON, R. (1967). *Social theory and social structure.* Glencoe, Ill.: Free Press, 1967.

MIKHAILOV, A. I., CHERNYI, A. I. and GILYAREVSKYI, R. S. (1966). 'Informatics—new name for the theory of scientific information.' *Nauchno-Tekhnicheskaya Informatsiya* (Scientific-Technical Information), 12, 1966, 35–39.

MIKHAILOV, A. I., CHERNYI, A. I. and GILYAREVSKYI, R. S. (1968). *Osnovy informatiki* [*Bases of informatics*]. Moscow: Nauka (Science) Publishing House, 1968.

MONTGOMERY, E. B. (*ed.*) 1968. *The foundation of access to knowledge: a symposium.* Syracuse, N.Y.: Syracuse University Press, 1968.

MOTE, L. J. B. (1962). 'Reasons for the variations in the information needs of scientists.' *Journal of Documentation*, 18 (4), 1962, 169–175.

MULLINS, N. C. (1966). 'Social networks among biological scientists.' Unpublished doctural dissertation, Department of Social Relations, Harvard University, 1966.

MURPHY, D. J. (1969). 'Defining management's needs is key to designing successful information systems.' *Automation*, 16 (5), 1969, 74–77.

NASATIR, D. (1967). 'Social science data libraries.' *American Sociologist*, 2 (4), 1967, 207–216.

NATIONAL COUNCIL FOR THE SOCIAL STUDIES (1963). *Social studies curriculum and methods: a topical bibliography. 1955–1962*, by L. S. Kenworthy. Washington, D.C.: National Council for the Social Studies, 1963.

NEELAMEGHAN, A. (1968). 'Discovery, duplication, and documentation: a case study.' *Library Science with a slant to Documentation*, 5 (3), 1968, 264–288.

NETHERLANDS—KONINKLIJKE NEDERLANDSE AKADEMIE VAN WETEN-SCHAPPEN—SOCIAAL-WETENSCHAPPELIJKE RAAD (1968). *De organisatie van de verspreiding van wetenschappelijke informatie bij de maatschappijwetenschappen.* (Handelingen van de Sociaal-Wetenschappelijke Raad, Nieuwe Reeks, no. 4.) Amsterdam: N.V. Noord–Hollandsche Uitgevers Maatschappij, 1968.

NEWMAN, J. W. (1958). 'Working with behavioral scientists.' *Harvard Business Review*, 36 (4), 1958, 67–74.

NICHOLS, R. F. (1944). 'War and research in social science.' *Proceedings of the American Philosophical Society*, 87, 1944, 361–364.

NORTHROP, F. S. C. (1947). *The logic of the sciences and the humanities.* New York: Macmillan, 1947.

NOVIKOV, Y. A. (1969). 'Psikhologicheskie problemy v informatike.' [*Psychological problems in informatics*] *Nauchrio-Teknicheskaya Informatsiya*, Series 2 (1), 1969, 6–9.

O'CONNOR, J. (1968). 'Some questions concerning information need.' *American Documentation*, 19 (2), 1968, 200–203.

ODUM, H. W. (1951). *American sociology: the story of sociology in the United States through 1950.* New York: Longmans, Green, 1951.

OFFICE OF THE MINISTER FOR SCIENCE—COMMITTEE OF THE MANAGEMENT AND CONTROL OF RESEARCH AND DEVELOPMENT (1961). *Report.* (Chairman: Sir Solly Zuckerman.) London: H.M.S.O., 1961.

OPPENHEIM, A. N. (1966). *Questionnaire design and attitude measurement.* London: Heinemann, 1966.

ORLANS, H. (1968). 'Making research more useful to government.' *Social Science Information*, 7 (6), 1968, 151–158.

OROMANER, M. J. (1968). 'The most cited sociologists: an analysis of introductory text citations.' *American Sociologist*, 3 (2), 1968, 124–129.

ORR, R. H., COYL, E. B. and LEEDS, A. A. (1964). 'Trends in oral communication, among biomedical scientists: meetings and travel.' *Federation Proceedings*, 23 (5), 1964, 1146–1154.

ORR, R. H. and LEEDS, A. A. (1964). 'Biomedical literature: volume growth, and other characteristics.' *Federation Proceedings*, 23 (b), 1964, 1310–1331.

OSGOOD, C. E. and WILSON, K. V. (1961). *Some terms and associated measures for talking about human communication.* Urbana, Ill.: University of Illinois, Institute of Communication Research, 1961. [*unpublished*]

OTTEN, K. and DEBONS, A. (1970). 'Towards a metascience of information: informatology.' *Journal of the American Society for Information Science*, 21 (1), 1970, 89–94.

PAGE, J. R. H. (1967). 'Planning and development of the European Space Documentation Service: an example of international collaboration', *in* A. de Reuck and J. Knight (*eds.*) *Communication in science: documentation and automation.* London: Churchill, 1967.

PAISLEY, W. J. (1965). *The flow of (behavioral) science information: a review of the research literature.* Palo Alto, Cal.: Stanford University, Institute for Communication Research, 1965. (Mimeo.)

PAISLEY, W. J. (1968). 'Information needs and uses.' *Annual Review of Information Science and Technology,* 1968, 3, 1–30.

PAISLEY, W. J. and PARKER, E. B. (1965). 'Information retrieval as a receiver-controlled communication system', *in* L. B. Heilprin, B. E. Markuson and F. L. Goodman (*eds.*) *Proceedings of the Symposium on Education for Information Science.* Washington, D.C.: Spartan Books, 1965, 23–31.

PAISLEY, W. J. and PARKER, E. B. (1967). *Scientific information exchange at an interdisciplinary behavioral science convention.* Palo Alto, Cal.: Stanford University, Institute for Communication Research, 1967. (Mimeo.)

PARKER, E. B. (1967). *Stanford Physics Information Retrieval System (SPIRES). Annual report.* Palo Alto, Cal.: Stanford University, Institute for Communication Research, 1967. (Mimeo.)

PARKER, E. B., LINGWOOD, D. A. and PAISLEY, W. J. (1968). *Communication and research productivity in an interdisciplinary behavioral science research area.* Palo Alto, Cal.: Stanford University, Institute of Communication Research, 1968. (Mimeo.)

PARKER, E. B. and PAISLEY, W. J. (1966). 'Research for psychologists at the interface of the scientist and his information system.' *American Psychologist,* 21 (11), 1966, 1061–1071.

PARKER, E. B., PAISLEY, W. J. and GARRETT, R. (1967). *Bibliographic citations as unobtrusive measures of scientific communication.* Palo Alto, Cal.: Stanford University, Institute for Communication Research, 1967. (Mimeo.)

PARSONS, T. (1946). 'The science legislation and the role of the social sciences.' *American Sociological Review.* 11, 1946, 653–666.

PATTERSON, A. M. (1945). 'Literature references in industrial and engineering chemistry for 1939.' *Journal of Chemical Education,* 22, 1945, 514–515.

PAYNE, K. B. (1954). *An analysis of the documentation of geography research to determine the serial publications most frequently used.* (Master's dissertation, Catholic University of America, 1954.) [*unpublished*]

PELZ, D. C. (1956). 'Social factors related to performance in a research organization.' *Administrative Science Quarterly,* 1, 1956, 310–325.

PELZ, D. C. and ANDREWS, F. M. (1962). 'Organizational atmosphere, motivation and research contribution.' *American Behavioral Scientist,* 6, 1962, 43–47.

PELZ, D. C. and ANDREWS, F. M. (1966a). 'Autonomy, coordination and stimulation in relation to scientific achievement.' *Behavioral Science,* 11 (2), 1966, 89–97.

PELZ, D. C. and ANDREWS, F. M. (1966b). *Scientists in organizations.* New York: John Wiley, 1966.

PEMBERTON, J. E. (1969). 'Library services for the sociocrat.' *International Library Review*, 1 (2), 1969, 277–281.

PEMBERTON, J. E. (1970). 'Access to primary materials in the social sciences.' *Aslib Proceedings*, 1970, 22 (1), 22–30.

PENNY, J. (1966). 'The documentation of management literature.' *Business (U.K.)*, 96 (1), 1966, 40.

PETERS, W. (1964). *A study of elementary classroom teacher participation in the selection and purchase of instructional supplies and equipment.* (Ph.D. dissertation, State University of Iowa, 1964.) [*unpublished*]

POOL, I. de S., MCINTOSH, S. and GRIFFEL, D. (1969). 'On the design of computer-based information systems.' *Social Science Information*, 8 (5), 1969, 69–118.

POOLE, J. B. (1969). 'Information services for the Commons: a computer experiment.' *Parliamentary Affairs*, 22 (2), 1969, 161–168.

PORAT, A. M. and HAAS, J. A. (1969). 'Information effects on decision-making.' *Behavioral Science*, 14 (2), 1969, 98–104.

PRICE, D. J. de S. (1956). 'The exponential curve of science.' *Discovery*, 17 (6), 1956, 240–243.

PRICE, D. J. de S. (1963). *Little science, big science.* New York: Columbia University Press, 1963.

PRICE, D. J. de S. (1965a).' 'Networks of scientific papers.' *Science*,' 149 (3683), 1965, 510–515.

PRICE, D. J. de S. (1965b). 'Is technology historically independent of science?' *Technology and Culture*, 6 (4), 1965, 553–568.

PRICE, D. J. de S. (1966a). 'The science of scientists.' *Medical Opinion and Review*, 1 (10), 1966, 88–91, 94–97.

PRICE, D. J. de S. (1966b). 'The science of science', *in* M. Goldsmith and A. McKay (*eds.*) *The Science of science.* Harmondsworth: Penguin Books, 1966.

PRICE, D. J. de S. (1967). 'Communication in science: the ends—philosophy and forecast', *in* A. de Reuck and J. Knight (*eds.*) *Communication in science: documentation and automation.* London: Churchill, 1967, 199–213.

PRICE, D. O. (1950). 'On the use of stamped return envelopes with mail questionnaires.' *American Sociological Review*, 15, 1950, 672–673.

PRITCHARD, A. (1969). 'Statistical bibliography or bibliometrics?' *Journal of Documentation*, 25 (4), 1969, 348–349.

QUINN, E. W. (1951). *Characteristics of the literature used by authors of books in the field of sociology.* (Master's dissertation, University of Chicago, 1951.) [*unpublished*]

READE, E. (1969). 'Contradictions in planning.' *Official Architecture and Planning*, 32 (10), 1969, 1179–1185.

REES, A. M. (1963). 'Information needs and patterns of usage', *in* Western Reserve University—School of Library Science—Center for Documentation and Communication Research *Information retrieval in action*. Cleveland, Ohio: Western Reserve University Press, 1963, 17–23.

REES, A. M. (1965a). 'The Aslib-Cranfield test of the Western Reserve University indexing system for Metallurgical literature: a review of the final report.' *American Documentation*, 16 (2), 1965, 73–76.

REES, A. M. (1965b). 'The art of teaching information science,' *in* L. B. Heilprin, B. E. Markuson and F. L. Goodman (*eds.*) *Proceedings of the Symposium on Education for Information Science*. Washington, D.C.: Spartan Books, 1965, 71–76.

REES, A. M. and SCHULTZ, D. G. (1967). 'Psychology and information retrieval,' *in* G. Schecter (*ed.*) *Information retrieval: a critical view*. Washington, D.C.: Thompson, 1967, 143–150.

REIN, M. (1969). 'Social planning: the search for legitimacy.' *Journal of the American Institute of Planners*, 35 (4), 1969, 233–244.

RIECKEN, H. W. (1967). 'Government-science relations: the physical and social sciences compared.' *American Psychologist*, 22 (3), 1967, 211–218.

RIECKEN, H. W. (1969). 'Social sciences and social problems.' *Social Science Information*, 8 (1), 1969, 101–129.

ROBERTS, C. R. and DAVIS, R. A. (1929). 'Reading interests of teachers.' *Educational Administration and Supervision*, 15 (2), 1929, 102–116.

ROBERTS, N.* (1970). *Current control of journal literature in economics in the United Kingdom*. [*unpublished*]
*The author is Senior Lecturer in the School of Librarianship and Information Science, University of Sheffield.

ROBIN, S. (1965). 'A procedure for securing returns to mail questionnaires.' *Sociology and Social Research*, 50 (1), 1965, 24–35.

ROEHER, G. A. (1963). 'Effective techniques in increasing response to mailed questionnaires.' *Public Opinion Quarterly*, 27, 1963, 299–302.

ROGERS, E. M. (1962). *Diffusion of innovations*. New York: Free Press of Glencoe, 1962.

ROKKAN, S. (*ed.*) (1966). *Data archives for the social sciences*. The Hague: Mouton, 1966.

ROSENBERG, V. (1967). 'Factors affecting the preferences of industrial personnel for information gathering methods.' *Information Storage and Retrieval*, 3 (3), 1967, 110–127.

ROSENBLATT, A. (1967). *The practitioner's use and evaluation of research*. (Paper presented at the 94th Annual Forum, National Conference on Social Welfare, Dallas, Texas, 1967.) [*unpublished*]

ROSENBLOOM, R. S., McLAUGHLIN, C. P. and WOLEK, F. W. (1965). *Technology transfer and the flow of technical information in a large industrial corporation.* 2 vols. Boston: Harvard University, Graduate School of Business Administration, 1965. (Mimeo.)

SALOMONSSON, O. (1969). 'Data banking systems for urban planning,' in Centre for Environmental Studies *Proceedings of the Conference on Information and Urban Planning, London, 1969.* Vol. 2. London: Centre for Environmental Studies, 1969, 7–48.

SARLE, R. G. (1958). *Characteristics of the literature used by authors of journal articles in business administration.* (Master's dissertation, School of Library Science, University of North Carolina, 1958.) [*unpublished*]

SAUNDERS, W. L. (1969). 'Economic success: the contribution of the information scientists.' *The Information Scientist,* 3 (3), 1969, 117–125.

SCHAUBER, A. (1952). *An analysis of the documentation of physics research to determine the serials most frequently used.* (Master's dissertation, Catholic University of America, 1952.) [*unpublished*]

SCHMOOKLER, J. (1962). 'Changes in industry and in the state of knowledge as determinants of industrial invention,' in Universities —National Bureau Committee for Economic Research *The rate and direction of inventive activity.* Princeton, N.J., National Bureau of Economic Research, 1962.

SCHMUCK, R. (1968). 'Social psychological factors in knowledge utilization,' in T. L. Eidell and J. M. Kitchel (*eds.*) *Knowledge production and utilization in educational administration.* University of Oregon, Center for the Advanced Study of Educational Administration, 1968.

SCHOBER, H.-W. and WERSIG, G. (1968). 'Information and documentation science: a discussion and theoretical treatment.' *TATUL Proceedings,* 4 (2), 1969, 26–40. [Translation of original in *Nachrichten für Dokumentation,* 19 (4), 1968, 116–124.]

SCHUTZE, G. (1968). *The social sciences: a bibliography of guides to the literature.* Woodhaven, New York, 1968. (Mimeo.)

SCHWARZ, P. A. (1969). 'Research needed to guide new policies and practices in international education.' *Yearbook of the National Society for the Study of Education,* 68 (1), 1969, 344–365.

SCOTT, C. and WILKINS, L. T. (1960). *The use of technical literature by industrial techonologists.* 2nd ed. London: Central Office of Information, 1960.

SELYE, H. (1966). *Symbolic shorthand system.* New Brunswick, N.J.: Rutgers State University, Graduate School of Library Service, 1966.

SHAPIRO, R. J. (1968). 'Creative research scientists.' *Psychologia Africana Monograph Supplement,* 4, 1968, pp. 180.

SHAW, R. R. (1956). *Pilot study of use of scientific literature by scientists.* Washington, D.C.: Washington National Science Foundation, 1956.

SHAW, R. R. (1959). 'Flow of scientific information.' *College and Research Libraries,* 20, 1959, 163–164.

SHEPARD, R. N. (1962). 'The analysis of proximities: multidimensional scaling with an unknown distance function.' I & II. *Psychometrika,* 27, 1962, 125–140, 219–246.

SHERA, J. H. (1951). 'Classification as the basis of bibliographic organization', *in* J. H. Shera and M. E. Egan (*eds.*) *Bibliographic organization.* Chicago: University of Chicago Press, 1951, 140–160.

SHERA, J. M. and EGAN, M. E. (*eds.*) (1951). *Bibliographic organization.* Chicago: University of Chicago Press, 1951.

SHILLING, C. W., TYSON, J. W. and BERNARD, J. (1963). *Factors associated with the citation of Russian research by American bioscientists.* (Biological Sciences Communication Project, Communique 15–63.) Washington, D.C.: George Washington University, 1963.

SHILLING, C. W., BERNARD, J. and TYSON, J. W. (1964). *Informal communication among bioscientists.* Washington: George Washington University, Biological Sciences Communication Project, 1964.

SINGER, J. D. *and others* (1969). *Beyond conjecture: data based research in international politics.* Chicago: Peacock, 1969.

SJOBERG, G. (1967). *Ethics, politics, and social research.* Cambridge, Mass.: Schenkman Publ. Co., 1967.

SLATER, M. (1963). 'Types of use and user in industrial libraries: some impressions.' *Journal of Documentation,* 19 (1), 1963, 12–18.

SLATER, M. (1968). 'Meeting the users' needs within the library', *in* J. Burkett (*ed.*) *Trends in special librarianship.* London: Clive Bingley, 1968, 99–136.

SLETTO, R. F (1940). 'Pretesting of questionnaires.' *American Sociological Review,* 5, 1940, 193–200.

SMITH, A. G. (1966). *Communication and status: the dynamics of a research center.* Eugene, Oreg.: University of Oregon, Center for the Advanced Study of Educational Administration, 1966.

SMITH, C. G. (1966). *Organisational factors in scientific performance in an industrial research laboratory.* Madison, Wis.: University of Wisconsin, Center for Advanced Study in Organization Science, 1966.

SMOKER, P. (1969). 'Social research for social action.' *American Behavioral Scientist,* 12 (6), 1969, 7–13.

STAVELEY, R. (*ed.*) (1957). *Guide to unpublished research materials.* London: Library Association, 1957.

STERN, H. (1969). 'Information systems in management science.' *Management Science,* 15 (6), 1969, 325–330.

STEVENS, N. D. (1969) 'Three early academic library surveys.' *College and Research Libraries,* 30 (6), 1969, 498–505.

STEVENS, R. E. (1953a). 'Characteristics of subject literatures.' *ACRL Monographs*, no. 6, 1953.

STEVENS, R. E. (1953b). 'The use of library materials in doctoral research: a study of the effect of differences in research methods.' *Library Quarterly*, 23 (1), 1953, 33–41.

STEVENS, R. E. (1966). *Reference books in the social sciences and humanities*. Champaign, Ill.: Illini Union Bookstore, 1966.

STORER, N. W. (1966). *The social system of science*. New York: Holt, Rinehart & Winston, 1966.

STORER, N. W. (1967). 'The hard sciences and the soft: some sociological observations.' *Bulletin of the Medical Library Association*, 55 (1), 1967, 75–84.

STORER, N. W. (1968). 'Modes and processes of communication among scientists: theoretical issues and prospects for investigation', *in Proceedings* of a Conference sponsored by Social Science Research Council and Institute for the Study of Science Affairs on *Theoretical issues in the study of science, scientists, and science policy*. New York: Columbia University, 1968.

STOUFFER, S. A. (1948). 'Studying the attitudes of soldiers.' *Proceedings of the American Philosophical Society*, 92, 1948, 336–340.

STRANG, R. (1942). *Exploration in reading patterns*. Chicago: University of Chicago Press, 1942.

SZWALBE, J. (1969). 'Niektore zagodnienia informacji w zakresie nauk spolecznych.' [*Selected information problems in social sciences.*] *Aktualne Problemy Informacjisi Dokumentacji*, 14 (1), 1969, 10–15.

TAPPER, C. (1965). 'Mechanized methods of documentation of interest to criminologists.' *Aslib Proceedings*, 17 (2), 1965, 60–70.

TAUBE, M. (1958). *An evaluation of 'use studies' of scientific information.* (Report prepared for the Air Force Office of Scientific Research, Contract No. AF 49 (638)–91, 1958.)

TAUBE, M. (1959). 'An evaluation of use studies of scientific information', *in* M. Taube (*ed.*) *Studies in co-ordinated indexing*, vol. 5. Washington, D.C.: Documentation Inc., 1959, 46–71.

TAUBER, M. F. (1964). 'Survey method in approaching library problems.' *Library Trends*, 13 (1), 1964, 15–30.

TAUBER, M. F. and STEPHENS, I. R. (*eds.*) (1967). *Library surveys*. New York: Columbia University Press, 1967.

THOMAS, E. J. (1964). 'Selecting knowledge for behavioral science', *in* National Association of Social Workers *Building social work knowledge*. New York, the Association, 1964, 38–47.

THORNE, R. G. (1954). *A survey of the reading habits of scientific and technical staff at the Royal Aircraft Establishment*. (Royal Aircraft Establishment Library. Memo 16, Sept. 1954.) (Duplicated report.)

TOBIAS, S. (1966). 'Lack of knowledge and fear of automation as factors in teachers' attitudes toward program instruction and other media.' *AV Communication Review*, 14, 1966, 99–109.

TREASURY—COMMITTEE ON THE CIVIL SERVICE (1968). *The Civil Service, vol. 1: Report of the Committee*. (Chairman: Lord Fulton) (Cmnd 3638.) London: H.M.S.O., 1968.

UNESCO (1963). *Education periodicals*. London: Unesco-H.M.S.O., 1963.

UNESCO (1966). *World list of social science perodicals*. 3rd ed. Paris: Unesco, 1966.

UNESCO—NATIONAL COMMISSION, NEW ZEALAND (1963). *Primary education: annotated bibliography*. Wellington, N.Z.: The Commission, 1963.

UNITED STATES—FEDERAL COUNCIL FOR SCIENCE AND TECHNOLOGY—COMMITTEE ON SCIENTIFIC AND TECHNICAL INFORMATION (1965). *Recommendations for national documents handling systems in science and technology*. 3 vols. Washington, D.C.: Federal Council for Science and Technology, 1965.

UNITED STATES—HOUSE OF REPRESENTATIVES—COMMITTEE ON GOVERNMENT OPERATIONS (1967). *The use of social research in federal domestic programs, II: The adequacy and usefulness of federally financed research on major national social problems*. Washington, D.C.: U.S. Government Printing Office, 1967.

UNITED STATES—NATIONAL ACADEMY OF SCIENCES—NATIONAL ACADEMY OF ENGINEERING COMMITTEE ON SCIENTIFIC AND TECHNICAL COMMUNICATION (1969). *Scientific and technical communication: a pressing national problem and recommendations for its solution*. Washington, D.C.: National Academy of Sciences, 1969.

UNITED STATES—NATIONAL BUREAU OF ECONOMIC RESEARCH (1962). *The rate and direction of inventive activity: economic and social factors*. Princeton, N.J.: Princeton University Press, 1962.

UNITED STATES—NATIONAL RESEARCH COUNCIL-COMMITTEE ON INFORMATION IN THE BEHAVIORAL SCIENCES (1967). *Communication systems and resources in the behavioral sciences*. Washington, D.C.: National Academy of Sciences, 1967.

UNITED STATES—NATIONAL RESEARCH COUNCIL—DIVISION OF MEDICAL SCIENCES—COMMITTEE ON BRAIN SCIENCES (1967). *Behavioral sciences indexing for the National Library of Medicine*. Washington, D.C.: National Research Council, 1967.

UNITED STATES—PRESIDENT'S SCIENCE ADVISORY COMMITTEE (1963). *Science, government, and information*. (The Weinberg Report.) Washington, D.C.: U.S. Government Printing Office, 1963.

UNITED STATES—SENATE COMMITTEE ON GOVERNMENT OPERATIONS/ SUBCOMMITTEE ON GOVERNMENT RESEARCH (1966). *Federal support of international social science and behavioral research.* 89th Congress, 2nd Session, 1966, 373 pp.

URQUHART, D. J. (1948). 'The distribution and use of scientific and technical information.' *Journal of Documentation*, 3, 1948, 222–231.

URQUHART, D. J. (1965). 'The ecology of inter-library loans.' *Library Association Record*, 67 (10), 1965, 341.

UYTTERSCHAUT, L. (1966a). 'Literature searching methods in social science research: a pilot enquiry.' *American Behavioral Scientist*, 9 (9), 1966, 14, 23–26.

UYTTERSCHAUT, L. (1966b). 'Pour une politique de documentation dans le domaine des sciences sociales.' *Synopsis*, 8 (104), 1966, 15–24.

VICKERY, B. C. (1961). 'The uses of scientific literature.' *Library Association Record*, 63 (7), 1961, 263–269.

VICKERY, B. C. (1968). 'Statistics of scientific and technical articles.' *Journal of Documentation*, 24 (3), 1968, 192–195.

VICKERY, B. C. (1969). 'Indicators of the use of periodicals.' *Journal of Librarianship*, 1 (3), 1969, 170–182.

WALFORD, A. J. (*ed.*) (1968). *Guide to reference material*, vol. 2: *Philosophy and psychology, religion, social sciences, geography, biography and history.* 2nd ed. London: Library Association, 1968.

WALLACE, D. (1954). 'A case for and against mail questionnaires.' *Public Opinion Quarterly*, 18 (1), 1954, 40–52.

WALLACE, J. F. (1964). 'Can information be available too early in a project?' *in* Institute of Information Scientists *Proceedings of the 1st Conference, Oxford, July, 1964.* Orpington, Kent: The Institute, 1966, 11–14.

WASHINGTON—JOINT BOARD OF COUNTY SCHOOL DIRECTORS (1967). *Assessment of education needs.* (Duplicated report.)

WASSERMAN, P, ALLEN, E. and GEORGI, C. (*eds.*) (1965). *Statistics sources: a subject guide.* 2nd ed. Detroit, Mich.: Gale Research Co., 1965.

WATKINS, J. W. N. (1957). 'Historical explanation in the social sciences.' *British Journal for the Philosophy of Science*, 8, 1957, 104–117.

WATSON, G. (*ed.*) (1967). *Change in school systems.* Washington, D.C.: National Training Laboratories, 1967.

WATSON, J. D. (1968). 'The double helix: discovery of the structure of DNA.' *Atlantic Monthly*, Jan., 1968, 77–99; Feb., 1968, 92–117.

WEBB, E. J. *and others* (1966). *Unobtrusive measures: nonreactive measurement in the social sciences.* Chicago: Rand McNally, 1966.

WENDER, R. W. (1969). 'Analysis of loans in the behavioral sciences.' *Special Libraries*, 60 (8), 1969, 510–513.

WESTBROOK, J. H. (1960). 'Identifying significant research.' *Science*, 132 (3435), 1960, 1229–1234.

WHITE, B. (1969a). 'Information for planning.' *Library World*, 70 (825), 1969, 223–226.

WHITE, B. (1969b). 'Current use of information in planning,' *in* Centre for Environmental Studies *Proceedings of the Conference on Information and Urban Planning, London, 1969, vol. 1.* London: the Centre, 1969, 85–116.

WHITE, B. (1969c). *Information in town and country planning: a research report.* London: Library Association. (Duplicated report.)

WHITE, C. M. (1964). *Sources of information in the social sciences: a guide to the literature.* Totowa, N. J.: Bedminster Press, 1964.

WHITE, O. and WILLIS, J. (1969). 'Background paper to the Conference on Information and Urban Planning', *in* Centre for Environmental Studies *Proceedings of the Conference on Information and Urban Planning, London, 1969, vol. 1.* London: the Centre, 1969, 7–19.

WIGHT, E. A. (1937). 'Methods and techniques of library surveys', *in* L. R. Wilson (*ed.*) *Library trends.* Chicago: Chicago University Press, 1937.

WILSON, J. T. (1952). 'Government support of research and its influence on psychology.' *American Psychologist*, 7, 1952, 714–718.

WINN, V. A. (1969a). *Access to information in the sociology of education: an information paper.* Oxford University, Department of Education, 1969. (Duplicated report.)

WINN, V. A. (1969b). *Information needs in the sociology of education: report of discussions amongst College of Education lecturers.* Oxford University, Department of Education, 1969. (Duplicated report.)

WOOD, D. N. (1969). 'Discovering the user and his information needs.' *Aslib Proceedings*, 21 (7), 1969, 262–270.

WOOD, D. N. and BOWER, C. A. (1969). 'The use of social science periodical literature.' *Journal of Documentation*, 25 (2), 1969, 108–122.

WUEST, F. J. (1965). *Studies in the methodology of measuring information requirements and use patterns*, Report no. 1: Questionnaire. Bethlehem, Pa.: Lehigh University Centre for Information Sciences, 1965.

WYNAR, L. R. (1968). *Guide to reference materials in political science.* 2 vols. Rochester, N.Y.: Libraries Unlimited, 1968.

WYSOCKI, A. (1969). 'Study of users' information needs: subject and methods', *in* International Federation for Documentation *On theoretical problems of informatics.* Moscow: All-Union Institute for Scientific and Technical Information, 1969, 80–92.

XHIGNESSE, L. V. and OSGOOD, C. E. (1967). 'Bibliographical citation characteristics of the psychological journal network in 1950 and 1960.' *American Psychologist,* 22, 1967, 778–791.

ZETTERBERG, H. (1963). 'The practical use of sociological knowledge,' *Acta Sociologica,* 7, 1963, 57–72.

Index

Abstracts, 9–10, 54, 58, 59, 89n, 103n, 113, 114, 126,
  coverage by, 88–9, 126, 127, 140–5
Accessibility, of information, 52, 55
Accumulation, of knowledge and literature, 38n, 45, 47–9, 55
Accuracy, 52, 53
ACKOFF, R. L., 20
Advertising and marketing, 22
ADVISORY COMMITTEE ON SCIENTIFIC POLICY (U.K.), 30n
ALBERT, R. W., 135
ALBRIGHT, L. E., 94
ALLEN, E., 89n
ALLEN, T. J., 10, 28n, 70, 72, 73, 77n, 83, 110–111, 146
ALPERT, H., 12n
ALTMAN, I., 62
ALTMAN, J. W., 89n
American Behavioral Scientist, 88n
American Documentation Institute (ADI)
  see American Society for Information Science
American Economic Association, 59
American Institute of Physics, 11
American Psychological Association 11, 13n, 71, 72, 76, 77, 80–1, 86, 93, 96–9, 111, 140, 141
American Psychologist, 12n
American Society for Information Science (formerly ADI) 6n, 7n
American Society for Metals Documentation Service Conference, 21n
American Sociological Association, 72, 133, 139
American University, 104
Analysis, units of, 125
ANDREWS, F. M., 28n, 86
ANDRIEN, M., 77n
ANDRY, R. G., 59–60
Annual Abstract of Statistics, 22
Annual Review of Information Science & Technology, 13n, 17, 18, 72, 73
ANTHONY, L. J., 145, 154

Anthropology, 59, 61, 120n, 134, 142
APPEL, J. S., 92–3
'Application criteria', 69
Applied research, *see* Social science research, application of
Architects, 110–111, 124
Archives, of data, 36n
ARIES CORPORATION, 80n
ARMSTRONG, SIR W., 122, 153
Aslib, 139n
Aslib Proceedings, 10
Assumptions, 32–3, 38n
Atomic energy, international policies in, 151
Atomic Energy Authority—Culham Laboratory Library, 122
Atomic Energy Research Establishment, Harwell, 23n
Attitudes, 104–5
Auerbach Corporation, 13n, 14, 18n
Author hierarchies, 136–8
Autobiographical material, 21–2

BAILEY, C. A., 13n, 14, 18n
BAIN, R., 129, 134
BARBER, A. S., 18, 47n
BARINOVA, Z. B., 74n
BARKER, A., 121
BARNES, R. C. M., 1n, 30
BARR, K. P., 126n
Bath University of Technology, 26n, 96, 124, 146
BECK, C., 89n
BECKER, H. A., 117n, 159
Behaviour, of users, 26, 27, 52, 90–2
Behavioural sciences, 5, 10, 52
  see also Social sciences
Behaviourism, 41, 42
  see also Psychology
BERNAL, J. D., 2, 3, 13, 24n, 25n, 74, 139n, 147, 157
BERGEN, D. P., 155
BERNARD, J., 75, 77n, 86
BEVIS, J. C., 25n
Bibliographic coupling, 48, 67, 76n
Bibliographical control, 54

Bibliographical tools, 7, 18–19, 87–
  96, 124, 142–5, 155
  and access to knowledge, 155
  coverage by 88n, 89, 126, 143–5
  list of, 88–9
  secondary, 88n, 92–6, 142–5
  tertiary, 88n
Bibliometrics, 125n, 128, 145
BIDERMAN, A. D., 12n
Biochemists, 76n
Biological sciences, 75–6, 87
BISCO, R. L., 13, 14, 36n, 37n, 60n
BIVONA, W. A., 94
BLOOM, M., 64, 67, 68–9
BOIG, F. S., 139n
BOLL, J. J., 137
Books, use of, 73–4, 126
  see also Reading habits, Published
    material, Libraries
BORKO, H., 18, 19, 31
BOTTOMORE, T. B., 88n
BOURNE, C. P., 6n, 18, 19, 27, 126n
BOWER, C. A., 130–1
BRADFORD, S. C., 139
Bradford's Law of scattering, 139n,
  142
Bradford-Zipf distribution, 139n
BRESSLER, M., 25n
Bristol University, 96
British Library of Political and
  Economic Science, 26n, 58
British Sociological Association, 99
BRITT, S. H., 18
BROADUS, R. N., 129
BROOKES, B. C., 139n
BROWN, M. J., 67, 103–4
Browsing, 43
BRYAN, H., 126
BUCKLAND, M. K., 139n
Building Research Station, 111
Business, sociological material in,
  38n
Business administration, 135
Business studies, 114–116

CNRS, see Centre National de la
  Recherche Scientifique (CNRS)
CAHALAN, D., 18
California, University of, 157
CAMP, W. L., 89n
CARTER, C. F., 66
CARTER, L. F., 126n
CARTER, L. J., 12n

CARTER, M. P., 66, 99
CARTWRIGHT, D., 66, 120n
Case histories, 18, 19–20
CAVANAGH, J. M. A., 11n, 27n
CAWKELL, A. E., 129n, 130
Center for Documentation and Com-
  munication Research, Western
  Reserve University, 61n
CENTRAL STATISTICAL OFFICE, 89n
Centre for Environmental Studies,
  108
Centre National de la Recherche
  Scientifique (CNRS), 59, 60–1
CHAFE, D. H., 21n
CHALL, L. P., 57
CHAMPION, D. J., 25n
CHERNS, A., 64, 66
CHERNYI, A. I., 8
Chicago University—Graduate Lib-
  rary School and Social Sciences
  Division 54n, 135
Citation analysis, 26, 48–9, 74–5,
  76n, 87, 135
Citation indexing, 7, 61–2
Citation studies, 129–143
  and evaluation of secondary
    literature, 143–5
  and obsolescence rate of literature,
    130–3
  and status, 136–9
  and type of material cited, 133–5
  see also Half-life
Citations and references, difference
  between, 129n
Classification, 34, 38, 51, 54–63,
  80–1, 102
  and retrieval of information, 60–1
  of users, 24–5
Clearinghouses of the Educational
  Resources Information Centre,
  89n
CLEVERDON, C. W., 61n
Clustering, 138
COHEN, N. E., 68n, 102
COHEN, S. I., 70, 77n, 83
Coding of literature, 56
COLE, J. R., 86
COLE, P. F., 139n
COLE, S., 86
Commerce, 132
  see also Economics
Communication, informal,   see
  Informal networks

Communication, oral, 77n
Communication artifacts, 74, 88n, 125–145, 154–5, 161
Communication input, index of, 86
Communication systems and resources in the behavioral sciences, 52–3
Communication theory, 5
Communications research, 84–6, 135
Communications technology, 159
  see also computers
Community work, 104–5
  see also Social work
Computers, 10–11, 36n, 37, 40, 52, 53, 57, 60, 102, 150, 152
CONNOR, J. H., 11n, 94
Consumer research, 22, 157
Controlled experiment, 29
COOPER, M., 94
COOVER, R. W., 18, 32
Correspondence, see Informal networks
COSATI, 12n, 14
Council of Europe—Demographic Conference, 1966, 75
Coupling, bibliographic, 48, 67, 76n
Coverage, by abstracts etc, 88–9, 126, 127, 140, 42–5
COX, F. L., 135
COYL, E. B., 77n
CRANE, D., 76n, 87
CRAWFORD, E. T., 12n
Criminology, 59–60
Critical incident technique, 31–2
CROS, R. C., 61n
CROSSLEY, C. A., 89n, 103n
CUADRA, C. A., 6n
Culham Laboratory, 122
CULLINGWORTH, J. B., 106, 107
Cumulativeness, 38n, 45, 47–9, 55
CURNOW, R. C., 26
Current awareness services, 47n, 55, 78, 95–6, 121–2
Current Contents . . ., 94
Curriculum materials, 117
'Cutting-edge' of science, 48

DNA, molecular structure of, 21, 158
DANIEL, R. S., 128, 130, 132, 140–2
DANNATT, R. J., 2, 23n
DANTINE, D. J., 116n
DARLEY, J. C., 12n, 120n

Data
  definition of, 4–5
  institutional, 36
  nontextual, 37n
Data archives, 36–7, 40, 60n
Data banks, 36–7, 58
Data Institute of Social Sciences, 103n
Data libraries, list of, 37n
Data systems, 116
DAVID, H., 120n
DAVIS, R. A., 13n, 14, 18n, 135n
DAY, M. S., 82
DEBONS, A., 9
Decision-making activities, 64, 65n, 149
Delays in announcement, indexing etc., 143–5
Demands, 1–3
  and publication programmes, 22
Demographic Conference, European, 1966, 75
DENUM, D. D., 37n
DEPARTMENT OF EDUCATION AND SCIENCE—COMMITTEE ON SOCIAL STUDIES, 64, 66
DESMOND, W. F., 126n, 127
DESROCHERS, E., 88n
DESSAUER, F. E., 7n
DEWS, J. D., 114–116
Diary method, 4, 18, 19, 22–3, 31
Disciplinary differences, 43–9
Disciplines, boundaries in, 5–6
'Discretion level', 108
Dissemination, 20
Documentalists, 90
Documentation, 51, 53, 54–63
  vocabulary, 91–2
Documentation Abstracts, 9
Documents on International Affairs, reprinting of, 22
DOIG, A. G., 88n
DONOHUE, J. C., 118n, 123
Duplicated research, cost of 151–2
Durham University, 95

EARLE, P., 130, 131–2, 139n
EAST, H., 145, 154
Eastern Regional Institute for Education, 116–118
Economics, 59, 89n, 90, 92, 132, 135, 143–4
  journals in, 92, 126

literature growth, 126–7
EDGERTON, H. A., 18
Education, 67, 88n, 89n, 117–120, 131, 132, 135, 142, 143
curricula, design of, 66, 117
sociology of, 99
see also Teachers
Educational administrators 81–2, 118–120
Educational research, 111n
use of data banks in, 37n
Educational Research Information Center (ERIC) 89n, 118
Educational technology, 117–118
Effectiveness, measure of, 31
see also Evaluation
EGAN, M., 18
EIDELL, T. L., 64, 67
ELLIOTT, C. K., 89n, 141
ELLIOTT, G. H., 135n
EMBREE, J. F., 120n
Empirical studies, 26n, 28, 71–4
Encyclopaedia of the Social Sciences, 58
ENGELBERT, H., 2n
Environmental variables, 24, 26–9
ERIC, 89n, 118
ERICSON, C. 117n
ERIE, 116–118
ETZIONI, A., 64
Evaluation, 18–19, 22–3, 113
of user studies, 29–33
Experts, assistance from, 90

FAIRTHORNE, R. A., 4, 5, 9, 125n, 139n, 148, 160
Feedback, 3, 11, 61, 73n, 79–80, 83
Field observations, 94–6
FISHENDEN, R. M., 1n, 14n, 30n
Flow of information, 38, 48, 74, 77
two step, 82–4
see also Informal networks
FLOWERS, B. H., 25n
FORD, M. M., 114n, 116
Foreign language materials, 74–6, 110
Formal communication systems, 154–5, 161
see also Informal networks of communication
FOSKETT, D. J., 46n, 54–5, 57
FOX, R. C., 47n
FRANZEN, R. B., 18

FREEMAN, R. R., 101
FUSSLER, H. H., 126, 141

GARDIN, J-C., 60–1
GARFIELD, E., 7n, 61, 62, 94
GARRATT, R., 130
GARVEY, W. D., 78, 80, 97, 98
GARVIN, P. L., 37n
Gatekeepers, 83–4
GATES, J. L., 89n
GEE, R. D., 89n
GELLNER, E. A., 34n
Geography, 89n, 131, 135, 136
GEORGI, C., 89n
GERALD, G., 25n
GEROULD, A. C., 136
GERSTBERGER, P. G., 28n, 77n
GERSTENFELD, A., 77n
GILCHRIST, A., 139n
GILYAREVSKYI, R. S., 8
GLASER, E. M., 105
GLASS, B., 7n
GLENNON, J. R., 94
GOLDBLUM, E. J., 94
GOODE, W. J., 25n
GOODMAN, F. L., 7n
GOTTLIEB, D., 89n
GOTTSCHALK, C. M., 126n, 127
GOULDNER, A. W., 64, 66, 69n
Government agencies, and user studies, 11
Government policies, and research in social sciences, 12, 120–2, 152–3
GRAHAM, W. R., 77n
GREENBERG, A., 25n
GRIFFEL, D., 37n, 49
GRIFFITH, B. C., 78, 80, 81, 97, 98
GRIFFITH, J. D., 143, 145
GROENMAN, S., 25n, 75, 100
GROSE, D., 36n
GUBA, E. G., 67
GULLAHORN, J. E., 25n
GULLAHORN, J. T., 25n
GURR, T., 92–3
GUSHEE, D. E., 10
GUTTSMAN, W. L., 48, 130
GYÖRE, P., 8

HAAS, J. A., 149
HALBERT, M. H., 20
Half-life, 74n, 130
HALL, J. L., 122n

HAMMER, D. P., 159
HANDY, R., 5
HANSON, C. W., 18, 25n
Hardness, of a science, 39, 45–6
HARMON, R. B., 88n
HARRIS, M. H., 40
Harvard University, 61n, 88n
HARVEY, J. M., 89n
HATT, P. K., 25n
HAUGHTON, R., 117n
HAVIGHURST, R. J., 104n
HEILPRIN, L. B., 7n
HEISKANEN, V. S., 64
HELMER, O., 66
HENKLE, H. H., 18
HERNER, M., 17, 30, 72, 143, 145
HERNER, S., 17, 19, 30, 72, 77n, 143,
    145
HERRING, P., 66
HERTZ., D. B., 23n
Hierarchies, 136–9
HINDLE, A., 139n
HOBBS, A. H., 129, 133–4
HOFFER, J. R., 68n, 102, 103
HOGEWEG-DE HAART, H. P., 55n, 75
HOLT, C. C., 126–7
HOROWITZ, I. L., 12n, 64
HOSELITZ, B. F., 88n
House of Commons Library, 121–2
HULME, E. W., 125n
HURT, P., 157
HYSLOP, M. R., 21n

INFROSS, see Investigation into the
    information requirements of the
    social sciences
Indexing, 55n, 59, 61
    citation, 7, 61–2
    see also Abstracts, Bibliographical
    tools
Industrial research, 14, 122
Informal networks of communica-
    tion, 35, 76–84, 148, 158, 161
    characteristics of, 78–80, 84, 97
    cost of, 80
    and social organisation, 80–1
Informatics, 8–9
Informatics Incorporated, 118–120
Information,
    definition of, 160–1
    flow of, 38, 48, 74, 77, 82–4
    storage of, 148
    surfeit of, 67, 149

uses made of, 148
Information centres, 89n
Information explosion, 78
Information officers, 94–5, 96, 124
Information retrieval, 10–11, 60–
    61n, 148
    analogy with education, 7n
Information science, theory of, 9, 10,
    156, 161
Information Science Abstracts, 9
Information Sciences, Technologies
    and Activities (ISTA), 9
Information services, 55, 92, 94–6,
    113, 114
    cost of, 150–3
Information systems, design of, 26–
    7, 155
'Informatology', 9
Innovations, 82, 97–9
Institute for Science Information,
    (ISI), 93–4
Interest profiles, 94–6
Interferon Scientific Memoranda
    (ISM), 80n
Inter-library loan service, 114
International Bibliography of the
    Social Sciences, 58
International Committee for Social
    Science Documentation, 54, 58
International contacts, 80
International cooperation, 54, 58,
    151, 156
International Union for the Scien-
    tific Study of the Population,
    Congress of, 100
Interpersonal contact,
    as predictor of productivity, 84–6
    see also Informal networks
Interviews, 4, 18, 21, 23n
Investigation into the information
    requirements of the social sciences
    (INFROSS), 23n, 26n, 96, 104n,
    113–114, 121, 146
Invisible Colleges, 48, 76–77n

JAHODA, G., 18, 23n
JAKOBOVITS, L. A., 136, 137
JANDA, K., 40, 95
JANSEN, A. J., 104n
JOHNS HOPKINS UNIVERSITY—CEN-
    TER FOR RESEARCH IN SCIENTIFIC
    COMMUNICATION, 72–3, 133
    —RESEARCH LIBRARY, 20

Journal of Documentation, 111
Journals
  clustering of, 138
  rejection rate of articles, 133, 139
  scattering of references across, 139–143
  status of 136–9
  see also Published material
JUDGE, P. J., 151

KENDALL, M. G., 88n, 139n
KENT, A., 126n
KEPHART, W. M., 25n
KESSLER, M. M., 67n
Keyword in Context Index, 7, 102
KIRKPATRICK, L. H., 135n
KITCHEL, J. M., 64, 67
KITTEL, D. A., 20
Know-how information, 79
KOBLITZ, J., 9
KOCHEN, M., 7, 9, 34, 71, 156
KUHN, T. S., 16n, 39, 40n, 43–5, 129n, 133
KURTZ, P., 5
KWIC (Keyword in context index) 7, 102
KYLE, B., 38, 54, 56

LAKE, D. G., 104
LANCASTER, H. O., 145
Language, *see* Foreign language, Terminology
Language sciences, 101
LANIER, L. H., 120n
LASSWELL, H. D., 83n
LAVER, F. J. M., 108n
Law, user studies in, 90
LAWLER, E., 130, 132
LAZARSFELD, P. F., 18, 64, 65n, 80
Learned societies, 59
Lecturers, *see* Teachers
LEE, N., 89n
LEEDS, A. A., 77n, 126, 139n, 140
LEEDS, R., 64, 67, 80, 116n
LEFTWICH, R. H., 59
LEGTERS, L. H., 12n
LEVIN, P. H., 107–8
LEVINE, S., 25n
LEVY, F., 60–61n
LEVY, N. P., 14n
LEWIS, P. R., 58, 59, 88n
LIBBEY, M. A., 21n

Libraries, 3, 20, 73–4, 95–6, 108–9, 113, 114, 130–2, 133n
  and reader instruction, 157
  and readership studies, 135
Library and Information Science Abstract, 9
Library science, and information science, 7, 148
Library surveys, 73–4, 126
LIN, N., 129, 133, 139
LINE, M. B., 3, 23n, 24, 27, 31, 50–1, 73n, 104n, 121, 130n
Linguistical problems, *see* Terminology
LINGWOOD, D. A., 73, 84–6
LINSKY, A., 18
Literature of the social sciences
  classification of, 54–63
  growth of, 126–9
  nature of, 34–53
  obsolescence rate of, 45–6, 55, 130–3
  primary and secondary, 88n, 92–6, 142–5
  statistics of, 26, 125–145
Literature searching, 88–96
  delegation of, 91
LIVESAY, M. J., 135
Loans, analysis, 130–2, 133n
LOCK, C. B. M., 89n
LOMPE, K., 120n
London Bibliography of the Social Sciences, 58
LONGWORTH, D. S., 18
LOUTTIT, C. M., 40–41n, 74, 127–9, 140, 141
LUCAS, P. G., 34n
LUFTMAN, K. A., 139n
LUNDBERG, C. C., 101n
LUNDBERG, G. A., 12n
LYNN, K. C., 126n
LYONS, G. M., 120n

MPs, 121–2
McCULLOCH, J. W., 67, 103–4
McDIARMID, E. W., 73n
McDIARMID, J., 120n
McINTOSH, S., 37n, 49
McKECHNIE, J., 89n
MACKENZIE, A. G., 157
McLAUGHLIN, C. P., 77n, 79n
MACRAE, D., 129, 132–3
MADGE, J., 36, 37n

MALTBY, A., 89n
Management, 65, 114–116
    literature, 116, 131
Manchester Business School, 114
MANDELBAUM, M., 34n
MANDELBROT, B., 139n
MANFIELD, M., 25n
MANTELL, L. H., 126n
MARK, F. M., 135
Marketing, 22
MARQUARDT, J. F., 135n
MARTIN, G. P., 135
MARTIN, M. W., 20
MARTYN, J., 1n, 30n, 139n, 151
MARUYAMA, M., 92
MASON, J. B., 88n
Mathematics, and hardness of a
    discipline, 45–6
MATTHEW, K. A., 111n
MAYER, M., 117
MEDAWAR, P. B., 50, 70
Median citation age, 130n
Medical sciences, 55n, 133n, 142–3
MEIER, E. L., 135
MEISTER, D., 11n
Members of Parliament, 121–2
MENZEL, H., 2n, 13, 14, 17, 18, 19,
    23n, 31, 32, 72, 74, 77n, 79n, 83,
    147
MERSEL, J., 118n, 123
MERTON, R., 16
Methods and methodology, 16–33,
    147, 149
    eclectic, 30
    evaluation of, 18, 22–3
    rationalisation of, 29–30
    of science, 12–22
    texts on, 18–19
microforms, 22
Michigan, University of—History of
    Education System, 61n
MIKHAILOV, A. I., 8
Mission orientation of research,
    11
Modelling, by computer, 37
MORRIS, W. A., 118n, 123
MOTE, L. J. B., 24–25n
MULLINS, N. C., 76n
Multi-authorship, 48
Multi-programming, 116n
Multistep flow of information,
    82–3
MURPHY, D. J., 116n

NASATIR, D., 36n
National aspects of information,
    11–13, 30, 120–2, 152–3
(National, see also under United
    States)
National Lending Library for Science
    and Technology (NLL) 30n,
    130–1, 132
Needs, 1–3, 19, 32, 50, 56, 61n, 95,
    101, 125, 147, 149,
    definition of, 160–1
NEELAMEGHAN, A., 152
NELSON, C. E., 129, 133, 139
Netherlands
    social science journals, 75
NETHERLANDS — KONINKLIJKE
    NEDERLANDS AKADEMIE VAN
    WETENSCHAPPEN—SOCIAAL-
    WETENSCHAPPELIJKE RAAD, 55n
NEWMAN, J. W., 116n
NICHOLS, R. F., 120n
Nomenclature, see Terminology
NORMAN, R. M., 18
NORTHROP, F. S. C., 34n, 39n
Northwestern University, 95
NOVIKOV, Y. A., 8, 9

O'BRIEN, G. M. St. L., 104
Observation, unit of, 32
Obsolescence, 45–6, 55, 61, 130–3
O'CONNOR, J., 2n, 3
ODUM, H. W., 133n
OFFICE OF THE MINISTER FOR
    SCIENCE—COMMITTEE ON THE
    MANAGEMENT AND CONTROL OF
    RESEARCH AND DEVELOPMENT,
    66
Office for Scientific and Technical
    Information (OSTI), 93n, 95, 96,
    104n, 108, 114n, 122, 124
OLSEN, W. C., 159
Operational definition, 3–5
Operations research study, 20
OPPENHEIM, A. N., 12
Optics, 40n, 133
Oregon, University of, Center for
    the Advanced Study of Educa-
    tion Administration, 81–2
ORLANS, H., 120n
OROMANER, M. J., 129, 134–5
ORR, R. H., 77n, 126, 139n, 140
ORR, S. C., 106, 107
OSGOOD, C. E., 130, 131, 136–8

OSTI, see Office for Scientific and Technical Information
OTTEN, K., 9

PAGE, J. R. H., 151
PAISLEY, W. J., 1n, 11, 13, 14, 16, 17, 18, 21, 30, 31, 71–2, 73, 74, 84–6, 125n, 130, 146, 147, 154, 155
PALMER, J., 122n
Paradigms, 16, 43, 44, 46, 64n, 133
PARKER, E. B., 11n, 18, 21n, 73, 84–6, 130
PARSONS, T., 12n
PATTERSON, A. M., 74
PAYNE, K. B., 135
PELZ, D. C., 28n, 77n, 86
PEMBERTON, J. E., 22
PENNY, J., 116
Periodicals, see Journals
Personal conversation, see Informal networks
PIETRZYK, A., 101
Planning, see Urban and regional planning
Planning Research, 110
Policy-making, and social science information, 120–2
Political science, 37n, 40–1, 87, 88n, 89n, 135
POOL, I. de S., 37n, 49
POOLE, J. B., 122 n
PORAT, A. M., 149
Postbehaviourism, 42
Practitioners, 63–70, 78, 101–124
and researchers, distinction between, 101n
Pre-prints, 35, 99
PRICE, D. J. de S., 43, 48–9, 64–65n, 67, 70, 76–77n, 126, 130
PRICE, D. O., 25n
PRICE, E., 102n
Primary literature, 89–92
and relationship with secondary literature 88–9, 143–5
PRITCHARD, A., 125n
Probation officers, see Social workers
Productivity, predictors of, 52–3, 84–7, 153
Professional associations, 11, 59
Project for the Evaluation of Benefits from University Libraries (PEBUL) 95–6

Psychiatric social workers, see Social workers
Psychiatry, and World War II, 120n
Psychoanalytic Quarterly, 75
Psychological Abstracts, 93, 98–9, 112, 127, 140–1
Psychologists
contribution to information science 8–9, 149
readership study of, 135n
Psychology, 4, 10, 35, 38, 39–41, 87, 92–3, 96–9, 111–113, 140–1
bibliographical tools, 88n, 89n, 140
citation studies in, 129–132, 136–7, 140–2
classification, 62
flow of information in, 96–9
foreign language material, 74–5
informal communication system in, 76–8
journals, 92–3, 98–9, 112–113, 127, 128, 131, 132, 136–9
literature growth, 126–7
variables in, 26–9
and World War II, 120n
Psychology of the user, 27–8, 148
Public communications, field of, 135
Publication trends, 22, 40–41n, 48–9
Publications (p roductivity), 84–7
Published material, 88–92
citation studies of, 129–145
demand for, 73–4, 88–96
growth of, 126–9
guides to, 58
obsolescence rate of, 45–6, 55, 61, 130–3
secondary, see Bibliographical tools

Questionnaires, 4, 18, 25n
QUINN, E. W., 135

Racism, and social workers, 104
RADER, G., 95
Random access, 116n
Random alarm device, 20
READE, E., 106–7
Reader instruction in university libraries, 157
Readership studies, 135
Reading habits, 20, 43–4, 67, 103–4
Recall ratio, 152
Recall, representativeness of, 47

Records, definition of, 4–5
Redondo Beach projects, 105
REES, A. M., 3, 9, 31, 61n, 149
REEVES, J., 89n
Regional planning, *see* Urban and regional planning
REIN, M., 38–39n, 68n
Reinforcement, 28–9, 79
Rejection rate (of articles), 133, 139
Relevance, 52, 53
Reliability, 22–3, 42
Reports, 119
Research, *see also* Social science research
duplicated, 151–2
on research, 123
Research productivity, and communication, 84–7
Research reports, 119
Researchers, and use of information 148–150
Response rate (to questionnaires), 25
Retrieval systems, 10–11, 38, 56, 60–1, 116n
Reviews, 89
RIECKEN, H. W., 12n, 64–5, 68
RIESTHUIS, G. J. A., 25n, 75, 100
RITVO, M. R., 104
ROBERTS, A. H., 101
ROBERTS, C. R., 135n
ROBERTS, N., 143–4
ROBIN, S., 18
ROEHER, G. A., 25n
ROGERS, E. M., 82
ROKKAN, S., 37n
ROSENBERG, V., 28n
ROSENBLATT, A., 67
ROSENBLOOM, R. S., 77n, 79n
Royal Society Scientific Information Conference, 13, 74
Royal Statistical Society, 59
RUBENSTEIN, A. H., 23n
RUSH, M., 121

SDI, *see* Selective dissemination of information
SALOMONSSON, O., 108n
Sampling, problems of, 23–6
SARLE, R. G., 135
Scattering, 139–143
SCHAUBER, A., 141
SCHMOOKLER, J., 126n
SCHMUCK, R., 117

SCHOBER, H. W., 9
School teachers, 116–118
SCHRANK, W. E., 126–7
SCHULTZ, D. G., 149
SCHUTZE, G., 88n
SCHWARZ, P. A., 123
Science, *see also* Social sciences philosophy of, 34–5
Science and technology
citation, study in, 129n, 130n, 139–140
classification systems in, 43–9, 56–7
financial support for, 11–12
obsolescence rate of literature in, 130n
reference scattering in, 139–142
relationship between, 64–5
user studies in, 12–15, 74
Science Citation Index (SCI), 130n
Scientific activity, views of, 43–9
Scientific literature
citation age, 132
growth rate of, 126–9
Scientific papers, 49, 86, 159
Scientific research, 43–9, 79, 129n
SCOTT, C., 14n
SEAR, A. M., 25n
'Search command', 95
Secondary literature, *see* Bibliographical tools
Selective dissemination of information (SDI), 8, 55, 94–6
SELYE, H., 126n
Serial literature, *see* Journals; Published material
SEWELL, W. H., 65n
SHAPIRO, R. J., 28n
SHAW, R. R., 22, 31
SHEPARD, R. N., 138
SHER, I. H., 62
SHERA, J. H., 55
SHILLING, C. W., 75, 77n, 86
SIMON, J. L., 126
Simulation, technique of, 37, 42
SINGER, J. D., 41
SJOBERG, G., 64
SLATER, M., 18, 25n, 145, 154
SLETTO, R. F., 25n
SMITH, A. G., 81–2
SMITH, C. G., 28n, 86
SMITH, T., 64, 116n
SMOKER, P., 42

Social engineers, 42, 65–6, 67, 69
Social organisations, and communication patterns, 80–1
Social planning, 38n
Social science research,
application of, 63–70, 78, 89n,
101–124
financing of, 153
government support for, 12, 120–
2, 152–3
nature of, 34–53, 148
problem-orientated, 69–70, 105
Social Science Research Council
(SSRC), 36n, 73n
Social science studies, reports on,
73n
Social sciences,
areas of study in, 5–6
characteristics of, 50
laboratory experimentation in, 42
pre-paradigmatic stage of, 44–5, 47
sources of material in, 35–43
Social sciences and physical sciences,
differences between, 43–50, 56,
63
Social scientists, applied, 101–107
Social studies, applied, 149
Social workers, 67, 101–105, 132
Sociologists, studies of, 72–3, 134
Sociology, 64–5, 88n, 99, 106, 107,
129, 135, 139
of education, 99
Sociology of Education Abstracts
(SEA), 93, 113, 114
Space research, 151
Stanford University—Institute of
Communication Research, 73
Statesman's Yearbook, reprinting of,
22
Statistical bibliography, 125n
Statistics, 88–89n, 110, 122, 131
literature in, 136–9, 145
Status, and communication, 81–2
see also Hierarchies
STAVELEY, R., 89n
STEPHENS, I. R., 73n
STERN, H., 116n
STEVENS, N. D., 73n
STEVENS, R. E., 135
Storage and retrieval systems, 10–11,
60–61n, 148
STORER, N. W., 43, 45–6, 65n, 76n
STOUFFER, S. A., 120n

Substitutability, 47, 114
SULLIVAN, D. J., 11n
Survey techniques, 18, 73–4, 126
Sweden—Board of Education, 111n
SWIFT, D. F., 93n
Systems engineering study, 20
SZRETER, R., 89n
SZWALBE, J., 55n

TAPPER, C., 60n
Target population, 23, 24–5
TAUBE, M., 18, 31, 157
TAUBER, M. F., 73n
Taxonomy, 58, 60
TAYLOR, R., 6n
Teachers, 111–118, 135n
college of education, 113–114
school, 116–118
university, 111–113, 114
Technological utilization, 52–3, 159
see also Computers
Technology, 64–5, 83
see also Science and technology
Terminology, 1–6, 46, 55, 56, 61,
105, 152, 160
Textbooks, in the natural sciences,
35, 43, 44
Theory, in information science, 9
absence of, 16–17, 29, 33, 70–1, 147
THOMAS, E. J., 69n
THORNE, R. G., 14n
Time-sharing, 116n
TOBIAS, S., 117n
TORPIE, R. J., 62
Translation, 74n, 75
Typologies, 16–17
TYSON, J. W., 75, 77n, 86

U.S.S.R., 7–8, 74n, 75–6
UNESCO, 54, 58, 88n, 89n, 93
United States, and the social
sciences, 104–5, 120, 152–3
United States—Federal Council for
Science and Technology—Com-
mittee on Scientific and Technical
Information (COSATI), 12n, 14
United States—House of Repre-
sentatives—Committee on Gov-
ernment Operations, 120, 153n
United States—National Aeronautics
and Space Administration, 11, 25n
United States—National Association
of Social Workers, 102n, 103n

United States—National Bureau of Economic Research, 28n
United States—National Conference on Social Welfare, 102, 103n
United States—National Council for the Social Studies, 89n
United States—National Library of Medicine, 55n
United States—National Research Council—Committee on Information in the Behavioral Sciences, 10, 37, 52, 72–3
United States—National Science Foundation, 12n, 14
United States—Office of Naval Research—Division of Medical Science, 55n
United States—National Science Foundation, 12n, 14
United States—Office of Naval Research, 120n
United States—Senate Committee on Government Operations—Sub-Committee on Government Research, 12n
University teachers, 111–113, 114
Unpublished material, use of, 89n, 110
Urban and regional planning, 106–111
URQUHART, D. J., 13, 30n, 74
Use, assessment of, 131n
Use studies, 88n
User behaviour, psychology of, 26–8, 148
User education, 157–8
User feedback, 3, 11, 61, 73n, 79–80, 83
User needs, see Needs
User orientated systems, 11
User studies, in the physical sciences, 12–15
User surveys, 11
UYTTERSCHAUT, L., 89–92

Validity, 22–3, 29–30, 31, 42, 57
Variables,
  definition of, 4
  dependent and independent, 26–9, 31
VICKERY, B. C., 126n, 130, 131–2, 139n

Vocabularies
  controlled, 160
  documentation, 91–2
  see also Terminology

WALFORD, A. J., 88n
WALLACE, D., 25n
WALLACE, J. F., 152
WARMAN, H. J., 136
WASHINGTON JOINT BOARD OF COUNTY SCHOOL DIRECTORS, 116–117
WASSERMAN, P., 89n
WATKINS, J. W. N., 34n
WATSON, G., 117
WATSON, J. D., 21, 158
WEBB, E. J., 30n
Weinberg Report, 12n
WENDER, R. W., 133n
WERSIG, G., 9
WESTBROOK, J. H., 129n
Western Reserve University—Center for Documentation and Communication Research, 61n
WHITE, B., 108–110
WHITE, C. M., 88n
WHITE, O., 106n, 107, 108n
WIGHT, E. A., 73n
WILENSKY, H., 65n
WILKINS, L. T., 14n
WILLIAMS, B. R., 66
Williams College, 73n
WILLIS, J., 106n, 107, 108n
WILSON, J. T., 120n
WILSON, K. V., 137
WINN, V. A., 93, 113
WOLEK, F. W., 77n, 79n
WOOD, D. N., 18, 130–1, 157
World War II, and social science research, 120–1
WUEST, F. J., 18, 23n
WYNAR, L. R., 88n
WYSOCKI, A., 1n, 18

XHIGNESSE, L. V., 130, 131, 136–7

York University—Institute of Advanced Architectural Studies, 111, 124

ZALTMAN, G., 21n
ZETTERBERG, H., 38–39n, 65n, 66